AA

HISTORIC PLACES
OF NEW ZEALAND

AA

HISTORIC PLACES

OF NEW ZEALAND

NZ HISTORIC PLACES TRUST · POUHERE TAONGA

Hodder & Stoughton

First published by Hodder & Stoughton Limited
46 View Road, Glenfield, Auckland, New Zealand

© 1990 maps: The Automobile Association (Auckland) Inc.
© 1990 text and transparencies: New Zealand Historic Places Trust

Produced for Hodder & Stoughton Ltd
by Weldon New Zealand
a division of Weldon Publishing.
372 Eastern Valley Way, NSW, 2068, Australia.
© 1990 edition: Weldon New Zealand

Compiled by John Wilson and Linda Pears,
New Zealand Historic Places Trust
Designed by Kathie Baxter Smith
Edited by Jo Rudd
Photography by Robert van de Voort, Profimage,
            New Zealand Historic Places Trust
            Tourist & Publicity Department
            Chris Lewis Photography
            Wally Bowater
            Kris Pfeiffer
            Conrad Sims
Monochromes reproduced by courtesy: Alexander Turnbull Library
                                    New Zealand Railways
Typeset by Savage Type Pty Ltd, Brisbane
Printed in Singapore by Kyodo Printing Co Ltd

ISBN 0 340 541 881

OTHER AA PUBLICATIONS

AA Road Atlas of New Zealand
Contains extensive map coverage of New Zealand's road system
plus useful travel information.
AA Guide to New Zealand
A practical and comprehensive reference for all travellers in New
Zealand. Many itineraries are covered by map and photographic
inclusions which makes it a valuable accompaniment to your
holidays.
AA Guide to Walkways North Island New Zealand
AA Guide to Walkways South Island New Zealand
These two illustrated editions are intended as portable guides to the
walkways system to encourage people of all ages to go 'for a walk'.
AA Guide to Tramping and Bushwalking in New Zealand
This interesting and informative publication not only provides
location, distance, facilities and recommendations for each walk or
tramp but also gives a brief historical outline of the area.
AA Guide to Day Tours in New Zealand
Day Tours has been produced to allow visitors and New Zealanders
alike to enjoy a variety of day trips to places of interest throughout
New Zealand.
AA Colours of New Zealand
AA Unique to New Zealand
The diversity of New Zealand captured in these 32 page photo-
graphic publications.

*Front cover: Erected at Waitangi in 1833–34 for the British
Resident, James Busby, the Waitangi Treaty House was the
scene, in February 1840, of the first signing of the Treaty
of Waitangi* Wally Bowater *Inset at left: Maori carving, Rotorua.*
*Half-title page: The first home of Michael Studholme when
he took up the Te Waimate run in 1854 was a tiny slab-
walled, thatch-roofed cottage, the Cuddy.*
*Title page: The lighthouse at Castle Point, first lit in
January 1913, was the last iron tower lighthouse
prefabricated in England to be erected in New Zealand.*
◄ *The charming little church at Onuku, a few kilometres
beyond Akaroa, stands on the site of an ancient kainga or
unfortified settlement.*

The AA Book of New Zealand Historic Places aims to tell readers what kinds of historic places are to be found in New Zealand and to encourage them to seek out such places when travelling. It is a book which intends only to point people in the right direction and to whet their appetites. For the informed traveller the landscape is an open book. It is not difficult to learn how to decipher its pages, sometimes blurred and indistinct, so that journeying around New Zealand becomes immeasurably enhanced.

This book does not direct attention only to picturesque places or dramatic buildings: historic places are not always 'sights' of a kind some travellers expect them to be, but behind the facade there is always a tale to be told. And many places will only come to life if visitors use their imaginations.

Hundreds of historic places are mentioned in this book and 93 colour and 19 monochrome photographs represent the wealth of tangible history New Zealand has to offer.

Many more places have had to be omitted, an indication of the depth and breadth of the New Zealand story. It is hoped that people's appetites will indeed be whetted and they will search out for themselves the places that space could not accommodate.

The Trust's mission is to care for and protect historic places, and to encourage interest in their preservation through activities such as publishing books and information leaflets. Other Trust books are:

> From The Beginning: The Archaeology of the Maori
> The Past Today: Historic Places in New Zealand
> Historic Buildings of Northland and Auckland
> Historic Buildings of Wellington
> Historic Buildings of Canterbury
> Historic Buildings of Otago and Southland
> Canterbury Historical Guide
> South Canterbury Historical Guide
> Waikato Historical Guide

NEW ZEALAND HISTORIC PLACES TRUST

Head Office
Antrim House, 63 Boulcott Street,
Wellington (PO Box 2629)
Phone (04) 724-341

Regional Offices

Pembridge, 31 Princes Street,
Auckland
Phone (09) 378-896

Antrim House, 63 Boulcott Street,
Wellington (PO Box 2629)
Phone (04) 724-341

Cranmer Centre,
Cnr Armagh and Montreal Streets,
Christchurch (PO Box 31-070)
Phone (03) 652-897

2nd Floor, Conservation House,
77 Stuart Street,
Dunedin (PO Box 1130)
Phone (024) 770-677

CONTENTS

▶ *The volcanoes of the Central North Island in the 1860s, when the Austrian scientist Ferdinand von Hochstetter visited them.* Historic Places Trust

Page 7: By its prominence on the city's skyline, Dunedin's First Church, designed by R.A. Lawson and built in 1868-73, still proclaims Otago's origins as a Presbyterian church settlement.

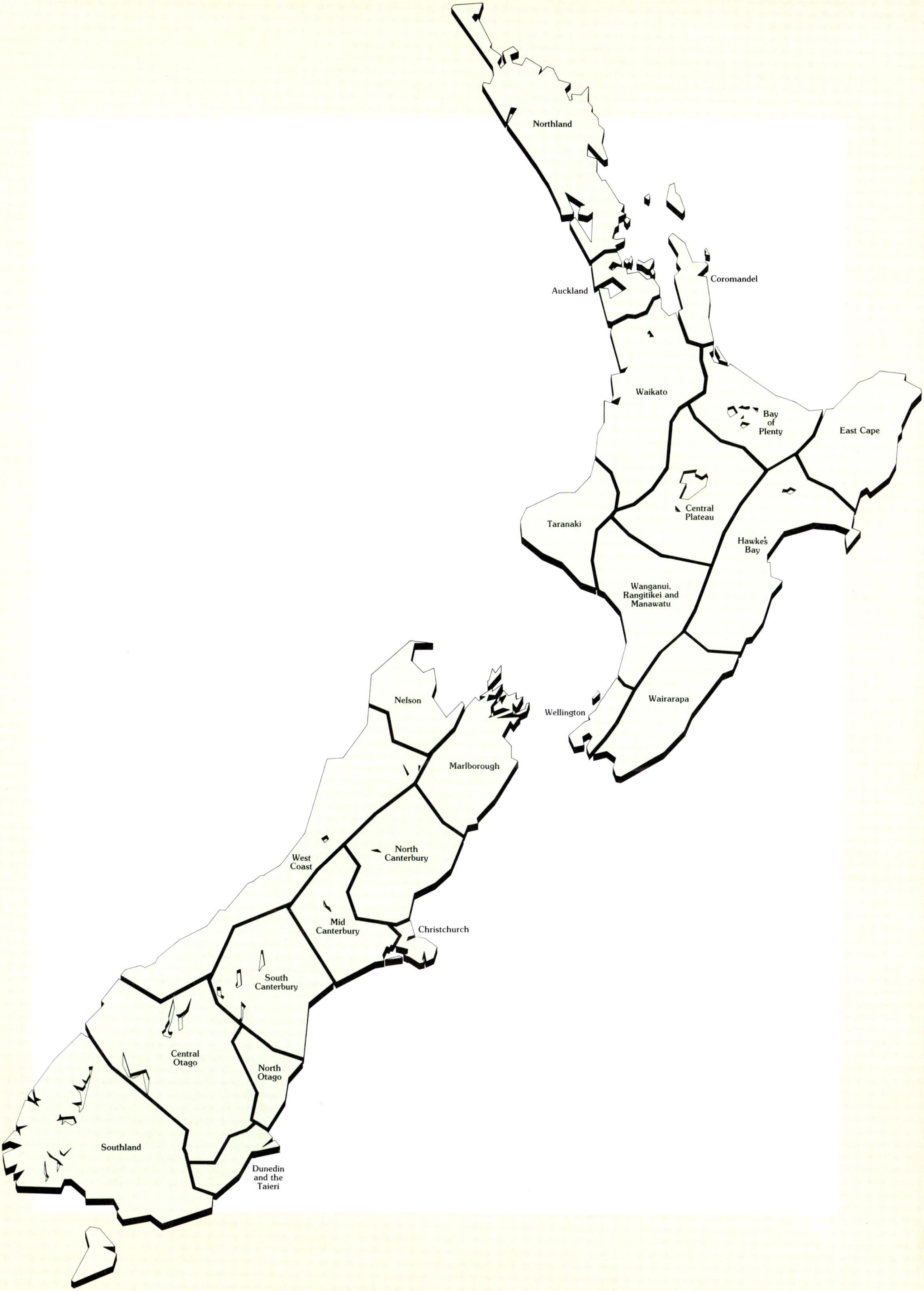

Northland

Auckland

Coromandel

Waikato

Bay
of
Plenty

East Cape

Central
Plateau

Taranaki

Hawke's
Bay

Wanganui,
Rangitikei and
Manawatu

Wellington

Wairarapa

Nelson

Marlborough

West
Coast

North
Canterbury

Christchurch

Mid
Canterbury

South
Canterbury

Central
Otago

North
Otago

Southland

Dunedin
and the
Taieri

FOREWORD

The New Zealand Historic Places Trust/Pouhere Taonga is pleased to join with the Automobile Association and Weldon Publishing in producing a new edition of this popular book about New Zealand's historic places.

I am sure that it will help build a greater understanding of the need to preserve our country's bicultural historic heritage.

The New Zealand Historic Places Trust was established by Act of Parliament in 1955 with a mission to preserve and protect heritage buildings and sites for all New Zealanders and visitors to appreciate.

As in other countries, many of our historic buildings and sites have already been lost through neglect or destruction. The task of securing long-term protection for the remaining national treasures represents an immense challenge. However, with the growing support of a large subscription-paying membership, annual grants from the Lottery Board and Government funding, the Trust's mission is an achievable one.

I am sure all readers will enjoy this book, and I hope that they take the opportunity to visit some of these magnificent and historically important places.

Geoffrey Whitehead
Director
New Zealand Historic Places Trust/Pouhere Taonga, Wellington

► *Hauling out kauri logs, Hokianga County, in the early years of this century.*
Alexander Turnbull Library

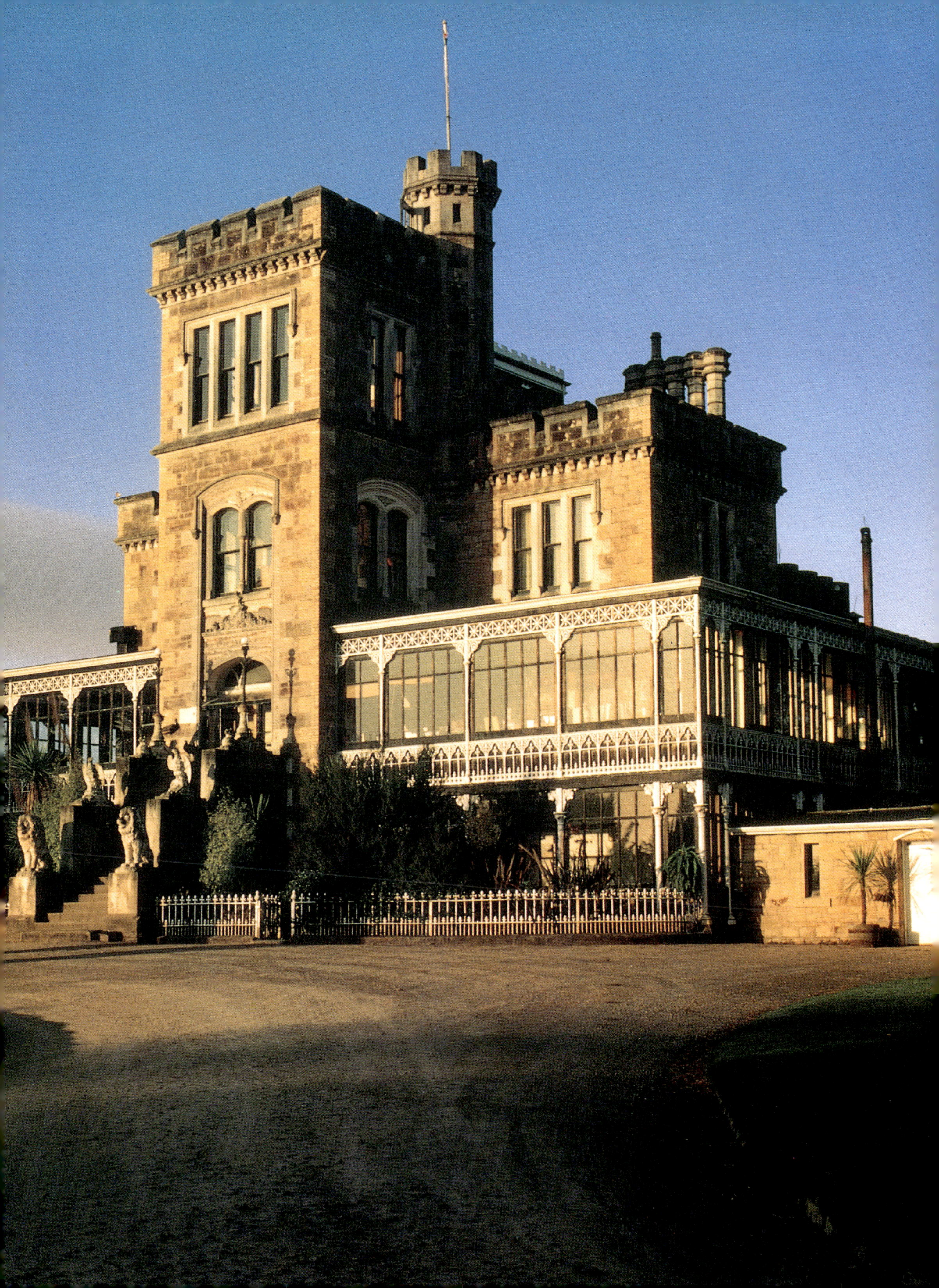

INTRODUCTION

The anniversaries of the year 1990, most importantly that of the signing of the Treaty of Waitangi in 1840, have prompted a surge of interest in New Zealand's history. More New Zealanders than ever, when travelling around their country, are conscious of its lengthening past and of the great interest of the story of human life in these islands. The reissue of this book (first published in 1984) should help focus this broadening interest in New Zealand's history on specific sites and buildings where events of the past unfolded and where the experiences of New Zealanders of past generations can be recaptured.

The following pages aim to tell readers what kinds of historic places are to be found in New Zealand and to encourage them to seek out such places. Much can be learnt about New Zealand's past by visiting its historic places. Our country has a story with many fascinating chapters, a story which all New Zealanders should know at least in broad outline. But visiting historic places is not just a serious matter of learning. It can be enjoyable as well, an interesting and sometimes exciting way of discovering our country's story. For the informed traveller, the landscape is an open history book. It is not difficult to learn how to decipher even its blurred and indistinct pages, so that one is able to 'read' the human landscape in a way that adds interest and enjoyment to journeys around New Zealand.

This book does not tell the story of New Zealand fully or systematically. Those who want to get as much as they can from their visits to the historic places mentioned are strongly urged to do some supplementary reading as well. For example, names of people important in New Zealand's history are mentioned at different points throughout the book, but there is space to give only very brief details about most of them. There are plenty of popular historical works in bookshops and libraries and leaflets have been published which provide additional detail about many historic places. The extra information to be gained will help greatly to bring historic places to life for those who visit them.

Some buildings or sites included in this book may at first glance look uninteresting. But the book's aim is to help travellers around New Zealand gain as true an understanding of our country's past as possible. It was necessary, therefore, to include some buildings or sites which may initially disappoint those who make an effort to visit them, but all have something interesting and important to tell about how New Zealand's story has unfolded.

Many of the historic places mentioned in this book will only come to life if visitors use their imaginations. This is especially true of the 'prehistoric' sites from which we can learn much about Maori life in New Zealand before the arrival of Europeans. It is not always easy to visualise people living, working — or fighting — on a site hundreds of years ago when all that can be seen today is a grassed-over ditch and bank, a faint terrace or a heap of old seashells. But it is important to make an effort of imagination to see such sites as they were when peopled by past generations. Most of the immediately interesting historic places belong to the past 150 or so years of life in New Zealand, since European settlement of the country began. Yet people were living here long before that and visiting old pa sites and similar 'prehistoric' places, however unglamorous they may seem, is a good reminder of this important fact.

▼ *The infant town of Gisborne in 1871.*
Gisborne Museum

New Zealand has been populated since at least 1000 A.D. Of the early 'archaic' or moa-hunter period of Maori culture, only faint traces remain — middens, usually heaps of discarded shells, and rock drawings in caves or under limestone overhangs, mostly in the South Island. Later, as moa became scarcer, and for other reasons only partly understood, Maori culture made a transition to its classic period during which shellfish, fish, smaller birds, fern-root and kumara grown in gardens were the main food sources. During the classic period the Maori built pa, places fortified for protection against attackers during tribal fighting. The ditches, terraces and banks of a great number of these pa remain and are the most obvious of our older historic places. Classic Maori sites are far more common in the North Island than the South — in some places like Taranaki and the Bay of Plenty the observant eye can see the remains of pa on many hills and ridges. In some places in the South Island there are pa sites of the later period.

The arrival of Europeans caused enormous changes in Maori life and as the nineteenth century advanced the Maori population declined dramatically. Inter-tribal wars became more devastating with the introduction of firearms, and diseases against which the Maori had no resistance were introduced. In the mid-nineteenth century some Maori, alarmed by these developments and the numbers of Europeans arriving in New Zealand, fought to resist the loss of their land to the European settlers and to preserve a distinct Maori identity. The sites of battles in these wars — which most historians now call the New Zealand Wars or the Land Wars — are some of the most interesting historic places in New Zealand. Armed conflict began in the 1840s with the Wairau Incident in Marlborough and the War in the North, came to a climax in the Taranaki and Waikato campaigns of the 1860s, then petered out in skirmishing in the 1870s in various parts of the North Island. With one exception — the site of the Wairau Incident — all the sites of battles and incidents in the New Zealand Wars are found in the North Island.

The efforts made by the Maori people after the wars to come to terms with defeat (although some had fought on the side of the Europeans, or remained neutral), to continue to resist the loss of their land and to retain what they could of their culture and distinctive ways of life give histori-cal significance to places like Parihaka, Maungapohutu, Ngaruawahia and Ratana, all mentioned in this book. Many historic meeting houses on Marae throughout the country also tell much about Maori history in the nineteenth and twentieth centuries.

The first Europeans to reach New Zealand were the navigators — Tasman, Cook, de Surville, du Fresne, d'Urville and others. Many monuments or plaques record where their ships came close to the New Zealand coast or where they actually landed.

After the navigators came sealers, whalers and timber and flax traders, exploiting some of the country's resources from the sea or from temporary coastal settlements. No traces remain of any of the temporary camps made by sealers from the 1790s on. But whalers, who began to establish shore stations in the 1820s, have left some lasting marks. Some present-day towns, on both islands, display trypots or whale bones from whaling days. In remote bays the remains of early shore whaling stations can still be found.

Christian missionary activity began in New Zealand with the visit of Samuel Marsden to the Bay of Islands in 1814. From

▲ New Zealand's largest concentration of Maori rock drawings, some of which date back to the days of moa hunting, is found in limestone caves and under limestone overhangs on the downlands of South Canterbury.

▲ *On Onawe Peninsula in Akaroa Harbour can be seen the remains of fortifications hastily raised by the local Maori in the early 1830s in a vain attempt to withstand attack by the North Island chief, Te Rauparaha.*

the first stations in Northland, missionaries gradually extended their activities inland and further south. The sites of some early mission stations are now marked by only a modern plaque or noticeboard or a few exotic trees; at others, buildings — mission houses or churches — have survived and these are among the most interesting, and the oldest, European buildings in New Zealand.

Other interesting early European historic places in New Zealand are associated with the discovery and exploitation of gold. The gold rushes were one of the most colourful episodes in New Zealand's history. Most goldmining sites are in Otago, on the West Coast of the South Island and on the Coromandel Peninsula. Gold was won in different ways — by washing alluvial deposits, by crushing quartz or by dredging — and goldmining sites show great variety. The story of goldmining is easy to follow by visiting historic places in the old gold rush districts.

New Zealand's story since the mid-nineteenth century is mainly one of settlement of the land, of breaking in farms from swamp and bush, and of building small towns and cities to serve the farmers and process and ship their products. The book draws attention to many buildings erected

by New Zealand's European pioneers — their houses, their farm buildings, their places of worship and their public buildings in towns and cities.

The settlers were tireless builders of churches. Some of the simple wooden structures of the earliest years have survived and are now much admired. In later decades larger churches of stone and brick, as well as wood, were built. These are now among New Zealand's most notable historic buildings.

As a farming country New Zealand has a great number of old farmhouses and farm buildings among its historic places. They include the great homesteads and wool-sheds of the pastoral age, notably in Hawke's Bay, the Wairarapa and the South Island, but also the humbler houses and cottages and farm buildings of smaller holdings established on cleared North Island bush country and on land subdivided out of the great estates. Butter, cheese and frozen meat have been the mainstays of the New Zealand farming economy and some places illustrate the history of processing these and other farm products.

This book is not concerned only with great houses or noble buildings or with places associated with famous people or important events. The humble cottage of a pioneering settler family, whose members toiled to establish and work a small farm, can tell us as much about our past as the mansion of a statesman or great landowner. In some respects, a small wooden post office built at the turn of the century in a backblocks township is as important as a historic place as Christchurch's imposing brick nineteenth century Chief Post Office.

Many different themes in New Zealand history are illuminated by the places mentioned in this book. The themes include exploration and the forging of transport and communications in a country with a rugged terrain and a long, wild coastline (light-houses, old tunnels and early viaducts); sports, entertainment and other leisure activities (sports grounds and theatres); and places of significance in New Zealand's literary and artistic life (the homes of writers and artists). We have tried not to restrict our choice of historic places to a few, conventional themes.

Included in this book are some buildings and sites which are privately owned. They were too important to leave out, but we cannot emphasise too strongly the need to approach some historic places with respect and to venture onto private property only with the permission of the owners. Maori buildings and sites in particular should be approached with respect for the customs of the Maori people. Meeting houses are not public places but belong to Maori communities, tribes or family groups and permission must be sought before they are visited. Most local Maori communities — and the owners of other historic buildings — welcome a sincere interest in their buildings. Genuine visitors should enquire at local public relations offices, museums, libraries or even the local store or hotel to make contact with the people who can give appropriate permission and guidance for a visit to a Maori meeting house, church or traditional site or to any privately owned European building.

Also included in this book are many museums and reconstructed historic villages. These are not strictly historic places, but we have included them because they provide a wealth of information about the local past of particular places. A visit to a pre-European pa site, for example, will be much more meaningful if the visitor already has knowledge about the Maori history of the area gained in a local museum. No West Coast goldmining town ever looked like Shanty Town, but a visit there can help to fire the imaginations of those who later visit abandoned, overgrown goldmining township sites.

This book merely scratches the surface. Hundreds of interesting sites and buildings have had to be omitted. Some omissions may aggrieve local people proud of a heritage which has not been included. It is hoped that this book will encourage people to search out for themselves historic places not mentioned here.

In this new edition the format and layout have been completely revised. The text, however, remains largely the same as it was in the 1984 edition although known errors have been corrected and changes in the historic places described have been noted. For example, some buildings have been demolished and others restored since the first edition was published.

The Historic Places Trust has an active publishing programme. This includes a series of regional historical guides which supplement this volume with more detailed information about the historic places of each region. The Trust also publishes an illustrated register series, which will eventu-

ally document every classified building in New Zealand, region by region.

If you would like more information about the Trust and its activities, or would like to join the organisation, please write to: The Director, New Zealand Historic Places Trust, PO Box 2629, Wellington or telephone (04) 724-341.

▲ *Canterbury Rowing Club clubhouse.*
Alexander Turnbull Library

KEY TO SYMBOLS

Homes and homesteads	⌂
Churches	⛪
Public buildings	🏛
Plaques and memorials	▲
Monuments and statuary	▮
Battle sites	✒
Redoubts	▣
Pa sites	⊓
Bridges	⌒
Ships and shipwrecks	⚓
Cemeteries and gravestones	⚱
Archaeological sites	∫
Museums	⚲
Coastal defences	◣
Maori art	☗
Farm buildings	▬
Towers and lighthouses	I
Industrial sites and buildings	⌐
Marae and meeting houses	⌂

NORTHLAND

In pre-European times Northland was the home of powerful tribes. Their traces on today's landscape range from the earthworks of fortified pa to heaps of seashells and other waste. There are also many places in Northland venerated in Maori tradition.

Captain Cook visited Northland, anchoring in the Bay of Islands in 1769; other Europeans were soon to follow. In the early nineteenth century, the region's harbours and bays attracted whalers and traders seeking flax and timber. Missionaries also arrived. Samuel Marsden preached the first Christian sermon in New Zealand on Christmas Day 1814. A year later Marsden founded the country's first mission station at now remote Rangihoua. Anglican, Wesley and Roman Catholic mission stations gradually spread across Northland. Throughout Northland are reminders of this missionary past — old buildings and plaques marking the sites of old mission stations. In the 1820s, 1830s and 1840s, increasing numbers of whalers and traders arrived and the unruly settlement of Kororareka (now Russell) flourished, to the distaste of the missionaries.

When the British Government finally felt obliged to act, to ensure British supremacy in New Zealand and to protect the Maori against unscrupulous Europeans, it was to Northland that the first British representative was sent; in Northland that the treaty with the Maori by which the British acquired sovereignty over New Zealand was signed; and in Northland that organised European government was established. Finally, in the mid-1840s, it was in Northland that Maori and European first engaged in prolonged conflict over land and the status of the two races in New Zealand.

After these stirring early years, Northland sank into relative obscurity in New Zealand history. Much of its subsequent nineteenth century history is linked with the area's resources of kauri, timber and gum, the latter providing a cash income for pioneering farmers as they established their farms.

THE FAR NORTH

At the end of the long Aupouri Peninsula is Cape Reinga, one of the best known traditional Maori sites. There, according to Maori belief, the spirits of the dead made their departure for the underworld. The lighthouse dates from only 1940–41, but it was the country's first automatic electric light. The population of the peninsula is still strongly Maori and there are a number of old buildings with Maori associations, among them the Ratana churches at Te Kao and Te Hapua.

At Houhora Heads, the Wagener Museum illuminates the history of the area. The old Houhora hotel and the recently restored Subritzky homestead, dating from the 1850s, add to the historical interest of a visit to Houhora. On the north side of the Houhora Heads, below Mt Camel, is an important archaic Maori archaeological site from which much has been learned about the diet of New Zealand's first Polynesians. On Ninety Mile Beach, in the sand dunes behind the beach, are large heaps of shells

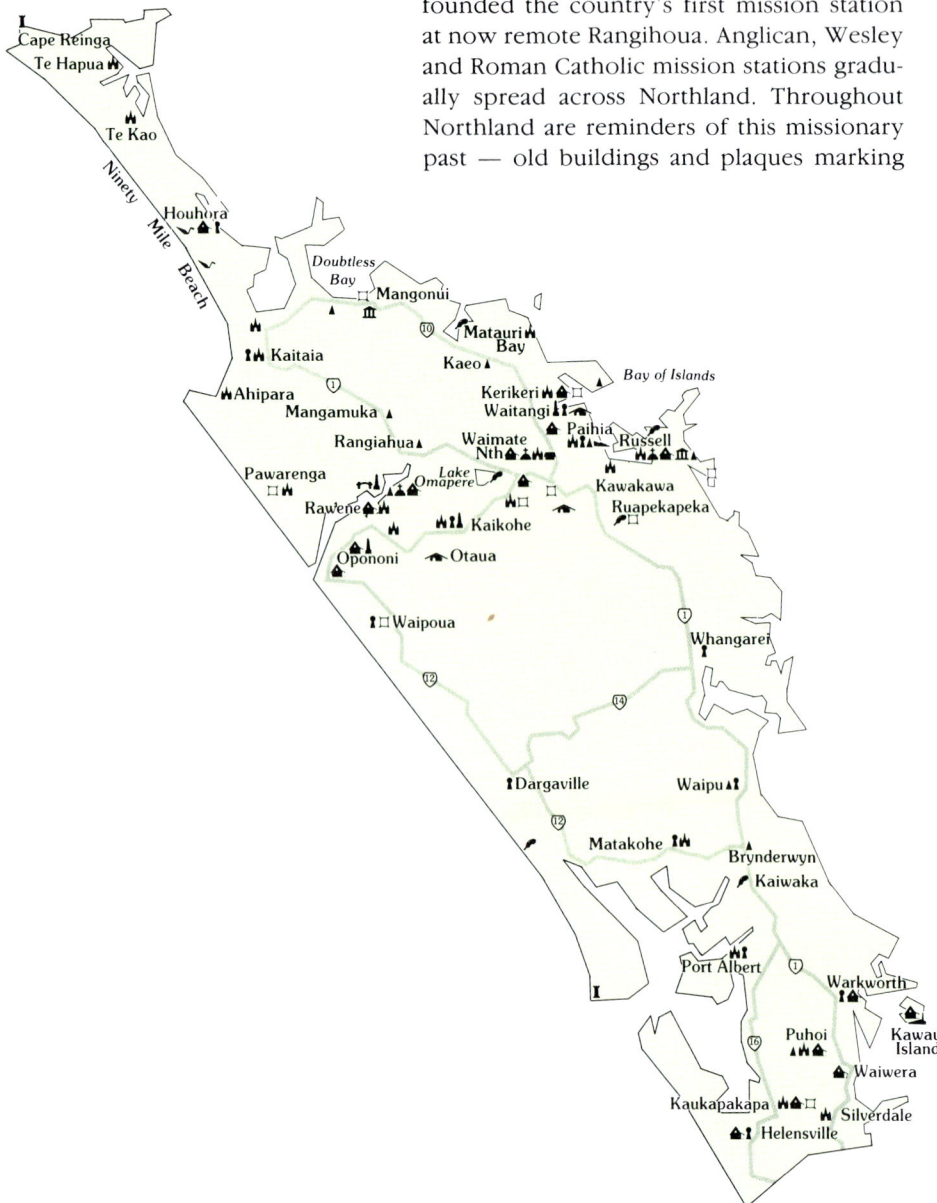

resulting from the gathering and drying of shellfish in earlier centuries.

A mission station was established in Kaitaia in 1834, on the site of which St Saviour's Church (1887) stood until it was destroyed by fire in 1985. There remain on the site old graves, including those of the missionaries who founded the station and of the local chief who afforded them protection. Other early churches close to Kaitaia are St Joseph's at Awanui (1887), St Clement's at Ahipara (1872) and one at Oturu (1867).

Late in the nineteenth century most of Kaitaia's inhabitants had some connection with gum-digging. Reminders of the gum-digging days can be seen at the Gumfields Historic Reserve near Kaingaroa, at the Far North Regional Museum at Kaitaia, and at the headquarters of the Aupouri Forest.

The legendary navigator, Kupe, is reputed to have made his first landfall at Taipa, Doubtless Bay, and a memorial by the river bridge marks his traditional landing place. It was in Doubtless Bay that the French navigator J.F.M. de Surville anchored in December 1769. He had sighted the New Zealand coast south of the Hokianga early in December, just two months after Cook had made his first landfall, but because of a storm de Surville and Cook remained unaware of each other's presence in New Zealand waters. A plaque on the headland at Patia Point records de Surville's visit. There are also several old pa on this headland. In the charming waterfront town of Mangonui is an 1892 courthouse which has been carefully restored.

Whangaroa Harbour was, in 1809, the scene of the burning of the British ship the *Boyd*, following an incident in which sailors were killed, apparently in retaliation for mistreating a Maori on board. The main activities at Whangaroa in the nineteenth century were timber-milling, shipbuilding, farming and copper-mining. Lane and Brown's shipbuilding yard at Totara North provides an interesting link with one of these early activities. Kaeo has historic links with the Wesleyan missionaries, and at Matauri Bay, the Samuel Marsden Memorial Church recalls Marsden's first visit to New Zealand in 1814 when he helped to prevent a clash between the local Maori and natives from the Bay of Islands.

THE BAY OF ISLANDS

The Bay of Islands has many historic places associated with the early days of European New Zealand. It also has a long Maori past which began, according to Maori tradition, when Kupe visited the bay. In succeeding centuries the Bay of Islands became an important centre of Maori population and the earthworks of many pa remain on coastal sites. At Whangaruru North, on Bland Bay, just south of the Bay of Islands, some fine earthworks of an early Maori pa, Whakaturia, can be seen.

► *Pompallier House, Russell, was built of rammed earth in 1841-42 to house the printing press of the Roman Catholic Mission. Later a tannery and then a private house, it is now preserved by the Historic Places Trust. Though it bears the name of the head of the French Mission, Bishop Pompallier never actually lived there.*
Wally Bowater

The bay was named by Captain Cook, who anchored off the island Motuarohia in 1769. His anchorage is marked by a plaque set in a rock in the cove in which he anchored. In the middle of 1772 the French navigator Marion du Fresne, in command of two ships, was killed in the Bay of Islands along with many of his men, possibly in reprisal for an unwitting violation of a tapu. The site of the killings can be visited (by foot from Manawaora Bay) at Te Hue Bay, on the Orokawa Peninsula.

At Oihi, near Rangihoua, a cross on the foreshore commemorates the first visit to New Zealand of Samuel Marsden. It can be seen on launch trips but can be reached overland only on foot. The headland pa above the beach which was occupied at the time of Marsden's visit is still discernible.

RUSSELL

In the 1830s Kororareka, as Russell was then known, emerged as New Zealand's first town. Frequented by whalers and traders, it gained a reputation as a wild place, but by 1839 it had acquired enough respectability for Bishop Pompallier to move his Roman Catholic mission there from the Hokianga. In the 1840s, it was at Kororareka that Hone Heke repeatedly cut down the British flagpole. In March 1845 the town was sacked by the Maori, although some buildings survived.

Peaceful Russell today belies its rowdy European beginnings, but a number of historic buildings remain from those early days. Christ Church, New Zealand's oldest surviving church, was built in 1835 and although altered in later years remains largely intact. Among the memorials in the churchyard is one to Tamati Waka Nene, a Maori chief who played a key role in early Maori-Pakeha relations in Northland. Some of the men who fell when the town was sacked in 1845 are buried there. Another building which survived the sacking of the town is Pompallier House, although Bishop Pompallier never lived in it. It was built of rammed earth in 1841–42 to house the printery of his mission. After Pompallier moved to Auckland the building served as a tannery before being converted, in the 1870s, to a dwelling. It was first acquired by the Government and restored in the 1940s before passing in 1967 to the Historic Places Trust. The printing press, which first came to New Zealand for use by the mission in

▲ Gilbert Mair, a former ship's carpenter, built the original Kororareka chapel in 1835. Extensively altered in 1871, it still stands as Christ Church, Russell, New Zealand's oldest surviving church building.

1841, was used in the Waikato by the Maori King Movement between 1891 and 1933.

Next door to Pompallier House is Clendon Cottage, built in 1852 by trader James Clendon who also built Clendon House at Rawene.

The former customhouse was designed by the Colonial Architect, W.H. Clayton, who was responsible for many early public buildings up and down the country. It was built in 1870 and is now the town's police station. The Duke of Marlborough hotel, another old building, still holds the country's first licence.

South-east of Russell, at Tikitikiore, is the site of a manganese mine worked from the 1870s into the 1890s. Miners' cottages are among the old homes which give Russell its historic character. The headquarters of the Bay of Islands Historic and Maritime Park, in Russell, provides information about many historic places in the area.

When Captain Hobson was setting up his government in New Zealand after the signing of the Treaty of Waitangi, he settled first on a site at Okiato, across the narrows from modern Opua, for his capital. He purchased land and gave it the name 'Russell' before deciding that his capital would be better located at Auckland. The name Russell was later transferred to Kororareka. Today Okiato enjoys permanent protection as a historic reserve.

WAITANGI

An event which occurred at Waitangi on 6 February 1840 is regarded by most New Zealanders as marking the birth of their nation. In 1833 the British Government, reluctant to assume full responsibility for New Zealand but increasingly concerned about lawlessness in the Bay of Islands, sent out a Resident, James Busby, who, lacking support from his superiors, served ineffectually as a 'man of war without guns'. His replacement William Hobson, sent out to become Governor of the new colony, arrived in the Bay of Islands on 29 January 1840. Within a week he had assembled a large number of Maori chiefs who were persuaded by the missionaries to sign a treaty under which they ceded sovereignty over New Zealand to Queen Victoria, receiving in return British citizenship and certain rights. The ceremony on 6 February was the first of many treaty-signing ceremonies as copies of the treaty were taken by Hobson's agents up and down the country so that chiefs not present at Waitangi on 6 February could also sign it. Many did, but some refused. Controversy still surrounds the Treaty of Waitangi. Some New Zealanders see the Treaty as a document whose promises to the Maori have been broken or ignored. To others the Treaty remains the sound foundation of New Zealand nationhood. Whatever interpretation is put on the

Treaty, 6 February 1840 was an important day in New Zealand's history and Waitangi is a key historic place.

The original part of the Treaty House is older than the Treaty. It was prefabricated in Sydney and sent out to New Zealand to be erected in 1833–34 for James Busby. In 1934 the then Governor-General Lord Bledisloe gave the Treaty House to the people of New Zealand. It has been restored and is open to the public. A kauri flagpole in front of the house marks the point to which it is thought the chiefs came forward to sign. Near the Treaty House is a carved meeting house and a canoe, Ngatokimata-whaorua, both built for the 1940 Centennial. Across from the Treaty House is the Te Tii Marae, where the chiefs camped on the night of 5 February 1840. A monument erected on the marae in 1880 has the articles of the Treaty engraved in stone. The present meeting house on the marae, Tiriti o Waitangi, was erected in 1918 to replace an earlier one.

PAIHIA

Paihia was the site of the third Church Missionary Society mission station, founded in 1823 by Henry Williams. The Church of St Paul was built in 1925 as a memorial to the Williams brothers, Henry and William, and is the fourth church to stand on the site. Several plaques and markers along the foreshore recall the early days of the Paihia mission. One marks the site of the launching of the mission vessel the *Herald* in 1826, and others identify where houses built for the Williams brothers once stood. It was at Paihia that William Colenso, in 1835, established a mission press, the site also marked by a plaque. Paihia has a museum of shipwrecks situated on board a fully rigged, three-masted barque, the *Tui*, where relics from many New Zealand shipwrecks are on display.

KERIKERI

The Kerikeri basin is one of New Zealand's outstanding historic places. After founding the country's first mission station at Rangihoua, Marsden decided to establish a second station in New Zealand. On his second visit he chose Kerikeri as the site for this station, in part because it was an important centre of Maori population. Kororipo, a pa of the Ngapuhi fighting chief Hongi Hika, was close to the chosen site. Today Kororipo is a reserve with notice-boards which explain the significance of the site. What give Kerikeri a special position among New Zealand's historic places are the Kemp House and the Stone Store, New Zealand's oldest surviving wooden and stone buildings respectively. The Kemp House was built in 1821–22, for the Rev. John Gare Butler who arrived in August 1819 to take charge of the new station.

◀ *New Zealand's oldest surviving building, Kemp House, Kerikeri, was built as a missionary's residence in 1821-22. In 1974 it was given to the Historic Places Trust by the Kemp family, members of which had lived in the house since 1833.* Wally Bowater

▲ *The sturdy Stone Store at Kerikeri was built in the 1830s as a storehouse for the mission station there. It is New Zealand's oldest surviving stone building.* Wally Bowater

More distant, towards Kerikeri Inlet from the basin, are the Edmonds ruins — the remains of the stone house of an early settler family. (The ruins are not easy to find.)

KAWAKAWA AND KAIKOHE

Inland from the Bay of Islands is a group of prominent volcanic cones, most of which were modified for use as pa by the Maori. Terraces can still be seen on many of them. One of the more prominent terraced pa sites in this area is at Pouerua, 15 km west of Kawakawa close to State Highway 1.

Puketona has a very early house, the Choat House, built by E.M. Williams and possibly once occupied by the first British resident in New Zealand, James Busby. At Pakaraka, on State Highway 1, is another Williams house, The Retreat, built for Henry Williams. Holy Trinity Church, Pakaraka, was built in 1851; Henry Williams and his wife Marianne are buried in the churchyard. The carved meeting house Tumatauenga at Otiria just west of Kawakawa is a modern building (1964), a memorial to the dead of World Wars I and II, significant in terms of the recent renaissance of Maori art, crafts and culture.

The Porowini Marae on which the house stands is much older. The Porowini hall, nearby, is of greater interest than its humble appearance might suggest. It was built in 1874, at Taumarere. Shifted to Otiria, it served as a hospital during the 1918 flu epidemic, and was then used by the Maori leader Sir Apirana Ngata as an office from which to administer his land development scheme for the North. At Taumarere is an 1870s church, resited here from Paihia.

Kaikohe has a historic church, the Aperahama Church, opened in 1885. The Hone Heke monument, erected in 1911 on Kaikohe Hill, commemorates not the fighting chief famous for cutting down the flagpole but his great-nephew of the same name. Kaikohe lacks the historic associations of other towns or townships in Northland but has the Kaikohe Pioneer Village, a museum collection of relocated and restored old buildings. They include the Waimate District runanga house and courthouse, a cottage, sawmill, jail and blacksmith's shop. On the marae at Otaua, southwest of Kaikohe, a restored 17 metre long Ngapuhi canoe, built in 1940 for the centennial celebrations, is on permanent display.

James Kemp, the mission blacksmith, and his wife moved into the house in 1833, and it remained in the hands of their descendants until 1974, when it passed to the Historic Places Trust. In 1981 the house was damaged by floodwaters and the opportunity was taken to restore the grounds and downstairs to the more spartan, austere appearance of the early missionary period. Upstairs the house still has the more comfortable feel of a Victorian family home. The Stone Store was built between 1832 and 1836 as a mission storehouse. Like the Kemp House, it eventually passed from the missionary society to the Kemp family. It served as a shop for many years and is now owned, like the house, by the Historic Places Trust.

On a rise above the Kemp House and Stone Store stands St James Church (1878).

THE WAR IN THE NORTH

In the mid-1840s, the Bay of Islands saw the first major clash of arms between Maori and Pakeha. This 'War in the North' is sometimes known as Hone Heke's War after one of the leading Maori antagonists. Some of the discontent of Hone Heke, Kawiti and other Maori who fought against the British stemmed from the decline of the Bay of Islands as trade went south to Auckland, the new capital. But there was also alarm at the loss of tribal lands and fear about the future place of the Maori in New Zealand.

At Russell, there is a memorial on Flagstaff Hill commemorating Hone Heke's repeated cutting down of the original flagstaff and the sacking of the township in 1845. The British campaign to subdue Hone Heke after the sacking of Kororareka took the war inland. The site of the first engagement, a pa on the shores of Lake Omapere, is alongside State Highway 1 about 5 km north-west of present-day Ohaeawai. A few weeks later another bloody battle was fought at Ngawha (Battle of Ohaeawai) where the Maori had converted a pa into an impregnable fort. The British attack was repulsed with heavy losses, but the Maori subsequently abandoned the pa. St Michael's Church, Ngawha, was built in 1871 as a memorial to British servicemen killed in the engagement. The metre high scoria wall which surrounds the church stands on the line of the outer fortifications.

After the Battle of Ohaeawai the Maori retreated to Kawiti's pa, Ruapekapeka (the Bat's Nest), south of Kawakawa. This pa was attacked by the British in January 1846 and captured on a Sunday when the Maori had assumed there would be a lull in the fighting. At Ruapekapeka, now a historic reserve, the lines of the fortifications can still be traced and a cannon is a stark reminder of the bombardment inflicted on the pa. The remains of another pa can be seen across the Kawakawa River from Opua.

WAIMATE NORTH

The Waimate North mission house is the only survivor of three built in 1831–32 by Maori carpenters under missionary supervision and using local materials. The first inland mission station, Waimate North was the site of New Zealand's first European

▼ *Maori and European vessels on the waters of the Bay of Islands off Kororareka (Russell) in 1849.*
Alexander Turnbull Library

▲ *The Mission House at Waimate North was built in 1831-32 by Maori carpenters working under missionary supervision. It was restored to its original appearance by the Historic Places Trust in the 1950s and is furnished in period.*
Wally Bowater

▶ *Surrounded by noble oak trees and graves older than the church itself, St John's Church at Waimate North was built in 1871, the third church on its site.*

farm. Between 1842 and 1844 the mission house served as Bishop Selwyn's 'palace' before reverting to a mission house, then a vicarage. In 1956 the house was taken over by the Historic Places Trust, restored to its original design and opened to the public. Its furnishings and displays recall the early days of the mission and the Selwyns' brief occupancy of the house. An archaeological walk with descriptive plaques crosses the central part of the mission settlement.

The Church of St John the Baptist, close by the mission house, was built in 1871 using timber from an earlier, 1839, church. In the churchyard are graves of the men killed in the 1845 war and of early missionary families. The Sunday School building dates from the 1880s. Also nearby are other signs of early mission occupation. Most of these are on private property but the country's oldest oak tree, replanted at Waimate in 1831, can be seen from the road. The site of the Bedggood farm buildings also dates from the mission period. The

blacksmith's shop, one of the Bedggood farm buildings, has been restored and on-site interpretation provided.

THE HOKIANGA

On the other side of Northland from the Bay of Islands is the sinuous waterway of the Hokianga Harbour. It has sites of importance in Maori tradition and history and a European history almost as long as that of the Bay of Islands.

The Hokianga was by tradition the point from which Kupe departed after exploring the New Zealand coast. There is a memorial to Kupe by the meeting house at Mangamuka. Kupe's landing spot is at Whanui on the North Head.

The Hokianga's European history began about 1820 when ships began calling to pick up kauri timber and later gum. Timber remained important to the Hokianga for many years, and many Hokianga towns were originally sawmilling settlements. But

there are few reminders left of the early days of trading or sawmilling. The Hokianga was also the scene of two early, ill-fated attempts at colonisation, one by the first New Zealand Company, led by Captain Herd, in 1827 and the second by the eccentric Frenchman Baron de Thierry in 1837. At Rangiahua, at the head of the Hokianga, a roadside plaque stands near the site of Baron de Thierry's house. The Hokianga was also an early mission field.

Horeke's most interesting historic building is the old Methodist mission house at nearby Mangungu, now owned by the Historic Places Trust. The Wesleyan Missionary Society established their second New Zealand station at Mangungu in 1828. Today's mission house was built in 1838–39, after an earlier house had burned down. On 12 February 1840, the lawn in front of the house was the scene of the second major gathering for the signing of the Treaty of Waitangi. In front of the house is a memorial cross to the early missionaries, erected at the time of the mission centenary, and also a historic cemetery. Horeke was the site of one of New Zealand's earliest shipyards and a plaque commemorates the building and launching of several vessels between 1827 and 1830.

Rawene was where Captain Herd, in 1827, purchased land for the first New Zealand Company settlement. Although the settlement was never started, the place was known for many years as Herd's Point. At Rawene is another house, probably dating from 1866–69, built for James Clendon, a British trader and official. Clendon's second wife, Jane Cochrane, lived until 1919 and the house, now owned by the Historic Places Trust, contains many items connected with the long residence of the family. Rawene's other interesting buildings include the Cochrane homestead, Hardimans Hotel, the Rawene Hotel and the Methodist church. Across the water from Rawene can be seen, in the settlement of Motukaraka, the superbly sited Church of the Assumption, which opened in 1910.

At Kohukohu is the remnant of a small bridge built of Sydney sandstone which may be the country's oldest surviving bridge, though its date of construction is uncertain.

North of the Hokianga, on Whangape Harbour is St Gabriel's, Pawarenga, one of Northland's many interesting Maori

churches. It was built in 1899 on the site of Makora Pa.

On the south side of the Hokianga Harbour, Omanaia has an 1884 Methodist church, where the unique carved headboards of the Hokianga can be seen in the graveyard. 'Opo' the dolphin who brought fame and fun to Opononi, is remembered in a foreshore statue. The Webster home, dating from about 1870, is an impressive survivor from the early days. In its grounds are two cannon from a ship wrecked on the Hokianga bar in 1856. At nearby Omapere is another old house, known as Captain Martin's. From Omapere, a walk along the beach leads to the South Head where there is an old signal station, surviving from the days when trading vessels plied the Hokianga.

Between the Hokianga and Dargaville stand the remaining forests of kauri, giving visitors an idea of what the Northland landscape looked like before most of the kauri was milled. At the Waipoua Forest headquarters, in the Maxwell Cottage, are displays illustrating the lives of kauri bushmen. In the lower Waipoua Valley are the remains

▲ *The Mangungu Mission House was built for the Methodist Mission on the Hokianga in 1838-39. The house was shifted to Onehunga in 1855 and did not return to Mangungu until 1972.*

of many pa and evidence of Maori gardening. In the same area the Waoku Walkway, reached south of Waima on State Highway 12, follows the line of an old coach road. The stone culverts and 'flushings' or fords illustrate how early roads were formed.

THE KAIPARA

The vast Kaipara Harbour stretches from Dargaville in the north to Helensville in the

south and, like the Hokianga, its waters were once busy with coastal vessels. Some of the Kaipara's historic places are connected with the kauri timber and gum trades; others were the scenes of early special settlements.

Dargaville began its life as a kauri timber port, founded in 1872. The Northern Wairoa Maori, Maritime and Pioneer Museum in Dargaville has displays covering ancient Maori life, Kaipara Harbour shipping and shipwrecks, and the gum industry. The museum is housed partly in a brick stable built in 1874.

On the coast north of Dargaville a plaque at Moremonui marks the site of a battle fought in 1807 between the Ngapuhi and the Ngati Whatua, thought to be the first in which the Maori used muskets. Access to the beach can be gained through Baylys Beach and Chase Gorge.

South of Dargaville, on the North Head of the Kaipara Harbour, is a reminder of the Kaipara's earlier importance as a timber exporting port. This is the North Kaipara Head lighthouse at Pouto Point, built of kauri in 1884 to make the crossing of the hazardous Kaipara bar safer. As shipping on the Kaipara declined, the need for the light diminished and it was finally extinguished in 1952. The lighthouse can be reached only on foot, a 6 km walk from the road end at Pouto.

In many of the small towns around the northern end of the Kaipara Harbour are reminders of the early days of kauri timber trading and pioneer farming. In Matakohe, the Otamatea Kauri and Pioneer Museum has displays which help visitors understand the kauri timber and gum industries and their place in Northland's history. A church in Matakohe and a memorial at Brynderwyn commemorate J.G. Coates (1878–1943), New Zealand's first native-born Prime Minister. He is buried in Matakohe. At Hukatere, south of Matakohe, is an old church, St Michael's on the Hill, built in 1861.

TOWARDS AUCKLAND

South of Whangarei, Waipu was the scene of one of New Zealand's better known special settlements. The stern Norman McLeod led a party of Scottish and Nova Scotian farmers to Waipu in 1853 to found a strict, self-contained community. The Pioneer Memorial Museum at Waipu contains relics of those days as well as artefacts of the earlier Maori occupants of the area. There is a monument to the early settlers in the town's main street and stained glass windows, memorials to McLeod, in a nearby church. Kauri was milled in the district and in the Mangawhai–Brynderwyn area there are remnants of bush-driving dams in the hills, but these are not easy to find and seldom impressive.

A few kilometres east of Kaiwaka is a marker indicating the site of a battle, Te Ika-a-Ranganui, fought in 1825, at which the Ngapuhi, using guns, decimated the Ngati Whatua, breaking their hold of the lower parts of Northland. Port Albert, like Waipu, traces its history back to a special settlement, planned from Birmingham in 1861, but the Albertland settlement never flourished. On a side road at Wharehine, a few kilometres south of Port Albert, is the tiny Minniesdale Chapel (1867) in a lonely setting. It can be seen from the road.

Another township with a distinctive past as a special settlement is Puhoi, founded by German-speaking Bohemians in 1863. Bohemian dances and other customs remain part of local tradition. A wayside shrine, unusual for New Zealand, is a memorial to the early settlers, and stands on the outskirts of the village. Puhoi has a lovely century-old church, the Church of St Peter and St Paul (1881), and a handsome two-storeyed colonial hotel. Just south of Puhoi at Waiwera, the homestead at the Wenderholm Reserve dates from the 1850s and is now open to the public.

On nearby Kawau Island is one of New Zealand's most historic houses, notable for its association with a formative figure in New Zealand history, Sir George Grey. The Mansion House was built in the 1840s for the manager of an early copper mine but from 1865 on it was greatly altered by the new owner. Grey, who bought the property in 1862 at the start of his second term as Governor, made it his home until 1888. Mansion House has been restored and is open as a house museum.

Also on Kawau Island are the remains of the short-lived copper mine; the copper ore was discovered in 1844 and mining ceased around 1851. There is a beautifully sited pumphouse and the remains of the old smelting house. The mine was one of New Zealand's earliest industrial enterprises.

At Warkworth there are the ruins of a cement works built in 1884, a pleasing courthouse, a typical Masonic Hall and a picturesque verandahed hotel.

On Highway 16, north of Kaukapakapa, the Omiru Reserve includes well preserved kumara storage pits and a summit platform. At Kaukapakapa are St Cuthbert's Church and Henley House. Warkworth has a district museum, and Helensville has a museum (located in a 1910 house), an historic courthouse and many fine wooden villas. Silverdale has a Pioneer Village.

▶▶ *Twice New Zealand's Governor and later its Premier, Sir George Grey is a dominant figure in New Zealand's nineteenth century history. His home on Kawau Island from 1862 to 1888, Mansion House, began life in the 1840s as the home of the manager of the short-lived copper mine on the island. Today, beautifully restored, it is a museum of Grey's life and colonial times.*
Kris Pfeiffer

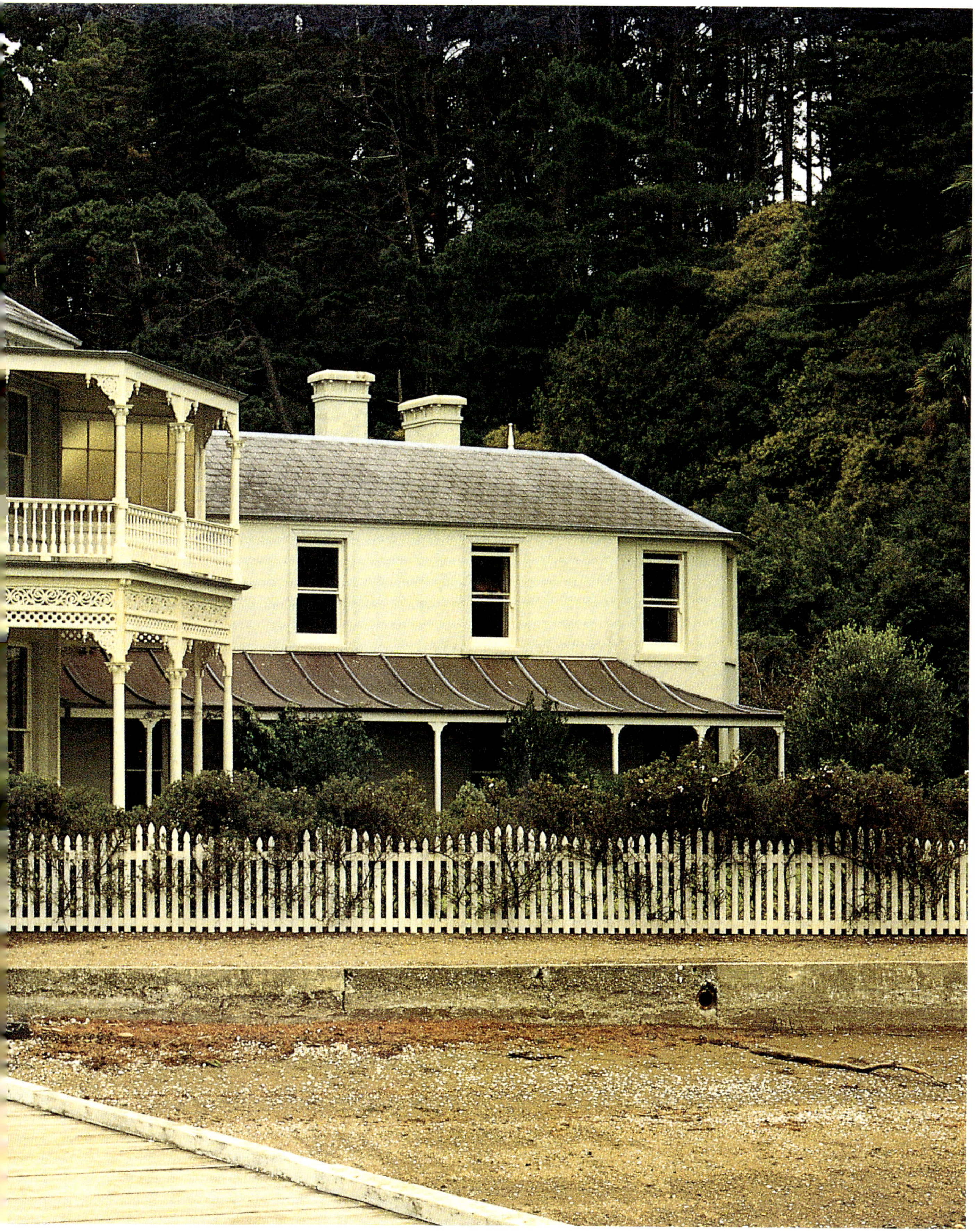

AUCKLAND

When Lieutenant-Governor Hobson chose the isthmus between the Waitemata and Manukau Harbours as the site of his new capital, he settled on a place long favoured by the Maori. The Maori name for the isthmus was Tamaki-makau-rau, which means 'Tamaki of a thousand lovers'. The area had good soils for growing kumara and easy access to food resources, and was at the hub of an extensive network of waterways. The volcanic cones provided secure places to dwell. Fashioning of forts on these cones began more than 500 years ago when prodigious earthworks formed terraces for defences and living space; some cones also had defensive ditches and banks. These man-modified cones are Auckland's most extraordinary legacy from the past. Nowhere else in the world are there so many well preserved stone-age sites in the midst of a modern city.

More remains of a pre-European Maori Auckland than of early European Auckland. After being persuaded by the Ngati Whatua to site his capital on the isthmus, Hobson founded the new town where downtown Auckland is today. Immigrant ships began to arrive in 1842.

In its early years Auckland was fed largely by Maori farmers who cultivated land in the Kaipara, Thames and Waikato districts. Auckland remained the capital only until 1865 when Wellington succeeded it. The loss of the institutions of government and the withdrawal of Imperial troops at about the same time were a setback; but Auckland was soon forging ahead, though not without further setbacks, on the basis of Coromandel and Thames gold and kauri timber. A number of old buildings have survived from the 1860s, 1870s and 1880s when Auckland began its climb to first place among New Zealand cities as a business and industrial centre.

EARLY AUCKLAND

Most of early European Auckland has been swept away by later development, including some original natural features. A plaque near the entrance to Bledisloe Wharf marks the position of Point Britomart where the British flag was raised on 18 September 1840 to mark the purchase of the site from the Ngati Whatua. William Hobson, New Zealand's first governor, who concluded the Treaty of Waitangi with the Maori and moved the colony's capital to Auckland, died in 1842. He is buried in the Symonds Street Cemetery. His grave can be visited at the western end of Grafton Bridge. Buried in the same cemetery is a colourful figure in New Zealand history — Baron Charles de Thierry. Another early cemetery can be found at Mt Victoria, Devonport. Buried in this cemetery is Eruera Maihi Patuone, the 'peacemaker', a leading Ngapuhi chief who was favourably disposed to the arrival of the Europeans and who, while living on the North Shore, helped by his mana to protect the city. When he died in 1872 the Government erected a monument in his memory.

For the first quarter-century of its existence Auckland was thought to be vulnerable to Maori attack and steps were taken to defend the city. In the late 1840s and early 1850s about 9.2 ha of land were enclosed by a stone wall. Within the wall were built the Albert Barracks, to accommodate upward of 1000 men. The barracks were

▲ *The Albert Barracks, Auckland, in the 1860s.* Alexander Turnbull Library

demolished in 1871 and Albert Park laid out on part of the land. The park's fountain and park keeper's cottage date from 1882, a flag-staff from 1894, the statue of Queen Victoria from 1899 and the Boer War Memorial from 1902. Older than any of these is the small section of the original barracks walls (about 50 metres) which still stands in the grounds of the University of Auckland.

Two statues in Auckland provide links with the city's early days, although one, that of Lord Auckland in Aotea Square, is a recent arrival. It was a gift to the city from Calcutta when the government of West Bengal was disposing of its colonial relics, including statues of former British governors. Hobson named the city after Lord Auckland in 1841. The other statue, in Albert Part, is that of Sir George Grey, who first came to Auckland as Governor in 1845.

On the slopes of One Tree Hill, in Cornwall Park, is one of Auckland's few very early buildings. Acacia Cottage was built in 1841 by John Logan Campbell and his partner William Brown. It first stood in O'Connell Street but was moved in 1920 to its present position opposite the kiosk.

THE VOLCANIC CONES

Two of the most impressive of Auckland's historic places are Mt Eden and One Tree Hill. On Mt Eden (Maungawhau) can be seen well preserved Maori earthworks. The pa was occupied possibly from as early as the twelfth century, and appears to have been abandoned in the seventeenth century after a battle. One Tree Hill (Maungakiekie) was the largest of Auckland's prehistoric Maori settlements. The hill was occupied before 1400; by the late 1600s it was the home of many hundreds of people. After the local Maori were defeated about 1730, the pa was abandoned. In later years an obelisk was built on One Tree Hill, in accordance with the wishes of a notable early Aucklander, John Logan Campbell, to show his respect for the Maori race. It is appropriate that it should stand where the impact of the Maori on New Zealand's landscape is so obvious. Earthworks are also visible on several other of Auckland's cones and on Browns Islands in the Hauraki Gulf. On Motutapu Island are sites, of interest to archaeologists, which were occupied before the eruptions which formed Rangitoto Island about 800 years ago. An important Maori traditional site is on the North Shore in the Devonport Reserve. A memorial marks the site of the landing place of the *Tainui* canoe, one of the traditional canoes which brought the Maori from the Homeland, Hawaiki. On the memorial is a replica of the carved stone bird, korotangi, which came on the *Tainui* and is now in the National Museum, Wellington.

▲ *Terraced Mount Eden from near Newmarket, about 1866.* Auckland Institute and Museum

OLD HOUSES

Two of Auckland's grander older homes have been opened to the public by the Historic Places Trust. Alberton, on Kerr Taylor Avenue, just off Mt Albert Road, was the family home of Allan Kerr Taylor, a young settler who arrived in New Zealand in 1849 and prospered from farming and timbermilling. The house was begun in 1863 but grew substantially through the years, notably in the 1870s when the exotic towers and balconies were added to the original, simpler farmhouse. The house has been restored and today shows how a prosperous land-owning family lived in nineteenth century Auckland.

Highwic, at 40 Gillies Avenue, is the home *par excellence* of a colonial gentleman of property. Alfred Buckland, the owner of a stock and station firm with interests in land and shipping, bought the property in 1862 and began building the grand house which became today's Highwic. Added to over the years, Highwic is New Zealand's best example of a large house in the Early English Gothic style. The house was acquired by the Auckland City Council and Historic Places Trust in 1978 and has been opened to the public, refurnished in a style appropriate to the days when it was a social centre for Auckland's 'upper crust'.

Other large houses of earlier times remain in private hands and can be seen from the street. The Pah, Hillsborough Road, built in imposing Italianate style as a private home in 1877–79, is now a Christian living centre for the temporarily homeless. Two streets of houses have remained reasonably intact since the nineteenth century. On Princes Street are grand townhouses built in the 1870s and 1880s. Renall Street, Ponsonby, is at the other end of the social scale. There, a number of old houses, the homes of artisans and working-class families, make a picturesque and historically interesting sight.

PARNELL

The inner suburb of Parnell contains a number of historic buildings, including early houses. Hulme Court, built of stone in 1843, has a Regency look which is not common in New Zealand. A little younger than Acacia Cottage, it is the city's oldest house still standing on its original site. Hulme Court is privately owned, it can be seen from the street.

Two old houses which may be visited are near neighbours on Ayr Street. Ewelme Cottage was built in 1863–64 as the Auckland home of the family of Archdeacon Vicesimus Lush. It was altered in 1882, when Mrs Lush made Ewelme her permanent home after her husband died, but has remained largely unchanged since then. One of Auckland's most charming early houses, Ewelme is a Historic Places Trust property and contains a fascinating collection of colonial furniture and household effects. Nearby, Kinder House is a two-storeyed stone building built in 1856, the home of pioneer churchman and artist John Kinder. It is open to the public and displays the work of the artist.

Many old houses on Parnell Road have been transformed into shops and boutiques. The historical purist might object, but the old buildings might not have survived but for this imaginative use of them. Other old houses in Parnell include the Old Deanery and Selwyn Court, built by Frederick Thatcher for Bishop Selwyn in the 1860s on St Stephen's Avenue, and stone houses at 330 Parnell Road and on Falcon Street.

On the edge of Parnell, St Stephen's Chapel stands on a small knoll overlooking Judges Bay. Built of kauri in 1857, the

▲ *Alberton, long the home of the prosperous Kerr Taylor family, was a simple colonial farmhouse until the 1870s, when the addition of towers, verandahs and balconies gave it a romantic, exotic air.*

▶ *A pioneer clergyman and his family lived in Parnell's Ewelme Cottage, which still contains many of the family's items of furniture and personal effects, giving the cottage a charming period air.*

▶▶ *Highwic, a fine example of an Early English Gothic house, was the home of the large Buckland family. The boys of the family shared a dormitory-like upstairs bedroom.*

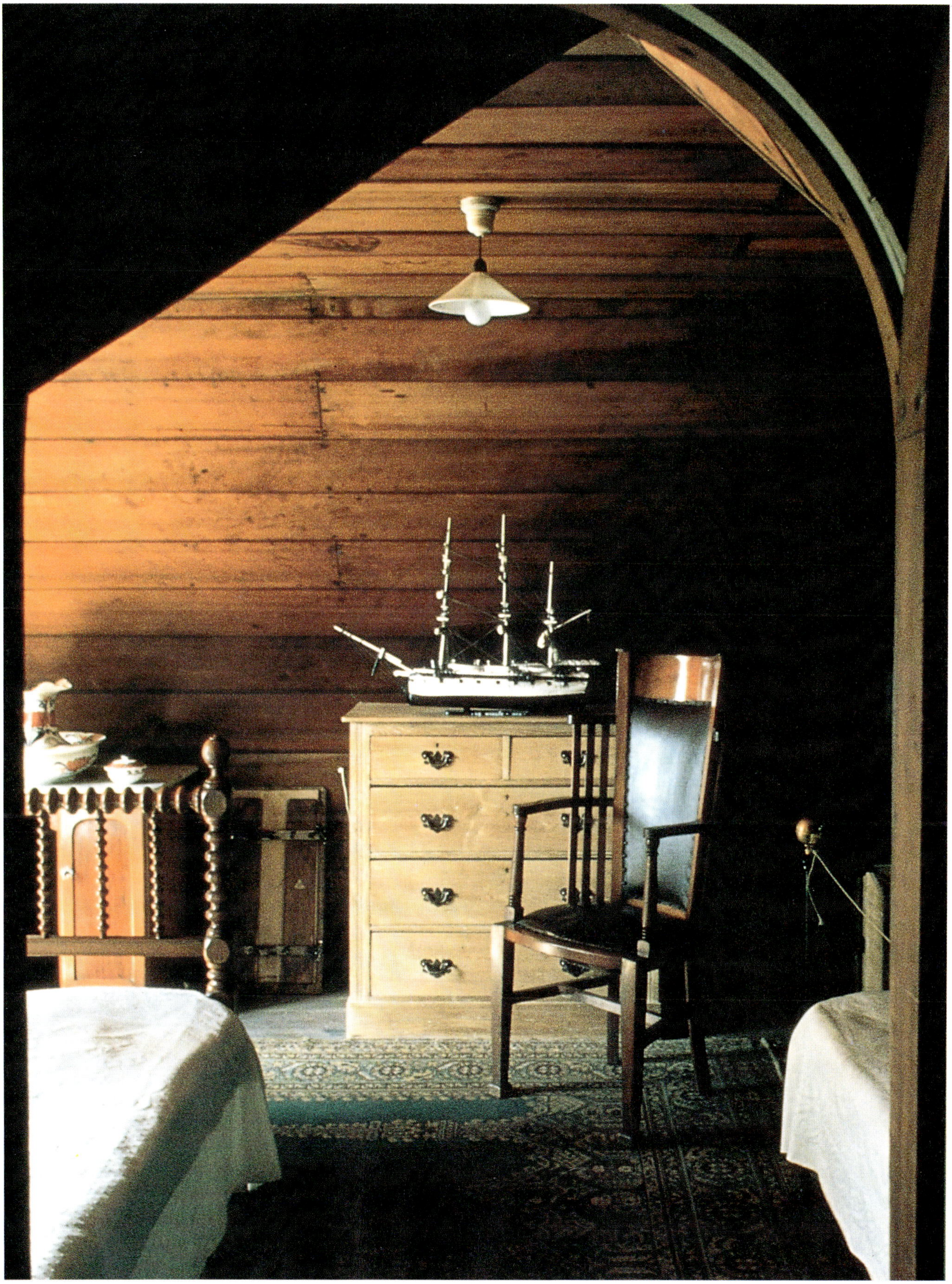

► *Auckland's Old Government House, official residence of New Zealand's early Governors, was a centre of the country's political life from 1856 until 1865, when Wellington became New Zealand's capital. Since 1969 the building has housed the senior common room of the University of Auckland.* Kris Pfeiffer

chapel replaced an earlier one on the site. Historic graves of early settlers are found in its churchyard. Younger and larger than St Stephen's, the Cathedral Church of St Mary was completed in 1897. A masterpiece of the Christchurch architect, Benjamin Mountfort, St Mary's has been described as 'one of the finest churches in the English-speaking world'. Amid considerable controversy the church was shifted across the road from its original site in 1982. Its lofty interior is notable for superb stained glass and memorial brasses. Parnell's Catholic Church of St John the Baptist (nearer town) was blessed by Bishop Pompallier in 1861.

Although beyond Parnell, St John's College, on St John's Road, Meadowbank, has many links with early residents of Parnell, above all Bishop Selwyn, its founder. Of the earliest stone buildings, only the former kitchen remains. The chapel (1847, extensively but sympathetically altered in the 1960s) and the college dining hall (1848–49) are by Frederick Thatcher.

On the waterfront at Mission Bay is another old stone building with church origins. The Melanesian Mission dates from 1859, when it was built as a college to which youths were brought from Melanesia. The Mission moved its headquarters to Norfolk Island in 1866. The old stone building then saw a number of different uses. It became one of the country's early flying schools, then in 1928 became a Melanesian Mission Museum. Unfortunately, the building was not suited to the proper conservation of valuable artefacts. After taking the building over in 1974 the Historic Places Trust decided to close the museum down and disperse the artefacts to other places of safer keeping. The building has been reopened as a restaurant.

OLD BUILDINGS

Although Auckland has been thoroughly redeveloped in recent years, a number of nineteenth and early twentieth century buildings have survived. From the days when it was New Zealand's capital, Auckland has retained its old Government House, designed by William Mason and first occupied in 1856. It is now the University Senior Common Room. Its imposing facade, facing Waterloo Quadrant, is a fine example of wood fashioned to mimic stone. Not far from the University is the old High Court Building, built between 1865 and 1868 of

brick with stone facings. It is notable for the many stone carvings, executed by Anton Teutenberg, on its exterior. Of the same vintage is the Northern Club on the corner of Princes and Kitchener Streets, built in the late 1860s of stuccoed brick but today picturesquely smothered in Virginia creeper.

Auckland has few outstanding nineteenth century commercial buildings left. One survival is the classical facade of the Bank of New Zealand, built of Tasmanian sandstone, which has graced Queen Street since the mid-1860s. Two important public buildings date from the 1880s. What is now the City Art Gallery was opened in 1887 as

the Public Library. Skilfully designed for a corner site on Wellesley Street, it is the finest building in the French Renaissance style in New Zealand, and contains an outstanding art collection. Also in the French Renaissance style is the former Customhouse on the corner of Customs Street West and Albert Street.

In the early twentieth century, Auckland acquired two celebrated public buildings linked by Queen Street. The Town Hall, by Aotea Square, was built between 1909 and 1911. Downtown, by the wharves, the Ferry Building was opened in 1912, on a site from which ferries have plied the waters of the Waitemata from Auckland's earliest days. The Harbour Bridge put most of Auckland's ferries out of business and this colourful chapter in Auckland's history is now kept alive by only a few remaining boats. Not far from the Ferry Building, Auckland's Chief Post Office was built between 1910 and 1912 in the English Baroque manner. One of Auckland's most exotic looking buildings, the University clocktower block, 1926, is a relatively recent addition to the Auckland skyline. Auckland Grammar School, a remarkable Californian mission style building (1913–16), can be seen from the southern motorway as it passes through Mt Eden. Between Khyber Pass Road and Mt Eden

Road the old bluestone prison catches the eye while across town are Oakley and Carrington Hospitals, both massive stone institutional buildings.

AUCKLAND'S CHURCHES

Among Auckland's older inner-city churches are second and third generation buildings, usually of stone, which replaced the wooden buildings of the pioneers. The site of the original St Paul's, Auckland's first church, was lost when Point Britomart was cut away. Today's St Paul's, on a different site in Symonds Street, dates substantially from 1894–95, although a new chancel was dedicated as recently as 1936 and the building is still incomplete. The foundation stone of the first St Patrick's Cathedral, Wyndham Street, was laid by Bishop Pompallier in 1846. The original church later became the transepts of the new building, but these were removed when further additions were made in 1907–8. St Andrew's Church, facing Constitution Hill, began its life in 1847–49 as a severe stone building; the addition of the tower and portico in 1882 turned it into something much grander. The porticoed Baptist Tabernacle was built in 1886 and on Khyber Pass Road the fine big kauri Church of the Holy Sepulchre, with its high spire, was built in 1880–81. On Remuera Road, the nave of the present St Mark's Church is the original church of 1860, but the building has been handsomely extended. On Mt Eden Road the nave of St Barnabas dates from 1847, and has stood on its present site since 1877. The old Synagogue in Princes Street has an unusual interior and dates from 1884. It has recently been restored to a new use as a bank.

In Ponsonby the St Mary's Bay area has had a long association with the Catholic Church, Bishop Pompallier having bought land there in 1853. On New Street, the St Mary's Convent Chapel dates from 1865, and the Bishop's house from 1894. The Ponsonby Post Office, 1912, on St Mary's Bay Road, is a curious example of one of the smaller buildings erected during a spate of post office building in the early 1900s.

AUCKLAND'S MUSEUMS

As befits the country's largest city, Auckland has one of its most important museums. The Auckland Institute and

◀ *Auckland's late nineteenth century Old Custom House is one of New Zealand's finest buildings in the French Second Empire style. The building has been restored for alternative commercial uses now it no longer serves as a Custom House.*

Museum is housed in a huge classical building in the Domain, erected in the 1920s as a memorial to the war dead. The museum's displays cover the full span of New Zealand's history. In the Maori gallery Nga Kahurangi, the meeting house, Hotunui, from the Thames district, was carved by members of the Ngati Awa tribe as a gift to the Ngati Maru tribe in 1878. The carved gateway, Rangitakaroro, came from Lake Okataina, near Rotorua. The war canoe, *Te Toki a Tapiri*, was built about 1836 near Wairoa. Among the important pre-European carvings in the museum is the Kaitaia carving, which is about 800 years old, and storehouse carvings, about 1780, from Te Kaha. The displays of 'Centennial Street' give a fascinating insight into European Auckland of the mid-nineteenth century.

Auckland Domain is Auckland's oldest park. A memorial palisade, erected in 1942, stands on the site of an ancient pa, Pukekaora, where a peace agreement was concluded in 1828 between the Ngapuhi and Waikato tribes. The first Maori king, Potatau, lived here briefly in the 1840s; Princess Te Puea Herangi, his descendant, planted a totara tree in his memory at the site in 1940. The Domain tea kiosk and band rotunda are relics from the 1913–14 Auckland Exhibition.

Auckland's other major museum is the Museum of Transport and Technology on the Great North Road. Centred on an 1876 pumphouse, its displays and working exhibits cover transport, agriculture and

◀◀ *French influence is evident in the architecture of the Auckland City Art Gallery, built in 1885-87 to house the city's public library. It is particularly admired for its contribution to the cityscape of a rapidly changing downtown Auckland.* Kris Pfeiffer

43

crafts such as printing. Old-time tram rides are available. A pioneer village represents the New Zealand scene in the early years of European settlement. The museum's aviation collection is housed at the Keith Park Memorial Airfield in Meola Road.

Those with an interest in maritime transport have an opportunity in Auckland to ride on a 1935 coal-burning steam tug, the *William C Daldy*. The vessel is cared for by a preservation society and sails from Marsden Wharf. Of significance in New Zealand's engineering history, the Grafton Bridge was opened to traffic in April 1910. It is believed to have been for many years the largest single-span concrete arch bridge in the world.

COASTAL DEFENCES

New Zealand has not, since European settlement, been invaded by a foreign power, but some New Zealanders have, at various times, been anxious about the country's defences. This anxiety prompted the building of fortifications and defence installations on headlands and islands to guard the approaches to the country's ports. The first of these were built as long ago as the 1880s, during the Russian scare. More were built during the First and Second World Wars. The remnants of coastal defences can still be seen at the approaches to all four of the country's main ports. At North Head, Devonport, are fortifications dating from about 1885. A disappearing gun was installed on nearby Mt Victoria in 1888. What remains on North Head are old gun emplacements, tunnels and ammunition galleries. A military fort of similar age, Fort Takapuna, is sited on restricted ground just over a kilometre away. Remnants of Second World War installations are at Stony Batter (Waiheke Island) and Home Bay (Motutapu Island). Bastion Point was the site of early Maori fortifications, but was first fortified by Europeans during Russian scares of the 1880s. The fortifications which remain date from 1939–45. Also on Bastion Point is the memorial to Michael Joseph Savage, New Zealand's first Labour Prime Minister, whose election victory in 1935 was a turning point in New Zealand's history.

At the end of the waterfront road at Achilles Point is a small memorial to the Royal New Zealand Navy cruiser HMNZS *Achilles* of Battle of the River Plate fame early in the Second World War.

SOUTH AUCKLAND

In recent years Auckland has sprawled south, new suburbs swallowing up farmland and small towns. Although they appear new, these suburbs retain historic buildings and sites from the days when they began their lives as rural villages. For some years after it was founded, until the end of the Waikato War in 1864, Auckland lived in fear of attack by the Maori of the Waikato. Towns were founded south, towards the Waikato, as defensive frontier settlements. Some, the fencible settlements, were semi-military in character. The fencible settlers, many on British Army pensions, were given a cottage and one acre of land on which to live. They were expected to earn their livings as civilians, but also to parade on Sundays and stand ready to defend Auckland against attack.

Fencible settlements were established at Howick and Onehunga in 1847, and at Panmure and Otahuhu in 1848. In Panmure's main street, a soldier's stone cottage has been resited and in Jellicoe Park, Onehunga, are an 1860 blockhouse and a replica fencible cottage. A few fencible cottages have survived, and there are other reminders in South Auckland of the days when it was a frontier between Maori and Pakeha.

Howick has retained something of a village atmosphere. At its centre is the lovely All Saints Church, built in 1847, on the instructions of Bishop Selwyn. Of the same age is Shamrock Cottage, originally the wet canteen of the fencible settlement. It became Howick's first hotel and is now a tea-room.

The Howick Colonial Village, in Pakuranga, is a collection of buildings of the period 1840–80, gathered together, laid out in authentic manner and restored. Next door is Bell House, now owned by the Historic Places Trust. Built in 1851 as a fencible officer's house and later used as a farmhouse it is now a restaurant.

A relatively modern building on Musick Point, Bucklands Beach, north of Howick, has historic interest. The art deco building was erected in 1942 as a memorial to Captain E.C. Musick, who in 1937 landed the first Pan American Airways flying boat on the Waitemata Harbour after a flight from San Francisco.

At Mangere is the only surviving stone church of the Selwyn period, St James,

◄ *Many of New Zealand's towns and cities gained handsome new post offices in the prosperous early years of this century. A large number of these fine Edwardian buildings have been demolished, but the 1912 building in Ponsonby still stands.*

► ► *One of the loveliest of the many churches built under the inspiration of Bishop Selwyn, New Zealand's first Anglican bishop, All Saints, Howick, was erected in 1847 and extended in 1862.* Kris Pfeiffer

▶ *This simple colonial cottage at Pukekohe dates from the 1860s, when the town was on the frontier between the warring settlers and Maori of the Waikato.*

Church Road, completed in the late 1850s. The old graveyard beside the simple stone building contains the graves of many locals.

The scoria walls in the neighbourhood are a legacy of the Hampton Park estate which saw more than 8 km of walls built to subdivide the land. The house erected at Hampton Park in 1855 burned down during the Second World War. The remains of stone stables can still be seen.

The Selwyn Church, on the corner of Massey Road and Hain Avenue, Mangere, began life in 1863 as Holy Trinity, Otahuhu. In 1928 it was shifted to its present site and somewhat altered. The tiny wooden Westney Road Methodist Church, on the approach road to the airport, was opened as long ago as 1856 and extended in 1887. The even smaller Mangere Presbyterian Church on Kirkbride Road, also wooden but rather less plain, was built in 1874. Christ Church, Alfriston, near Papakura, with an unusually dominant tower and spire, was built in 1877. St Paul's, Chapel Road, East Tamaki, was built probably in 1886. St James' Church, Church Road, Ardmore, was built in 1893 with more elaborate exterior decoration than the simpler earlier churches. In the graveyard are graves older than the church itself for it replaced an 1861 building which burned down. On the Clevedon-Kawakawa Bay Road is the tiny but fascinating Te Tokotoru Tapu Church built around 1912 along the lines of a traditional meeting house.

In South Auckland are a number of interesting houses of the later nineteenth and early twentieth centuries, most privately owned. Many can be seen from the road. One important house open to the public is the Massey homestead, Franklynne, on Massey Road, built in 1852–53 of brick. In 1890 the house was purchased by W.F. Massey, Prime Minister of New Zealand from 1912 to 1925. The house has recently been restored for use as a community cultural centre. The Nathan homestead on Hill Road in Manurewa was built in 1924 to replace an earlier homestead. It is now used as a community and cultural centre. The McNicol homestead, on the Clevedon-Kawakawa Bay Road, is a two-storeyed house with verandah and balcony, built as the second home of a pioneering family in 1878. The house is now leased by the Clevedon Historical Society.

The area's old school buildings include the Mangere Central School and school-

house, the Flatbush School at East Tamaki (now used by the local community) and a relocated 1880s schoolhouse at Pakuranga.

TOWARDS THE WAIKATO

The towns further south share with the fencible settlements their 'frontier' origins. But while the fencible settlements never saw action, the more southern outposts were involved in clashes of arms. In the 1860s, when the Waikato War broke out, skirmishing occurred north of the Waikato River and some of the area's historic places relate to this fighting. All Souls Church, North Road, Clevedon, was built in 1861 and opened by Bishop Selwyn. In 1863 the church was used to accommodate soldiers building the Galloway Redoubt, faint traces of which can still be seen between the church and its vicarage. In Papakura, the original St John's Presbyterian Church, 1859, is now the church hall. In 1863 it was fortified against attack. The Pukekohe East Presbyterian Church was built in 1862–63. Within months, it had been stockaded and was, in September 1863, the scene of a fierce engagement between settlers and attacking Maori. St Bride's Anglican Church at Mauku, built in 1859, was also stockaded in 1863. The loopholes cut into its walls can still be seen. During 1863 several redoubts were built north of the Waikato River. At Pokeno, the site of the Queen's Redoubt can be visited and just north of the town is a small military cemetery. At Tuakau, the Alexandra Redoubt is in a better state of preservation and the layout of the fort can be traced. A memorial stands inside the redoubt.

These sites associated with Maori and Pakeha fighting might tempt visitors to think that the history of the area began when it was first settled by Europeans in the 1840s. But at the site of the Pukekiwiriki Pa, on Red Hill Road towards Hunua, the remains of pre-European fortifications can still be traced.

Pukekohe preserves a pioneer cottage which was garrisoned in 1863, in Roulston Park. It is now furnished with pioneer furniture and relics. A museum at Waiuku has relics of the New Zealand Wars. The Glenbrook Vintage Railway, near Waiuku, provides visitors with an opportunity to relive the age of steam trains.

WAIKATO

Many stories have been written about the farmlands of the Waikato. The region supported a large population in pre-European times and was the scene of early missionary activity and of early Maori adoption of European farming methods. It was also the scene of Maori efforts to resist the tide of European settlement.

The story of the fighting in the Waikato is closely related to that of the Maori King movement. The first European traders on the New Zealand coast were welcomed by the Maori as providers of European goods, above all muskets and ammunition for use in tribal warfare. With the founding of European settlements, Maori farmers found markets for their produce. But, as the tide of European immigration began to flow more strongly, increasing numbers of Maori became suspicious about Pakeha intentions and fearful about the future of their race. There were clashes of arms in the 1840s and throughout the 1850s resistance grew to the sale of land. It led eventually to an effort to set up a Maori nation under its own king to ensure the survival of Maori culture and the retention of land in Maori hands.

The belief that the Maori King posed a subversive challenge to the authority of Queen Victoria reinforced impatience at the reluctance of some Maori to sell land. Finally the Government took steps, first in Taranaki then in the Waikato, which provoked the Maori to fight to prevent the loss of their land and of their identity as a people. This is the background to many of the Waikato's historic places.

THE WAIKATO WAR

The eagerness of many settlers to acquire more Maori land eventually led to war. To most Aucklanders it was particularly galling that the rich lands of the Waikato were closed to them.

Later, after some Waikato Maori had gone to Taranaki to assist Wiremu Kingi (who had taken up arms to prevent the loss of his tribal land at Waitara), the decision was finally made to invade the Waikato.

In July 1863 Imperial Troops crossed the Mangatawhiri Stream, which the Maori had warned would be taken as a declaration of war. The first major engagement was at Meremere. From a fortified position, a Maori force held up the British advance for almost three months but was ultimately obliged to evacuate when the British landed troops from armed steamers further up the river. The British then constructed a redoubt on the Maori fortifications. The earthworks on the site, reached by driving up through the power station village, are still distinct, although overgrown.

In Mercer, an iron gun turret from the gunboat *Pioneer* forms the base of the town's war memorial. Another gun turret from the same vessel stands on the Point at Ngaruawahia.

After the British had taken Meremere, the Maori retreated to fortifications at Rangiriri. There, an outnumbered Maori force took their stand against 1500 British troops. The position was stormed by the British on 20 November 1863 in the Battle of Rangiriri. The British captured two outly-

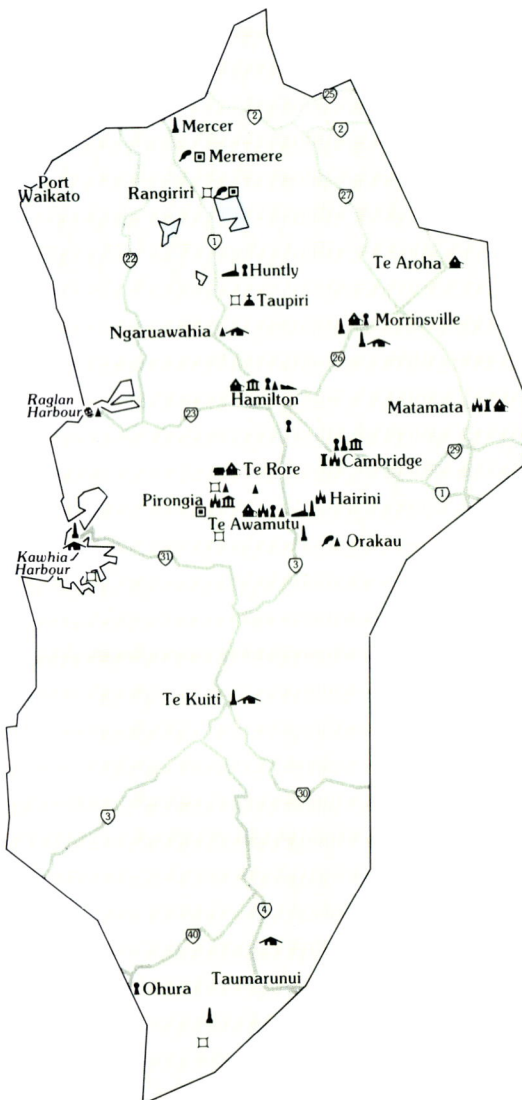

◄ *A roadside obelisk near Kihikihi marks the site of the Maori fortification at Orakau where the last major engagement of the Waikato War was fought in 1864. The spirit of Maori resistance at Orakau is renowned in New Zealand history.*

ing pa but the strong central redoubt held out until the next day. Part of this redoubt, although pierced by the Great South Road, has been preserved and the grassed-over ditches and banks give an impression of the formidable task the British undertook in attempting to drive the Maori from their defences. After the battle, a redoubt was built on part of the Maori earthworks to house a British garrison. The redoubt took its name from Wiremu Te Wheoro who occupied it on behalf of the Government in 1868–69, during the Te Kooti campaigns.

After Rangiriri, the British troops moved against little resistance up through Ngaruawahia to where Te Awamutu now stands. The major Maori fortifications at Paterangi (no traces now remain) were out-flanked and the Maori village at Rangiaowhia attacked. The British encoun-tered final Maori resistance at Orakau, where a band of 300 Maori under Rewi Maniapoto, held out for three days against great odds. The British, suggesting that the women and children should leave the pa, were told the women would fight as well as

▶ *One of the best-preserved earthworks to have survived from the Land Wars period, the Alexandra Redoubt near Pirongia was built by the Armed Constabulary towards the end of the period of conflict.*

the men. On the third day the surviving Maori broke from the pa, many escaping across the Puniu River into what became the King Country. (A monument to Rewi Maniapoto can be seen at Kihikihi.)

The Maori were defeated and the Waikato lay open for confiscation and European settlement. But, in resisting the British invasion of the Waikato, the Maori gave New Zealand one of the most stirring chapters in its history. The sites which can be visited are not impressive as monuments, but there are few places of such significance and interest.

NGARUAWAHIA

Ngaruawahia, at the confluence of the Waipa and Waikato Rivers, can lay claim to an important place in New Zealand history because of its association with the King Movement. At Ngaruawahia in 1858 the Waikato Chief Te Wherowhero was proclaimed the first Maori King as King Potatau. Five years later, in 1863, the Maori were forced to abandon Ngaruawahia without a fight after losses at Meremere and Rangiriri. Nothing survives in Ngaruawahia from the days when it was the capital of the Maori King, although a memorial to King Potatau stands at the confluence of the two rivers.

In the twentieth century, Ngaruawahia assumed a new importance because of the activities of Princess Te Puea Herangi. A granddaughter of Tawhiao, the second Maori King, she was determined that a Maori identity should survive, and decided to re-establish a Maori presence at Ngaruawahia. In 1921 she bought back land on which a new marae, Turangawaewae ('a place to stand'), was built.

Turangawaewae is now one of the most important marae in the country with several notable and historic buildings on it. In a whare waka are kept the great canoes important to the river tribes. Access to Turangawaewae is restricted, but the marae can be viewed from nearby roads or across the Waikato River. The home marae of the Maori Queen is at Waahi, but it can be visited only in appropriate circumstances.

Between Ngaruawahia and Huntly is Mt Taupiri, the sacred mountain of some Waikato tribes. On a spur is the site of a pa which was the scene of a tribal engagement in the early eighteenth century. The crest of the spur is now sacred as the burial place of Maori kings and of leading Tainui chiefs. On

the western bank of the Waikato is the site of Kaitotehe Pa, and the site of an early mission station.

Huntly was established in European times as a coalmining town, and a museum in a restored mine manager's residence illustrates Huntly's coalmining and brick-making industries. A relic of early industry at Ngaruawahia is a concrete building,

erected in the late 1870s as a store for a flour mill.

PIRONGIA

Pirongia, an 1864 military settlement, has two sites of great historic interest. The older is the pa Matakitaki, north of the township. A roadside plaque records that it was the scene of a battle in 1822, when musket-armed Ngapuhi overwhelmed the tradition-ally armed Waikato tribes. From the plaque, a short walk across farmland leads to earth-works.

On the other side of Pirongia from Matakitaki is the well preserved Alexandra Redoubt, built by the Armed Constabulary in 1869, when Pirongia was garrisoned during the Te Kooti campaigns. There is still a full two metres of escarpment from the bottom of the ditch to the top of the bank. It is easy here to appreciate how redoubts were built.

The first Anglican mission on the central Waikato was established in 1835 at Mangapouri, near Pirongia, at the junction of the Puniu and Waipa Rivers. The most notable of Pirongia's old buildings is the Public Library, built as a schoolroom in 1864 and taken over by the local Mechanics Institute as early as 1871. Part of a school building more than 100 years old survives as a play centre.

▼ Dedicated in 1856 when Hairini, then known as Rangiaowhia, was a thriving Maori settlement, St Paul's survived the controversial British attack on the settlement in the 1860s and was renovated in the mid-1870s. Little else remains of the once-busy Maori village which surrounded it.

HAMILTON

Hamilton began life as a military settlement, established immediately after the Waikato campaign when soldiers were settled on plots of confiscated land. When the settlers arrived, most of the Maori had retreated south beyond the Puniu River, but there had been Maori villages and pa in the area for a long time. The pa called Te Rapa and Kirikiriroa have both disappeared. On City Council land on River Road are the remaining earthworks of the riverside pa Miropiko.

The landing place of the first of Hamilton's European settlers is marked on the riverbank. Redoubts were built in 1864 at East and West Hamilton to protect the infant settlement. Hamilton took its name from Captain John Hamilton R.N., who was killed at the Battle of Gate Pa near Tauranga. He lies buried in the Tauranga mission cemetery; his sword and medals are on display in the Hamilton City Council Chambers.

In 1982, the hulk of the gunboat, *Rangiriri*, was retrieved from the bed of the Waikato River. A paddle-steamer built in sections in Sydney in 1864 and assembled at Port Waikato, it was ordered to tow barges on the river and brought Hamilton's first settlers to their new home. It had spent 90 years under water and silt.

In the Waikato Art Museum is a fine example of the craft used on the Waikato River before the days of river steamers. The canoe Te Winika was begun in the 1830s and completed about 1840. The museum has many other artefacts which illuminate Hamilton's Maori past, including wooden carvings which have been recovered from swamps in the district.

Two Hamilton schools have grown up around interesting old houses, the Waikato Diocesan School for Girls around Bankwood, a homestead of the 1890s, and the Southwell School in a homestead built in 1879. On Victoria Street are some interesting commercial buildings of the 1870s and 1880s, notably the old Bank of New Zealand, built in 1878. The Clydesdale Agricultural Museum at Mystery Creek, 16 km south of Hamilton, has displays which bring the rural ways of pioneering days to life. The stables and blacksmith's shop are 'working exhibits' which serve the Clydesdale horses whose name the museum has adopted.

CAMBRIDGE

Cambridge, like Hamilton, began life as a military settlement immediately after the Waikato Campaign. An obelisk and plaque mark the site of the redoubt built in 1864 at the limit of navigation for British gunboats on the Waikato River. Unlike Hamilton, Cambridge has remained a small town. One of its loveliest old buildings is St Andrew's Anglican Church, built in 1881, with high gables and a tall spire.

Cambridge's old school, a fine building with four projecting gables, the oldest parts of which date back to 1874, has been remodelled and remains in use. Public buildings of historic interest in Cambridge include the post office and Town Hall. The town also has two appealing old hotels and two band rotundas. The water tower is a monument to early efforts to provide Cambridge with proper amenities. Historical artefacts are displayed in a museum housed in the former Court House, itself a building of historic interest.

TE AWAMUTU

Te Awamutu, which lies just north of the confiscation line, for many years the frontier between Maori and Pakeha, has a European history long preceding the Waikato War. It was the site of the Otawhao Mission, established in 1839, at which a pioneer missionary, the Rev. John Morgan,

laboured for more than two decades. A plaque in Selwyn Park marks the site occupied by the mission until the outbreak of the Waikato War in 1863. St John's Church, opened in 1854, was built at Morgan's initiative. Between 1864 and 1867, it was a garrison church and in the cemetery are the graves of combatants, though most are no longer individually marked.

Later, the first co-operative dairy factory in the North Island was established at Te Awamutu. A plaque marks the site. Part of the old wooden Te Awamutu School, built in the late 1870s, survives on a new site as the Te Awamutu Little Theatre. The Te Awamutu and District Museum houses Maori and European colonial artefacts, including the famous carving Uenuku, and relics of the New Zealand Wars.

At Hairini, formerly Rangiaowhia, is an interesting old church, St Paul's, dedicated in 1856. It fell into disrepair but was renovated in the mid-1870s and is today a reminder of the Anglican mission station established at Hairini in the 1840s. Nothing remains of the thriving Maori village of Rangiaowhia which was captured by the British in 1864.

South of Te Awamutu is the Kakepuku Reserve. On a mountain of traditional significance to local Maori are the remains of a fortified pa, terraces and pits. The reserve is interesting to visit, but not easy of access. Some of the terraces and pits are on private property.

EAST OF HAMILTON

East of Hamilton, lowlands stretch across to the Piako and Waihou Rivers. The tribes occupying these lowlands had links with the tribes of the Waikato Valley proper in pre-European times and supported the King Movement. Near Morrinsville, at the Rukumoana Pa, a marble statue of the third Maori King, Mahuta, stands next to a Maori meeting house. The original meeting house once stood at Maungatautari, south of Cambridge, where important discussions leading to the establishment of Maori kingship took place. Close by is a carved meeting house, Werewere, which also has connections with the King Movement.

In Morrinsville itself there is a museum and a pioneer cottage, furnished in turn-of-the-century style. The cottage dates probably from the early 1870s and was moved to

► *In 1880-81 a local landowner, J.C. Firth, fearing a resurgence of fighting between Maori and Pakeha, had a massive concrete blockhouse built to protect his holdings. Today the tower is at the centre of a local museum.*

its present site from Kiwitahi to serve as a nucleus for the museum.

In Matamata there is further evidence of the links between the Maori of the Upper Thames Valley and those of the Waikato. Matamata was the home of the great Ngati Haua chief Te Waharoa (1776–1838); his son was Wiremu Tamihana, known in New Zealand history as the Kingmaker, who played a key role in the Maori King Movement. A cairn marks the place where he died in 1866. Near the cairn is the Firth Tower, a massive concrete blockhouse erected in 1880–81 by J.C. Firth, a local landowner and businessman, at a time when a resurgence of fighting was feared.

At Kuranui, a short distance from Morrinsville, one of the niu poles still stands. These poles were erected by adherents of the Pai Marire faith, founded in Taranaki in the early 1860s by the prophet Te Ua Haumene. The poles served as focal points for ritual observances. Most were pulled down in the 1860s in an effort to stamp out the Pai Marire faith which was stiffening Maori resolve to resist the loss of their land. The niu at Kuranui, erected probably in early 1865, is known as Motai after the hapu of Ngati Raukawa associated with the site.

Te Aroha, founded in 1880, is an interesting place in the history of tourism in New Zealand. It was developed as a spa based on its hot springs, and quaint kiosks and other buildings still stand in the Domain, notably the Cadman House, opened in 1898. The Historic Places Trust has declared the area an historic precinct. Gold was mined near Te Aroha between 1880 and 1921, but more important goldmining sites arc found further north, at Paeroa and Waihi. At Waiorongomai historic goldmining tracks are being managed by the Department of Conservation.

WEST OF HAMILTON

The coast west of the lower Waikato Valley is indented by three harbours: Raglan, Aotea and Kawhia. North of the three harbours, Port Waikato, at the mouth of the Waikato River, was the site between 1838 and 1854 of the Maraetai mission station, which was moved about 12 km up the river in 1854. In 1863, during the Waikato War, Port Waikato was founded for the assembly of pre-fabricated ships and for the trans-

▶ *Famous as a Te Kooti house, donated by that fighting chief to the Ngati Maniapoto with whom he took refuge after being defeated by settler forces, Te Tokanganui a Noho in Te Kuiti was built and carved in 1878.*

shipment of military supplies to river steamers.

Kawhia Harbour has an important place in Maori tradition and history. On the shores of the harbour is the traditional last resting place of the *Tainui* canoe. Above Te Piu Beach, and behind the meeting house, Auau-ki-te-rangi, on the Maketu Marae, two stones mark this sacred spot. A monument on a hill near the marae marks the site of Ahurei, the whare wananga founded by Hoturoa, the captain of the *Tainui* canoe. At Kawera is an ancient pohutukawa tree which, according to legend, was used to moor the *Tainui*. Kawhia was important in later Maori history as the homeland of the Ngati Toa tribe and the place from where Te Rauparaha led the tribe south to Kapiti. At an old pa on Waiharakeke Inlet, dit-

ches, banks, terraces and pits can still be discerned.

The early Polynesian inhabitants of Raglan have left a fascinating indication of their presence in the form of carved rocks, about 6 km from the town on the road to Whale Bay. The concentrations of Maori population on the Raglan and Kawhia Harbours attracted early missionaries. A memorial in the main street of Raglan records the founding of the Wesleyan mission station in 1835 at Te Horea, on the northern side of the harbour. European settlers began to arrive in Raglan in the mid-1850s.

THE KING COUNTRY

South of the Waikato lies the King Country. After their defeat in the war of 1863–64 and

▲ *Taumarunui, the King Country railway town, in the early years of this century.*
Alexander Turnbull Library

the confiscation of large tracts of their land, many Waikato Maori retreated south beyond the confiscation line into the then-forested King Country. There the Kingite Maori lived in semi-hostile isolation for nearly 20 years, until King Tawhiao emerged in 1881 to make peace at Pirongia. After the King Country was opened to settlement, timber milling and railway building were, for many years, the principal industries.

The railway reached Te Awamutu in 1880. Seven years later Te Kuiti began its European history as a railway construction camp. But Te Kuiti's greatest historic interest stems from the 17 years (1864 to 1881) that the Maori King Tawhiao lived in the village of Te Kuititanga. In 1872 Tawhiao afforded hospitality to Te Kooti, after his final defeats in the central North Island. Te Kooti remained with the King Movement Maori until his pardon in the early 1880s. In 1878 Te Kooti's followers built a meeting house, Te Tokanganui a Noho, which, after Te Kooti was pardoned, was presented to the local Ngati Maniapoto in recognition of their hospitality. The

house has fine carvings and was restored in the early 1970s.

At the southern limit of the King Country is the town of Taumarunui, on the Wanganui River. Once the site of a Maori village, it was a key link in pre-European canoe routes. At Maraekowhai, on an historic reserve at the junction of the Ohura and Wanganui Rivers, are two niu poles dating from the days when the area was a Hau Hau stronghold.

North of Taumarunui on the Te Koura Marae is a carved monument, made of totara, known as Tawhaki Piki ki te Rangi. A meeting house built in 1904 stands on the marae next to the monument. The first European settled in Taumarunui in the 1870s, but it was not until the era of railway construction that the town began to grow. The line between Te Kuiti and Taumarunui was opened in 1903. In Taumarunui, the Crocker Stationary Engine Collection recalls the age of steam. A museum at Ohura on the Stratford to Taumarunui line, built between 1901 and 1932, illustrates the timber milling, railway construction and farming past of the district.

COROMANDEL

The Coromandel Peninsula is a large area of densely forested hills, rugged and steep, with fast-flowing streams that tumble through gorges to the sea. When Cook visited its waters in 1769 to observe the transit of Mercury, the region was well populated and traces of pre-European settlement can still be found. But the real story of Coromandel is one of kauri and gold. The extensive kauri forests noted by Cook were exploited from the early nineteenth until well into the twentieth century and considerable evidence remains, if one knows where to look. Kauri gum was also a highly prized product of the Coromandel. Yet it was for gold that the region is perhaps best known. Gold was discovered on the Coromandel Peninsula in 1852 and was its most valuable resource for almost a hundred years. Many reminders and relics of that important chapter in its history can be seen in the buildings, museums and mining sites of Waihi, Thames and Coromandel townships.

THAMES

Thames, built right on top of a goldfield, has fascinating goldmining relics but the history of the area predates the interest in gold. The Totara Pa cemetery (where some of the headstones commemorate important chiefs) is on the site of a pa built by the Ngati Maru tribe in pre-European times. Some earthworks are still visible and a noticeboard explains the history of the site. The Thames area was visited by Captain Cook who sailed up the Firth of Thames in November 1769. A cairn near Netherton records this visit.

But it is gold that gives Thames its famous history. The first major rush occurred in 1867. For several decades the mining and crushing of quartz for gold provided Thames with its livelihood. The Hauraki Prospectors' Association has reopened some old mine tunnels in Thames and restored a stamper battery on the site of the Golden Crown mine. These are open to the public.

Another survivor from goldmining days is the Thames School of Mines, opened in 1886. It included an assay room and furnace, laboratory, small battery, lecture rooms and a mineral museum. Keeping water out of the shafts and tunnels below Thames was always a problem, and the remains of the steam-operated Big Pump, installed in 1898, are among the relics that can still be seen. Appropriately for a mining town, hotels are among Thames's other interesting old buildings. The Lady Bowen (originally The Wharf) was built in the 1850s or 1860s on Auckland's North Shore and shipped to Thames in 1868. The Brian Boru dates from the early years of this century.

There is also much in Thames of early industrial interest because plant and equipment was built in the town for use in the mines. The firm of A. & G. Price opened in

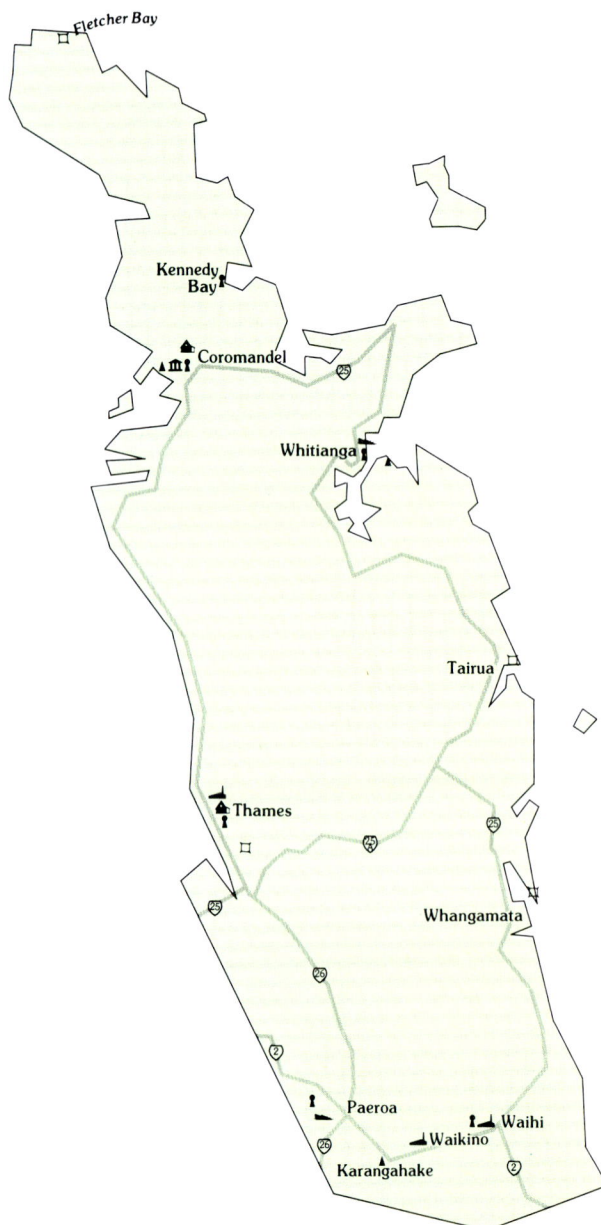

Map of the Coromandel Peninsula showing Fletcher Bay, Kennedy Bay, Coromandel, Whitianga, Tairua, Thames, Whangamata, Paeroa, Waihi, Waikino and Karangahake.

Thames in the 1870s to undertake heavy engineering on the goldfields and some old buildings of these works remain. The historic Judds foundry was demolished in the 1980s. The Thames Historical Museum is housed in an old Methodist church and displays relics of the old pioneering days.

COROMANDEL

Coromandel (the harbour which has given its name to the whole peninsula) takes its name from HMS *Coromandel* which anchored there in 1820 to load kauri spars. The town's interesting buildings relate to its later prosperity as a goldmining town. A plaque on a bridge at the town's northern exit records the first discovery of gold in the district in 1852. Like Thames, Coromandel had a School of Mines. The building now houses a small museum, with photographs and mining relics on display. Under the management of the Coromandel School of Mines, the Government in 1898 opened a battery which had a single stamp for crushing specimen ores and also a five-stamp battery for general crushing. This Government battery can still be visited. Other interesting old buildings in Coromandel include the Courthouse, built in 1873 for the gold warden and now serving as Council Chambers, and the mine manager's house, built in the 1880s.

OTHER COROMANDEL TOWNS

The main historic interest of Whitianga stems from the visit made by Captain Cook to Mercury Bay at the end of 1769. A plaque at Cook's Beach marks the approximate spot from which Cook observed the transit of Mercury on 10 December 1769 and a memorial to him stands on the Shakespeare Cliffs near the beach. Traces of the pa which Cook observed remain near Whitianga Rock.

Whitianga was a kauri timber port but it is not easy to find reminders of early timber days. Deep in the bush are the remains of old kauri driving dams and timber milling equipment, but they are difficult to locate. On the Tarawaere Stream in the Kauaeranga catchment east of Thames, a dam of the 1920s in a reasonable state of repair can be visited without difficulty.

At the ferry landing in Whitianga is a stone wharf, built in the 1830s, when many ships were calling at Coromandel ports to pick up kauri. In 1840 the *Buffalo* was wrecked in Mercury Bay and relics from the wreck are preserved along the foreshore. Displays in the Mercury Bay District Museum in Whitianga recall the days of kauri timber milling and gum digging.

North of Coromandel and Whitianga are more small towns with timber milling or

▲ *View of Castle Hill and Coromandel Harbour in the 1860s.*
Alexander Turnbull Library

goldmining pasts, like Kauotunu, the scene of a rush in 1889. At the tip of the Peninsula is Moehau Mountain, a place of traditional significance to the Maori. A walkway from Fletcher Bay, which partly follows an old pioneer bridle path, has traces of pre-European pa in the form of trenches, embankments and terraces along its course. The area's Maori past is also recalled at a private museum at Kennedy's Bay. Other pa sites still visible are at Paku, near Tairua, and on the north head of the Whangamata Harbour on the east coast of the Coromandel peninsula. Tairua and Whangamata were once timber ports, and around the turn of the century gold was mined from the hills behind them.

PAEROA-WAIHI

At the southern end of the Coromandel Range are Paeroa and Waihi, both with important places in New Zealand goldmin-

way. The *Settler*, an old river packet, sailed the Waihou until 1936. In 1960 it was burned out at Kawau Island but has been restored and now again plies the river on which it spent much of its working life. Visitors can ride on the *Settler* and on other restored vessels.

At Karangahake is a Goldfields Walkway developed by the Department of Conservation. This takes the walker through an old railway tunnel (which is illuminated) and past the sites of some big mines, including the Crown where the use of the cyanide process to extract gold from crushed quartz was pioneered.

At Waihi are some spectacular monuments to the technological achievements of the heyday of mining on the Coromandel goldfields. The Martha Mine, which operated from 1881 into the 1950s, was one of the most highly productive gold mines in New Zealand, thanks in part to the use of the cyanide process. On Union Hill, Waihi, stand huge cyanide tanks which were erected about 1905 for use in this process. The Number 5 Pumphouse of the Martha Mine, also built in the early years of this century, is now a huge concrete ruin. The cyanide tanks and pumphouse are among New Zealand's most impressive monuments to early industrial enterprise.

The 1912 Waihi strike, an important event in New Zealand's trade union history, is recalled at the local museum.

Visitors who enjoy reliving the days of steam can take a ride on the Goldfields Steam Train.

▲ *Coromandel's Courthouse, built in 1873, is typical of many country courthouses which, by their slightly grand architecture, proclaimed the presence of the law in New Zealand's small towns. Most are no longer in use as courthouses, but many have been retained for alternative public uses.*

◀ *The name of the Brian Boru Hotel in Thames, built in 1905 to replace an earlier building which burned down, reflects the Irish origins of many of New Zealand's nineteenth century immigrants. Its architecture is typical of that of many early New Zealand hotels.*

ing history. At the Gold Camp, a short distance out of Paeroa, are displays of mining equipment. The Paeroa Historical and Arts Society maintains an early Paeroa Street.

The Waihou River, which flows close to Paeroa, was an important waterway until the 1930s, when roads in the area were improved. Near Paeroa, on the site of an old depot of the Northern Steamship Company, is a Maritime Park which recalls the days when the river was the district's main high-

BAY OF PLENTY

Maori lore claims that the Bay of Plenty was the landing place of several of the great Polynesian canoes that journeyed from far-off Hawaiki. Their names live on: *Te Arawa, Mataatua, Takitimu* and *Tokomaru* are some of the canoes that made their first landfall here.

From the time of Cook's visit in 1769 there is no record of any European vessel dropping anchor on these shores until 1828, when the mission schooner *Herald* called in at Tauranga. Flax traders arrived in the 1830s and the settlers followed. Fighting in the New Zealand Wars spilled over into the Bay of Plenty in the 1860s leaving several battle sites and other places of interest to present-day visitors.

Inland is the city of Rotorua, the Rotorua lakes and a thermal region which contains many important sites of traditional Maori significance. The region is a major tourist attraction and also the hub of an increasingly prosperous timber industry.

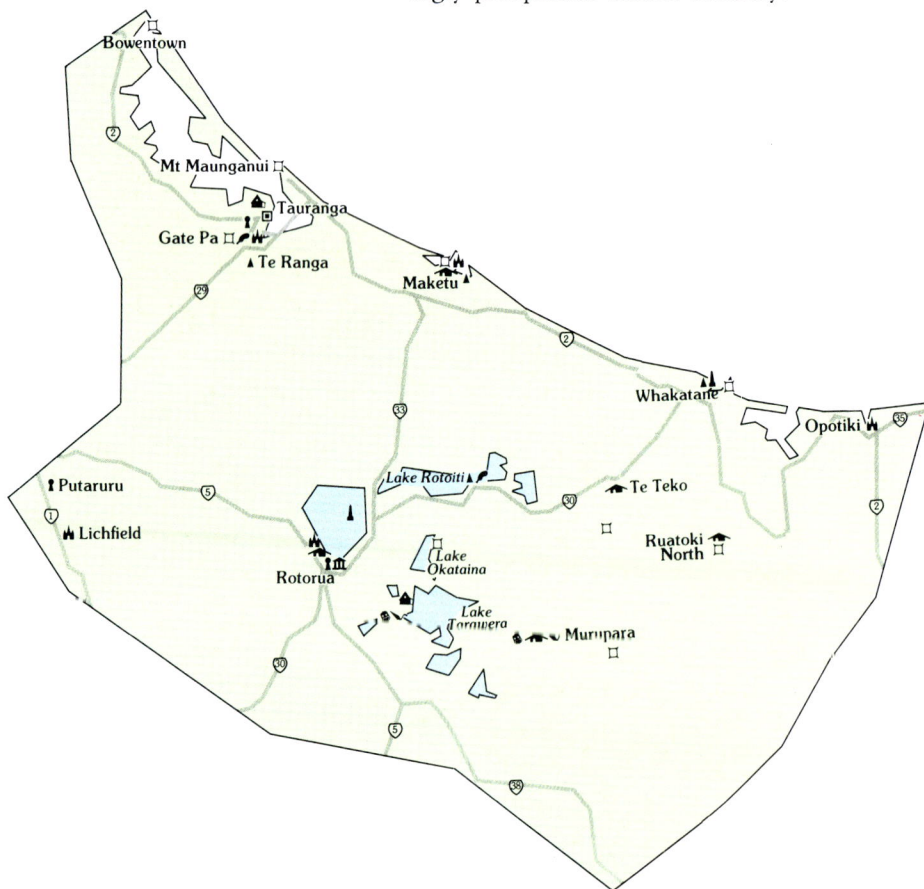

BAY OF PLENTY PA

The Bay of Plenty was named by Captain Cook, but it was a bountiful area even before it got this name, for when Cook sailed up the Bay of Plenty coast in 1769 he noted a large number of pa. The earthworks of many of these pa are still clearly visible. On a headland overlooking the north-western entrance to Tauranga Harbour are the magnificent terraces of a pa, Te Kura a Maia, probably several hundred years old. The pa is an historic reserve and of easy access by road. The earthworks of ancient fortifications on Mt Maunganui are also still visible. There was a large group of pa on the hills above Papamoa at the south-eastern end of Tauranga Harbour which, by tradition, is very old. Many other pa and archaeological sites in the Bay of Plenty remind today's visitors of the district's long Maori past.

TAURANGA

Tauranga's most interesting building is The Elms, a mission house built in 1847 and the most important surviving early mission building outside Northland. The mission itself was founded in 1835 but soon foundered because of troubles with local Maori. It was reopened in 1838. In 1839, the mission library, which still stands in the grounds of the mission house, was built. In the 1830s Archdeacon Alfred Brown began an association with Tauranga which lasted until 1884, although his mission work had virtually ceased by the 1860s. The mission house became his private home in 1873. Today the mission house, still privately owned, is open to the public, its furnishings recalling Tauranga's early days.

One reason for the mission's eclipse in the 1860s was war. Troops were sent to Tauranga at the beginning of 1864 and at Gate Pa, on the outskirts of today's town, the British suffered heavy losses. Gate Pa is a reserve and St George's Church, built in 1900, stands on the site of the pa itself. The battle at Gate Pa was followed by a further engagement in June at Te Ranga where the British revenged their loss. A commemorative plaque stands on the site of the rifle pits at Te Ranga, on the Tauranga-Rotorua highway. On two bushed knolls in the centre of Tauranga are a military cemetery and the

▲ *Little changed from when it was built in 1847, The Elms Mission House, Tauranga, became the private home of Archdeacon Alfred Brown in 1873 and is still in private ownership, though open to the public.*

◄ *Redoubt on the site of Gate Pa, scene of a notable battle during the Land Wars.*
Alexander Turnbull Library

WHAKATANE

▲ *The village of Ohinemutu on the foreshore of Lake Rotorua has impressive examples of nineteenth century Maori carvings on its public buildings, which include a fine lakeside church.*

▶ *The Church of St Stephen the Martyr in Opotiki was built in 1864, a year before the missionary stationed there, Carl Volkner, was killed in a controversial incident in the Land Wars.*

earthworks of the Monmouth Redoubt. Guns also remain on the site of the redoubt.

The Tauranga Historic Village replicates a turn-of-the-century town, with old buildings shifted onto the site. There is a model of a Maori pa, and the exhibits also touch on early mining and engineering as well as the early days of transport. In operation are a steam train and an old steam tug, the *Taioma*.

The small coastal town of Maketu has traditional significance for the Maori as the place where the *Arawa* canoe came to rest. It is from this canoe that the Bay of Plenty tribes trace their descent. A cairn at the river mouth marks the traditional last resting place of the canoe. The town became a flax trading post in the late 1820s, and a mission station was founded there in 1842. During the Bay of Plenty fighting in the 1860s the Pukemaire Redoubt was built on an old pa site behind the mission station, where St Thomas's Church, built in 1868, stands. In the graveyard of St Thomas's is a memorial to an Arawa chief who was killed in intra-tribal fighting in 1864. Two interesting meeting houses stand on the site of an ancient pa.

One of the great figures of Maori legend is Toi, an explorer who, searching for his lost grandson, Whatonga, abandoned his quest on arriving at Whakatane and decided to settle. There Whatonga, himself searching for his grandfather, was eventually reunited with Toi. On Kohi Point, near Whakatane, in the Kaputerangi Historic Reserve, are several pa sites, one of which is traditionally regarded as Toi's pa. Archaeological evidence suggests the site was first occupied some time between the late ninth and early eleventh centuries. The fortifications which can be seen today are believed to have been built in the fifteenth century. There are several pa sites along the ridge out to Kohi Point and, although some are obscured by undergrowth, terraces, pits and defensive ditches and banks can be seen in several places.

Whakatane gained its name from an incident when the *Mataatua* canoe arrived and there is a plaque at the Whakatane Heads marking the landing place. When the canoe beached the women remained aboard while the men went ashore to explore. While the men were away, the canoe drifted off the beach. Paddling a canoe was a man's job, and the paddles were tapu to women, so they sat helpless until Wairaka, with the cry 'Whakatane' — I will act as a man — seized the paddle and saved the canoe. There is a model of the *Mataatua* canoe beside the Pohaturoa Rock in the centre of Whakatane.

Whakatane's European history began, like Maketu's, with flax traders who established themselves in the early 1830s. In 1867, during the Te Kooti disturbances, Whakatane was garrisoned, then attacked and sacked by Te Kooti in March 1869. A memorial on the main road to Opotiki marks the place where a mill owner, Jean Guerrin, defended his mill but was eventually killed by the attackers.

Opotiki has an historic church associated with an incident in the Bay of Plenty disturbances of the 1860s. In 1859 a German Lutheran missionary, the Rev. Carl Volkner, founded a mission at Opotiki. In 1864 he built the church which survives, but a year later he was captured and killed by the Hau Hau leader, Kereopa. After this incident the church was surrounded by a redoubt. In 1875 it was rededicated as the Church of St Stephen the Martyr.

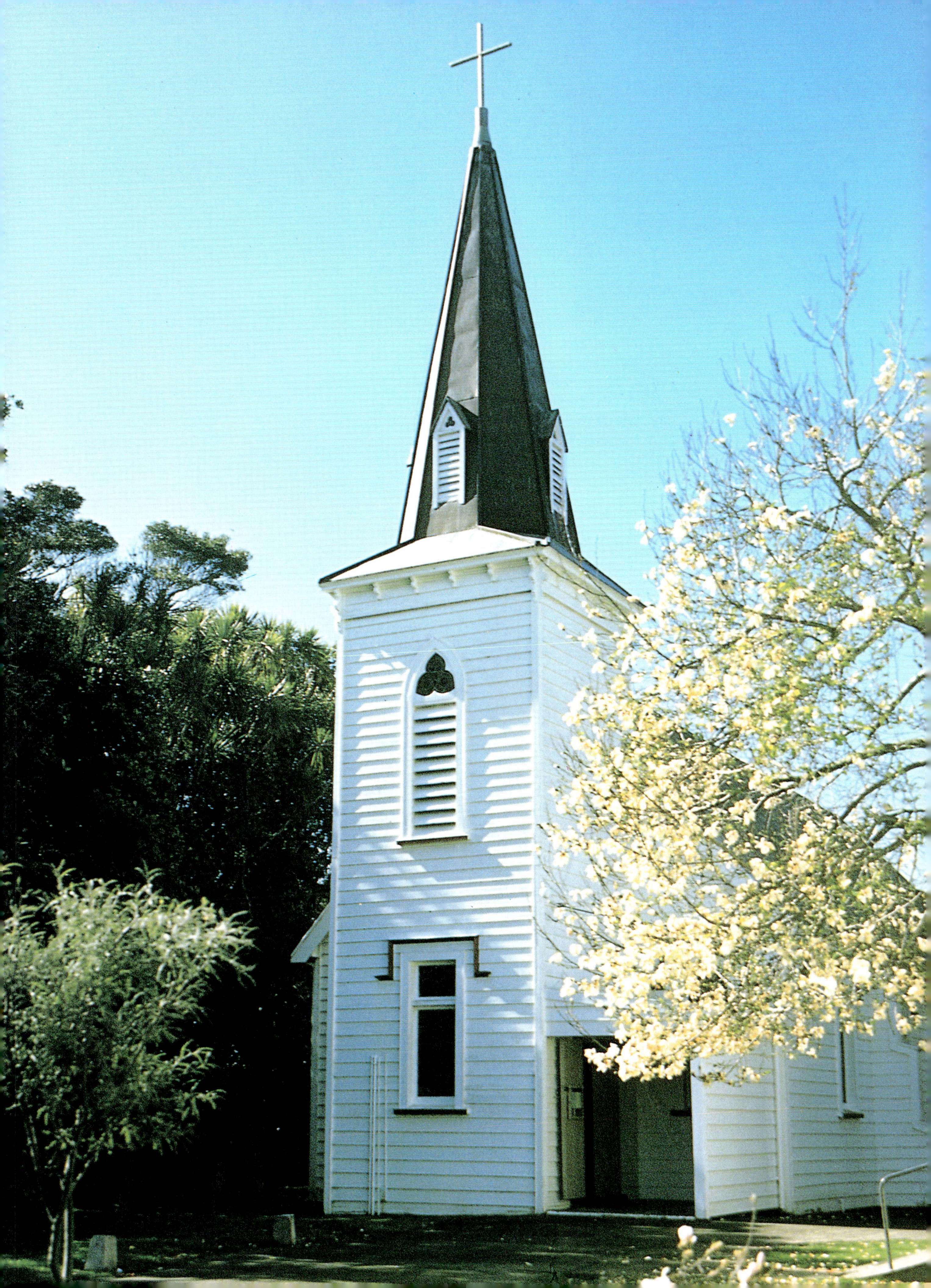

▶ *Rotorua's grandiose Tudor-style Bath House was built in 1906-07 as part of the Government's effort to promote Rotorua as a spa. It now houses the local art gallery and museum.*

INLAND BAY OF PLENTY

Inland from Whakatane, on the Kokohinau Marae in the small town of Te Teko, is the important Ngati Awa meeting house, Ruataupare, built by Te Kooti in 1882 in gratitude to the people who supported him in his conflict with the Government. It was renovated in the 1920s and is today being carefully preserved. In the Rangitaiki Valley south of Te Teko are concentrations of old pa whose earthworks are still visible.

South of Taneatua, in the Ruatoki area, many pa sites can be seen on the lower hill slopes. The area is well known for the many meeting houses of the Tuhoe. Many more pa sites are evident near the Waimana Plains adjacent to State Highway 2, and in the Waiotahi Valley.

Near Murupara, the main highway passes the Kaingaroa rock shelter, where there are images of canoes cut into the soft volcanic rock. The Whirinaki Valley was an important centre of Maori life in the nineteenth century; meeting houses built by Te Kooti and a number of pa can be seen in the valley and on the Te Taupiri ridge.

ROTORUA

The Rotorua district is the heartland of the Arawa tribe and there are many reminders of the district's long Maori past. Around Lake Okataina are several pa sites and at one, Te Koutu, well preserved rua (kumara storage pits) can be seen. The model pa above the Whakarewarewa Reserve in Rotorua, palisaded and with buildings characteristic of the pre-European era, gives an idea of how these and other now-deserted sites once looked. Near the Tarawera landing are Maori rock drawings depicting a canoe, a frequent motif in ancient rock carvings in the area. On Mokoia Island, in Lake Rotorua, which was once terraced and cultivated, there is an ancient stone statue of Rongo, the god of agriculture.

The historic path known as Hongi's Track between Lakes Rotoehu and Rotoiti is part of the route that the Ngapuhi chief, Hongi Hika, dragged his canoes in order to attack the Arawa on Mokoia. Just off the track is a sacred tree, Hinehopu, and a stone memorial to a chief who was killed in 1823.

At Ohinemutu, an old Maori settlement around which Rotorua has grown, there is a Maori village catering for tourists. In the village are several items of genuine historic interest among them the carved meeting house, Tamatekapua, which was erected in 1878, but substantially rebuilt in 1939–43. Some of the carvings are older than the house itself and may date back to about 1800. St Faith's Church, Ohinemutu, was built in 1910. It is Tudor on the outside, but decorated in traditional Maori fashion within. Relics of the New Zealand Wars are displayed in the church.

At Te Wairoa are the excavated ruins, partly reclaimed, of a village buried in the

Mt Tarawera eruption of 1886. Before then, with a two-storey hotel, the village had been the starting point for tourists visiting the Pink and White Terraces, also obliterated in the eruption. The Te Amorangi Trust Museum has Maori, missionary and pioneer material housed in an old farmhouse and its adjacent workshop.

Rotorua has, for more than 100 years, been a popular tourist centre. The finest monument to the town's history as a tourist resort is the Tudor-style bath house, built in 1906–07 as part of the Government's effort to develop Rotorua as a spa. In the building is a museum, with a Maori collection and a furnished colonial cottage.

Rotorua was formerly an important centre for the milling of native timber. At Putaruru, on State Highway 1, a timber museum displays machinery, artefacts and photographs which illustrate the history of the timber industry in the central North Island. Lichfield, just south of Putaruru, boasts an intriguing little stone building. Built in 1888, it served first as a pub, but in 1945 was converted for use as a church.

EAST CAPE

The historic interest of Gisborne and the coast north of Poverty Bay is both Maori and European. The area has a long Maori history, and pa sites and meeting houses are among its historic places. In 1769, the hills behind Gisborne were the first part of New Zealand sighted from the *Endeavour* on James Cook's first voyage and there are sites on the East Coast linked to Cook. In the early nineteenth century shore whaling stations were established and it was also a scene of missionary activity, the Turanga mission station being opened in 1842. In the 1860s the district became caught up in warfare and Te Kooti raids.

In the later nineteenth and twentieth centuries the East Coast remained an area of importance for the Maori and one distinctive in New Zealand for its large Maori population. Large stations on the hills and smaller farms on the more fertile river flats have provided the area's economic foundation since European settlement, though the area was notorious for its bad roads until well into the twentieth century. Coastal shipping continued to play an important role in the area's economy for longer here than in most other parts of New Zealand. These many woven strands make the district one of great historic interest.

MEETING HOUSES

The most striking legacy of the long Maori history of the East Coast is its meeting houses. None now standing dates from pre-European times, but some have survived from last century. In Gisborne itself, Poho o Rawiri, built in 1935, is one of the largest meeting houses in the country. It is not built according to traditional design but incorporates some old carvings. Above the meeting house is a small Maori church.

At Manutuke, south-west of Gisborne, the carved meeting house of Te Mana o Turanga, completed in 1883, blends traditional Maori arts with more popular folk art elements. Some of the slabs are older than the house itself which stands near the site of the house, Te Hau ki Turanga, built in 1842 and now in the National Museum, Wellington. Also in Manutuke is the finely painted meeting house, Poho o Rukupo, recently restored, which has strong associations with the Maori battalion which fought in World War II. Next to Poho o Rukupo is a church, the third on the site, dedicated in 1913. Its plain, plastered brick exterior gives no hint of its richly carved interior.

Just north of Patutahi, at Waituhi, the meeting house Rongopai was built in the mid-1880s. Inside, the house is not carved but has remarkable paintings executed in a transitional style. Maori decorations and motifs were used, but European influences are apparent, making the paintings a unique expression of folk art.

The other evidence of the importance of the district to the pre-European Maori, besides these later meeting houses, is the large number of old pa sites on the hills bordering the Waipaoa River flats. Most are indistinct and difficult to locate.

GISBORNE

'Young Nick' (Nicholas Young) sighted New Zealand from the *Endeavour* early in October 1769. On 9 October, Cook landed at Kaiti Beach, the first recorded occasion on which a European stepped onto New Zealand soil. The memorial on the approximate site of the landing was unveiled in 1906. On Kaiti Hill there is a lookout with a plaque which notes the first landing on the shore below. A statue of Nicholas Young in Young Nick's playground is a tribute to the cabin boy who first sighted New Zealand.

In the second half of the 1860s, the Gisborne district became caught up in the last phases of the New Zealand Wars, when the Hau Hau and Te Kooti prolonged the fighting against the European newcomers.

A tragic episode of these later wars was Te Kooti's attack on 10 November 1868, on the settlement of Matawhero. Te Kooti's forces killed 33 Europeans and 37 Maori. Many of the victims were buried in the Makaraka cemetery. A short time afterwards, Te Kooti's forces were defeated at Ngatapa Hill, west of Gisborne, and in a shameful episode 120 of his captured followers were summarily executed. Ngatapa

Pa is still an impressive place. The site of the blockhouse built in Gisborne in 1869 after Te Kooti's attack on Matawhero is marked by a plaque.

In 1842 the Turanga mission was founded by William Williams. Links with the Williams family are provided by a house, Te Rau Kahikitea, which was built in 1876 by Bishop W.L. Williams, and a memorial window in the Waituhi church.

The site of the first Maori church built in Gisborne in 1864 is marked by an old cemetery in Hirini Street. The church stood next to an early Poho o Rawiri marae, which was moved when land was excavated for the inner harbour basin. Only the graves in the Hirini Street cemetery remain as reminders of the earlier importance of this spot.

The Presbyterian church at Matawhero was built in the mid-1860s as a schoolroom. It was the only building in the vicinity to survive Te Kooti's 1868 raid. It became a Presbyterian church in 1872, and although altered and extended at various times up to 1904, remains one of the most historic buildings in the Gisborne area.

The Gisborne Museum and Arts Centre has a comprehensive photographic display

▲ *The Tokomaru Bay freezing works, which are now just ruins.*
Alexander Turnbull Library

► *One of the finest painted Maori meeting houses in New Zealand, Rongopai, in the small settlement of Waituhi near Gisborne, was built by the followers of the fighting leader Te Kooti in the 1880s in anticipation of a visit by him to the East Coast which never eventuated.*

►► *The restored Wyllie Cottage in Gisborne, built in 1872, is a classic of simple colonial architecture. It stands next to the Gisborne Museum.*

of Gisborne's history and also material relating to the Maori in the pre-European and contact periods. A whaleboat and trypots make it one of the few places at which the story of East Coast shore-based whaling can be followed. Next to the museum is the restored Wyllie Cottage, built in 1872 and shifted onto its present site in 1886. It is Gisborne's oldest complete house.

Gisborne also has a museum of transport and technology at the A & P Showgrounds on the outskirts of the town. One of Gisborne's stately homes, Ulverstone, built in 1911, is now an art gallery and reception centre. At Matawhero there is a private collection, at the East Coast Fertiliser Company, of horse-drawn implements.

Until the 1920s the sea was the usual way of getting to and from Gisborne and other East Coast towns. A plaque marks the

site of the old passenger wharf used by travellers in those days. Another relic from the days when sea transport was important to Gisborne is a house which was once the bridge of a ship, the *Star of Canada*, wrecked in 1912 on Kaiti Beach.

Fifty kilometres inland from Gisborne, the Otoko Walkway follows the line of an old railway up the Waihuka River. Sights along the way include an old tunnel and the monumental concrete piers of a bridge. The line was built between 1899 and 1917, when its last few kilometres were opened. It was never completed to Opotiki as planned and closed in 1959. There are reminders along the walkway of the pick-and-shovel days of railway construction and at Rakauroa is a museum in an abandoned railway station with displays and exhibits recalling the heyday of the branch line.

▶ *The meeting house Tukaki at Te Kaha is, like the great majority of Maori meeting houses, named after an ancestor of the tribe. Like many other East Coast meeting houses, Tukaki was built this century under the inspiration of Sir Apirana Ngata.*

THE EAST CAPE

Whangara, between Gisborne and Tolaga Bay, is a place of traditional importance to the Ngati Porou. A carved meeting house has a tekoteko (figure at the peak of the gable) of Paikea riding a black whale. Whangara also has an early European missionary church.

At Anaura Bay and Tolaga Bay, north of Gisborne, are two more Cook landing sites. A plaque on a cairn at Anaura Bay commemorates Cook's visit on 20–22 October 1769, when he took on water. After leaving Anaura Bay, Cook anchored for six days at Tolaga Bay, to the south, where he had a friendlier reception from the local Maori. Cook's Cove, Tolaga Bay, is accessible by foot along a walkway. There is a plaque at the cove, where Cook took water, wood and greens on board the *Endeavour*.

At both these bays there is abundant evidence of pre-European occupation of the area. The Anaura Bay Walkway passes rectangular holes in the ground which are the remains of kumara storage pits.

The Spencer Scenic Reserve, at the entrance to the Hikuwai Valley, also has evidence of storage pits. A fine example of an old pa may be seen from the Tauwhareparae Road, in the Mangaheia Valley. South of Tolaga Bay, in private ownership, is the site of Te Raroa, the fighting pa of Porourangi, ancestor of Ngati Porou.

A derelict house built by one of the earliest European farming families in the area is a feature of the Spencer Scenic Reserve. At Anaura Bay the Waipare homestead, built of kauri in the 1880s, is a fine example of a large East Coast station homestead. An old coach road to Gisborne passes through Te Raroa Station, near Tolaga Bay.

At Tolaga Bay a long wharf remains from the days when sea transport was vital to East Coast communities. Tokomaru Bay was a major export port between 1911 and 1953. Here, and at Hicks Bay, there is evidence of old freezing works. Other old port towns like Waipiro Bay, Tuparoa and Port Awanui are now all but deserted.

Along the road around the East Cape are many places important in Maori history and tradition. About 3 km from Ruatoria, at Mangahanea, is a marae of great importance to the Ngati Porou, the meeting house of which was built in 1896, incorporating some older carvings. The Ruatoria district has strong links with an important Maori leader of the early twentieth century, Sir Apirana Ngata.

The Ngata homestead is at Waiomatatini, a few kilometres from Ruatoria. It is still a private house, but can be seen from the road. Near the homestead is the Porourangi meeting house, built in 1888 and shifted to its present site in 1936.

The Anglican Church of St Luke at Waiomatatini was erected by the Williams family to commemorate Major Ropata Wahawaha, who fought against Te Kooti. Tikitiki, across the river from Waiomatatini, has a Maori memorial church, built in 1924–26, to honour the dead of World War I. The arch in front of the church is a memorial to Arihia, the first Lady Ngata.

▶ *The east window of St Mary's, Tikitiki, a church renowned for the quality of its Maori decorative work, shows the figures of two Maori captains, P. Kaa and H. Kohere, both killed in action in 1917, kneeling at the feet of the crucified Christ. The background detail is New Zealand flora surrounded by Maori designs.* Graham Stewart

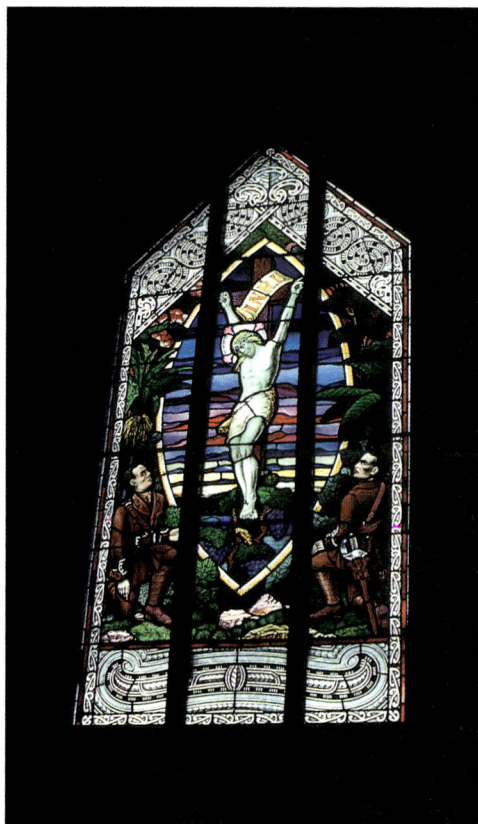

EASTERN BAY OF PLENTY

At Te Araroa, just before Hicks Bay, there is an enormous pohutukawa tree on the foreshore, Te Waha o Rerekohu, which is over 600 years old and of traditional significance to the Maori. From Te Araroa a road leads to the East Cape where there is a lighthouse, built in 1906 on an island off the coast and later shifted onto the mainland. Hicks Bay has an important meeting house, Tuwhakairiora. The carvings inside date from 1872 although the house itself was erected on its present site later, as a memorial to Ngati Porou who died overseas. On the peninsula immediately north of Hicks Bay there is a well preserved fortification.

Beyond Hicks Bay, the coastline runs south and west towards the Bay of Plenty. The landscape and historical associations are similar to those of the coast between Gisborne and Hicks Bay, although it is the territory of Te Whanau-a-Apanui. The Potikirua coastline has many pa along it. Whangaparaoa is of traditional importance to the Maori as the place of first landfall of the *Arawa* and *Tainui* canoes on the voyage from Hawaiki. At Raukokore are two old and picturesquely sited churches.

Te Kaha was once a whaling station, but there are few reminders in the settlement of this, even though open-boat whaling was still being pursued here as late as the 1930s. The finely carved Tukaki meeting house is one of the important houses of Te Whanau-a-Apanui. The remains of a pa at Te Kaha are visible, but on private land. Other old pa are along the sides of the Motu River, the Waiaua Valley (traces only) and elsewhere in the vicinity.

► *The meeting house Te Mana o Turanga, one of the finest carved houses in the country, stands on the Wakato Marae, Manutuke. The house was opened in 1883.*

CENTRAL PLATEAU

The volcanic plateau of the Central North Island, with its high mountains and the broad expanse of Lake Taupo, is the homeland of Ngati Tuwharetoa. Better known for the magnificence of its unusual scenery than for its sites of historic interest, there are nevertheless such sites to be found in the region. They are associated with the history of the Tuwharetoa, with early mission activity in the area, with skirmishing towards the end of the New Zealand Wars and with the development of transport links and of tourism. The Tongariro National Park was the first in the country, the nucleus of today's park having been given to the people of New Zealand by the Tuwharetoa chief Te Heuheu Tukino IV in 1887.

TAUPO

The central North Island was drawn late into the discord between Maori and Pakeha, but has interesting historic sites related to those hostilities. The settlement of Taupo dates from the establishment at Tapuaeharuru, in 1869, of an Armed Constabulary post. A redoubt was built for defence against Te Kooti and occupied for about 15 years, although there was never any fighting at Taupo. The post was abandoned in 1885, but the remains of the redoubt, built of earth and pumice and regularly refashioned, can be seen in a reserve in Taupo on the eastern bank of the Waikato River below its outfall from Lake Taupo. A small ammunition magazine, built of pumice in about 1874 and rebuilt in 1969, stands on the site. Taupo has a regional museum with Maori and early European artefacts on display. Four kilometres north of Taupo is the Huka Historic Village, where craftspeople work and there are many buildings and artefacts of historic interest.

The road from Taupo to Napier follows roughly the old Maori track to the coast. From 1865 to 1874, a road was built along this line, with military posts and blockhouses down its length. The line was a frontier between the Urewera country where Te Kooti was active between 1870 and 1872 and the more settled areas. Some 17 km along the road from Taupo is the Opepe Reserve where a detachment of soldiers was surprised by Te Kooti in June 1869. Nine were killed in the encounter. Today there remain only the graves of the nine victims and, in the bush, a five-metre-long water trough fashioned from a totara log which was in use at the time of the fighting. About 45 km along the road to Napier is the Runanga historic reserve, containing the remains of another military post occupied by the Armed Constabulary in the 1870s.

WAIHI

The shores of Lake Taupo (and other parts of the central North Island) are the ancestral home of the Ngati Tuwharetoa. One of the tribe's main centres is Waihi, a private village at the southern end of the lake. At Pukawa, near Waihi, a large hui (meeting) took place in 1856 at which chiefs from all over the North Island met to debate the loss of land to settlers. At this hui the Waikato Chief Te Wherowhero was chosen to be the first Maori King.

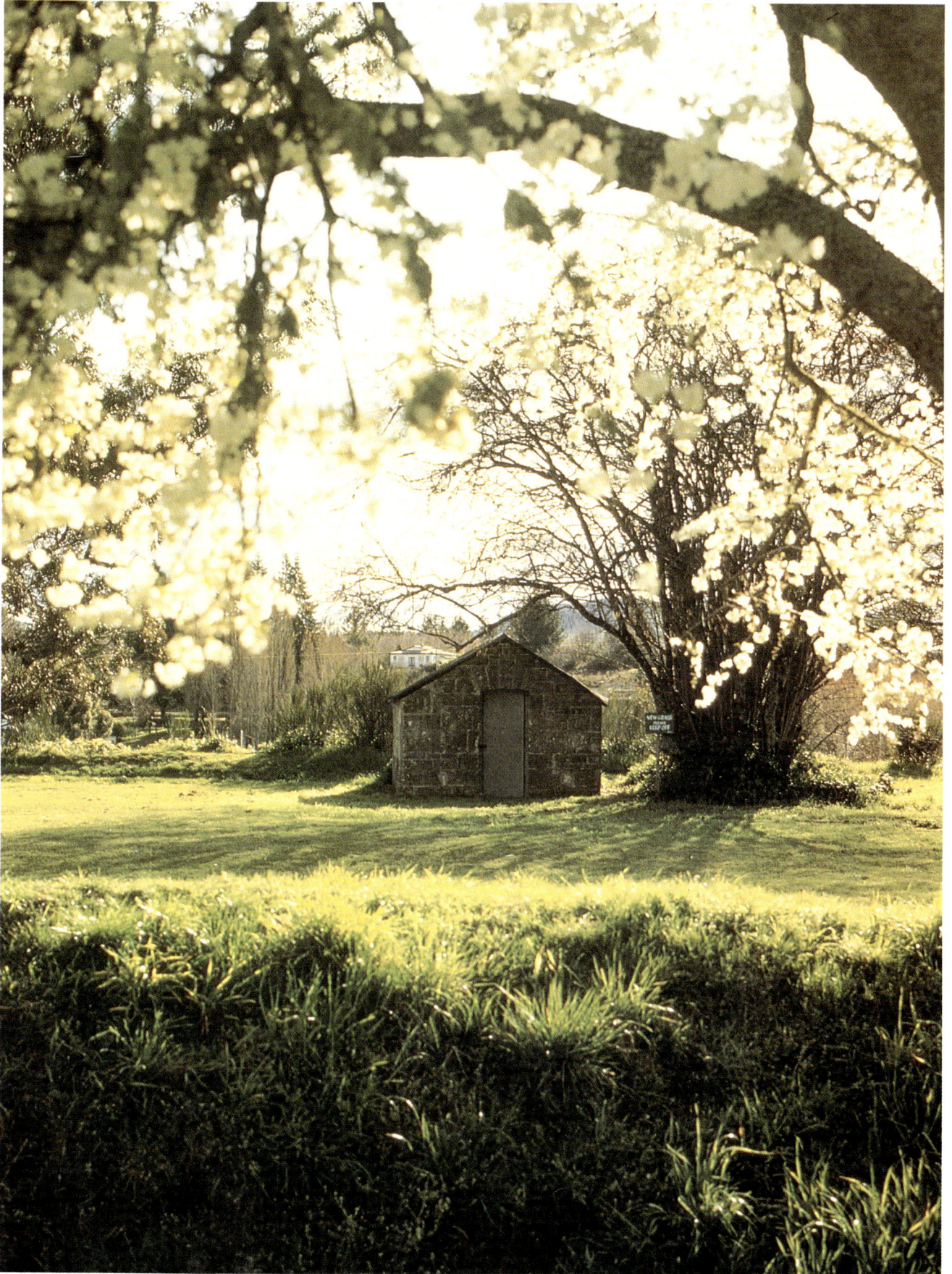

► *The last major engagement of the Land Wars of the 1860s was fought in the central North Island at Te Porere. Te Kooti and his small force were driven from the redoubt they had built in October 1869 but escaped into the nearby bush. Te Kooti was never captured.*

In Waihi is the Te Heuheu mausoleum, where some of the paramount chiefs of Tuwharetoa are buried. Nearby is the meeting house, Tapeka, opened in 1959. Pukawa was the site of an early mission station occupied by Thomas Grace and his family. It was abandoned in 1863. An interesting homestead, still occupied by descendants of the missionary, was built in the 1880s and can be seen from the lake.

TURANGI

Turangi, which grew up in recent times as a hydro-electric construction town, was a Maori village in the nineteenth century. In the visitor centre are items of archaeological interest found during the construction of the power project. The older part of Turangi lies along the banks of the Tongariro River, its growth keeping pace with the development of the trout hatchery and fishing. Rainbow trout were first released into the Tongariro River in 1898 and later releases have led to the river becoming internationally acclaimed for its fish. The hatchery to the south of the town provides historical information about the fishing, as well as a chance to see trout in the spawning stream.

TOKAANU

Tokaanu is an old settlement. Te Kooti made it his headquarters during the New Zealand Wars and later it was policed by the Armed Constabulary. The Tokaanu Hotel was opened in 1874 and the present hotel holds the oldest licence in the Taupo area. St Paul's Anglican Church is a memorial to the missionary, Thomas Grace, and his wife Agnes, who were the first Europeans to live in the area. The church is decorated with tukutuku (woven panels) and Maori rafter patterns. A shattered bell in the porch was brought to the district by Mr Grace. Near St Paul's is the Roman Catholic Church, St Mary's, also decorated with Maori art, and a 1931 meeting house, Puhaorangi.

TE PORERE

South-west of Turangi is the scene of the last major engagement of the Land Wars. In 1869 Te Kooti, having been driven from the

East Coast and Bay of Plenty, built a redoubt at Te Porere below Mount Tongariro. Here, on 4 October 1869, Te Kooti and his small force were attacked. In the confusion of the battle Te Kooti escaped into nearby bush. He was never captured and until pardoned in 1883 lived in the King Country. Today both the main redoubt and lower earthworks which formed an advanced line of protection are still clear and protected in a historic reserve.

On the shore of Lake Rotoaira at Opotaka are the excavated sites of partly restored dwellings from which visitors can gain an impression of how the Maori of the area lived in the early nineteenth century.

MAIN TRUNK RAILWAY

An interesting chapter in the history of the central North Island was the building of the North Island Main Trunk Railway around the western edge of the volcanic plateau. The section of line from Taumarunui to Taihape was not completed until 1908–09. Today the line is a monument to the skills of early New Zealand surveyors, engineers and workmen. Among the sights of historic as well as engineering interest on the line are the Raurimu spiral and several great viaducts. One point on the line was the scene of the tragic Tangiwai disaster in 1953. The foundations of the railway bridge, swept away by a lahar flood from Mt Ruapehu, can still be seen in the bed of the Tangiwai River, west of Waiouru.

WAIOURU

Waiouru is the home of the Queen Elizabeth II Army Memorial Museum, where visitors can learn much to help them appreciate historic sites elsewhere in the country, such as the pa and redoubts of the New Zealand Wars. The museum displays relics and records of New Zealand's military history and hostile encounters that have taken place in New Zealand and by New Zealanders overseas. The old Waiouru homestead still stands inside the army camp.

TARANAKI

Much of Taranaki's historic interest stems from its having been the scene of the outbreak of the main phase of the New Zealand Wars in the early 1860s. Several places in Taranaki are connected with events leading up to and during the fighting of that decade. The province's long Maori history before the disruptions, first of tribal wars in the early nineteenth century, then of the arrival of European settlers, is still plainly evident in many ancient pa and other sites. Whalers had settled on the North Taranaki coast by the 1830s, but large-scale European settlement of Taranaki began with the founding of the New Zealand Company settlement at New Plymouth in the early 1840s. Several buildings survive from the earliest two decades of European settlement of Taranaki. After the difficulties of their early years, the European settlers began to prosper later in the nineteenth century and the province subsequently earned an important place in the history of the dairy industry. The symbol of the province — Mt Taranaki — is a mountain of great traditional significance to the Maori of the region.

MAORI TARANAKI

When European settlers arrived in Taranaki in 1841 to found New Plymouth, there were few Maori living there. Taranaki was favourable to Maori ways of life in pre-European times, but tribal wars in the early nineteenth century had driven the North Taranaki tribes south as far as what is now the western end of New Plymouth. Many Te Atiawa people left the area, settling on both sides of Cook Strait. Some of North Taranaki's Maori historic places are where fighting occurred during these tribal wars; others were important centres of Maori population.

The remains of a large number of old pa can still be seen in Taranaki. Some of these pa are the sites of still-remembered events in Maori history; some later gained added historical significance as the sites of battles during the Taranaki campaigns of the New Zealand Wars. Their importance today is evidence of the long Maori history of Taranaki.

There are also many places in Taranaki of traditional significance to the Maori. The tribes of Taranaki link their identity with Mt Taranaki, as other tribes link theirs with mountains in their own territories.

Some pa sites are within the boundaries of modern New Plymouth, although most traces of Maori living have been obliterated. Along the walkway which follows the Te Henui Stream are Pukewarangi, Parihamoi and Puketarata. On all these sites some earthworks are still visible; Pukewarangi is the most picturesque and easily accessible of the pre-European pa in New Plymouth. The site of the Otaka pa is now occupied by a cool store. In the 1830s the pa was bravely defended by a remnant of the Te Atiawa against the invading Waikato. The grave of a Te Atiawa chief, Pohorama Te Whiti, is on the site.

Mokau

Tongaporutu

Pukearuhe

Urenui

Waitara

New Plymouth

Oakura

Whangamomona

Puniho

Pungarehu
Parihaka

Mt Taranaki

Douglas

Stratford

Opunake

Kapuni

Normanby

Manaia

Hawera

Manutahi

Patea

Waverley

Immediately north of New Plymouth, near the mouth of the Waiwakaiho River, is Rewarewa, the largest and most historic pa close to today's city. The ditches and banks which defended an area protected also by a river cliff are still quite obvious. Some of the sites of pre-European pa are still occupied by marae. On the north bank of the river in Waitara is the Owae Marae, also known as Manukorihi. The meeting house, Te Ikaroa a Maui, was built in 1936.

Inland from Waitara is one of Taranaki's most historic sites. The pa Pukerangiora was a major stronghold of Te Atiawa. In the tribal wars of the 1820s and early 1830s it was taken by the Waikato forces, then recaptured. During the Taranaki campaigns of the New Zealand Wars, in the early 1860s, part of the pa (Te Arei) was refortified by Maori opposed to the sale of the Waitara block. The pa was eventually taken by British forces under General Pratt who had a long sap (protective trench) dug towards the fortifications. Parts of the sap and its associated redoubts can be seen on the slopes below the pa. Situated within the present reserve are a well preserved section of sap and the remains of a British redoubt built in 1865.

The historic pa Okoki, near Urenui north of Waitara, has associations with Te Rauparaha, and in the twentieth century

with Te Rangi Hiroa (Sir Peter Buck). A memorial to Sir Peter stands on the historic reserve and a stone on the edge of the Urenui golf course marks his birthplace.

Along the coast north of Urenui can be seen the earthworks of some spectacular cliff-top pa. South of the White Cliffs is the pa Ruataki, close by the settlement of Waiiti. A long narrow ridge was turned into a series of defendable platforms by ditches and banks. Another pa, Katikatiaka, in a similar situation at the north end of the White Cliffs, was a stronghold of the Ngati Tama people and guarded the northern approaches to Taranaki.

At Tongaporutu on the north Taranaki coast, there are early Maori rock carvings on the walls of sea-carved caverns, which can be reached by taking time and care. Further north again, at Mokau, is a stone held by tradition to be the anchor stone of the *Tainui* canoe. It has been set in concrete at Maniaroa, a pa which has been used subsequently as an urupa (burial ground).

Some of the ancient pa south of New Plymouth are still obvious features on the landscape, but others are faint and many have been destroyed.

Inland from Oakura, on a promontory protected by a loop in the Oakura River, are the ancient fortifications of Koru. Terraces, ditches, banks and pits are still visible in the

▲ *Redoubt, with a wooden watchtower, at Manaia in South Taranaki, built during the Land Wars.*
Alexander Turnbull Library

bush now covering the site. Especially interesting are stone walls, formed of river boulders, used to face the fronts of terraces.

Tataraimaka, another ancient pa which is still reasonably obvious, sits on a coastal headland and is protected in a historic reserve. Nearby are the earthworks of St George's Redoubt built in 1863. On the marae at Puniho is a sacred rock called Toka-a-Rauhotu which, according to legend, guided Taranaki on his journey from the central North Island after being driven away by a jealous Tongariro for aspiring to the love of Pihanga. The rock is set on a concrete base and is still the focus for ceremonial observances by local Maori.

THE TARANAKI WARS

The roots of war in Taranaki go back to the early days of settlement, when the European immigrants landed in an area largely depopulated, but still claimed by different tribes and hapu. The New Zealand Company claimed to have purchased a large tract of Taranaki land, but this was disputed. The settlement seemed set to prosper when a Land Commissioner, William Spain, awarded the Company a tract of more than 60,000 acres, to the great disquiet of Te Atiawa people, many of whom were returning to the area. In 1844, Governor FitzRoy reversed Spain's award of this large tract to the Company. Delighted Maori who were opposed to selling land erected a 'pou tutaki' (*pou*, pole; *tutaki*, to bar or block) to remind the settlers of the limit prescribed for their settlement. The original pole was burned in the 1870s but later replaced with a replica which still stands by the roadside beyond the Waiwakaiho River.

Over the next 15 years insufficient land passed into European hands to satisfy the increasingly frustrated settlers. Meanwhile, conflicts erupted among the Maori between those who wanted to sell land to the Europeans and those who did not. A stone cross by a roadside near New Plymouth marks the Puketapu feud, one of these conflicts.

War broke out in Taranaki in 1860, when Governor Gore Browne insisted on purchasing a block of land at the mouth of the Waitara River against the will of a large part of Te Atiawa led by Wiremu Kingi. When the survey of the block was thwarted, martial law was proclaimed, the disputed block occupied, and the Maori dwellings and cultivations on it destroyed. The Waikato, Taranaki and Ngati Ruanui were drawn into the conflict. Both north and south of New Plymouth are the sites of engagements and fortifications of the two Taranaki campaigns. On many of the sites earthworks are still visible, although faint in some cases.

The battle of Waireka, the first major engagement of the first war, was fought about the pa, Kaipopo, on 28 March 1860, near the present-day settlement of Omata. A plaque marks the site. The Waireka Redoubt was built in July 1860 and was the scene of skirmishing for some weeks. It survives as faint depressions in a paddock and its shape can still be seen from the air. Remnants of the Omata stockade are still prominent. Between New Plymouth and Waitara are several battle sites. The first Taranaki Campaign ended with the seige of General Pratt at Pukerangiora.

The second Taranaki War broke out in 1863 when Governor Grey re-occupied the Tataraimaka and Omata blocks. Just west of the church in Omata is a memorial to several farmers who were ambushed and killed at the beginning of this war.

At Tataraimaka, by the important ancient pa, St George's Redoubt was built in 1863. Mataitawa Redoubt, near Lepperton, was built in October 1864. A large rectangular fort, it had defending angles built out at each corner to provide flanking fire along the faces. A relic of the wars in New Plymouth is the Albuhera Cottage (privately owned, but visible from the street), built in 1863 for troops in New Plymouth for the second Taranaki Campaign. Another reminder of the fighting is the memorial on Marsland Hill, once the site of a pa.

At the end of the 1860s, after its two wars were over, Taranaki saw another hostile incident. Pukearuhe is at the southern end of the White Cliffs. A pa was built there on the terrace above the sea possibly around 1500 AD. In 1863 a blockhouse and redoubt were built on the site to prevent hostile Ngati Maniapoto from moving towards the European settlements in Taranaki. Skirmishing persisted in the area for some months, and the redoubt was occupied for most of the 1860s. In 1869 the Gascoigne family, the missionary John Whiteley and two other men were killed at Pukearuhe in an isolated act of hostility. The concrete remains of soldiers' housing

can be found, and nearby is evidence of the earthworks of the redoubt. The most prominent feature is the memorial erected to commemorate the killing of Whiteley.

North of Pukearuhe is a historic site dating from the late nineteenth century. To expedite the passage of stock up and down the coast, a 50-metre tunnel was cut through the sea cliffs and it is still possible to walk through this tunnel.

NEW PLYMOUTH

The first immigrants of the New Zealand Company arrived at New Plymouth in 1841. The settlement grew only slowly, partly because some local Maori were reluctant to sell land. Their reluctance eventually drove the settlers and their Government to provoke war over the Waitara purchase. Some of New Plymouth's historic places date from before the years of war.

The whalers, New Plymouth's first Europeans, arrived in the late 1820s. An obelisk at the foot of Pioneer Road marks the spot where the first Company settlers came ashore on 31 March 1841. St Mary's Church was begun in 1845–46, but only a small part of the original stonework survives; the church now has more additions than original buildings, but is still of great historic interest. In the churchyard are memorials and headstones which tell much of New Plymouth's early history. The

► *The building known today as The Gables, from its architectural style, was first built as a cottage hospital as part of Governor Grey's efforts to bring the benefits of European civilisation to the Maori of Taranaki. It was shifted to its present site in 1904 and has been restored.*

graves include those of men who died during the Taranaki Wars. In the nearby vicarage garden are the graves of Maori killed at Mahoetahi in November 1860.

Other early buildings in New Plymouth also have a religious character. The Holy Trinity Chapel, built on Bishop Selwyn's initiative, was opened in 1845. The tiny Henui Parsonage, the remaining stone portion of an 1845 addition to an even earlier house, is a charming piece of colonial architecture. The wooden Whiteley Mission House, built in 1847–48, was originally part of the Grey Institute, established with

Governor Grey's assistance because he was impressed with the work of the local Methodist mission. The building is an attractive example of simple colonial architecture.

The Gables, in Brooklands Park, does not stand on its original site, but is one of New Zealand's most historic buildings. It was designed by Frederick Thatcher and built in 1847–48 to serve as a cottage hospital, as part of Governor Grey's efforts to bring the benefits of European civilisation to the Maori. It is the only survivor of four such hospitals.

On the outskirts of New Plymouth is a

wooden farmhouse, a simple building of historic interest as the first home of a young settler who became a leading politician. Harry Atkinson arrived in New Plymouth in the early 1850s, one of a remarkable group of settlers, all members of the Richmond or Atkinson families, who decided in England to embark on a new life in New Zealand. Hurworth is the only survivor of the houses and farm buildings the members of this group built on their bush sections on the fringes of the new settlement. The house, now owned by the Historic Places Trust, is open as a typical example of an early farmhouse of a working settler. The stone Richmond Cottage also has associations with the two families.

Some buildings and sites of historic interest in New Plymouth date from after the wars. On Pendarves Street is a group of houses from the 1860s. The earliest surviving parts of the Egmont flour mill date from 1866. Its Powderham Street facade, executed in a handsome Italianate style in wood, was added after the building ceased to be a mill. A pump at Ngamotu reminds visitors of the discovery of oil here in 1865, the first well in the British Empire to show oil.

In Te Henui Cemetery, opened in 1861, are buried many of New Plymouth's early settlers. A notable individual grave is that of the historian and writer, S. Percy Smith.

The Taranaki Museum has extensive holdings of pre-European artefacts and the European history of Taranaki is also illustrated by displays.

▲ *The wooden farmhouse at Hurworth is the only survivor of several built in close proximity by members of the Richmond and Atkinson families who pioneered bush sections on the outskirts of New Plymouth in the 1850s. The builder of Hurworth, Harry Atkinson, later became Premier of New Zealand.* Kris Pfeiffer

PARIHAKA

In the late 1860s, the centre of Maori resistance to European acquisition of their land in Taranaki shifted south. Between 1866 and 1907, the village of Parihaka, inland from Cape Egmont, was the home of two prophets, Te Whiti O Rongomai and Tohu Kakahi, who, after the Maori had been defeated in the wars of the 1860s, endeavoured to retain Maori land by campaigns of civil disobedience. The followers of Te Whiti and Tohu ploughed paddocks which Pakeha settlers claimed were theirs, tore out survey pegs and attempted to impede road building across disputed land. So serious did the threat seem to the Government that in November 1881 troops marched on Parihaka, confronted the Maori assembled at the village and arrested the unresisting Te Whiti and Tohu and many of their followers. The episode is remembered today by many European New Zealanders with shame. Only a few buildings remain at Parihaka, but Te Whiti's tomb and a meeting house which is a memorial to Tohu can be seen. The place remains one of great importance to many Maori.

▼ In Patea is a striking model of the Aotea canoe in which the ancestors of the Maori living in the district, led by the canoe's captain, Turi, first came to New Zealand.

A European structure of historic interest near Parihaka is the Cape Egmont lighthouse. First erected on Mana Island in 1864, it was re-erected on Cape Egmont in 1881 at the height of the Parihaka 'troubles'. It is the only lighthouse in New Zealand built under armed guard.

PATEA

In Patea, founded as a military settlement in the 1860s, there is an imposing old house, Beaconsfield, built of kauri in 1881, which still looks elegant despite the loss of its verandah. It is being restored. A more recent construction is the large model of the legendary *Aotea* canoe, erected in 1933 to commemorate Turi, captain of the canoe. Patea has a District Museum housing Maori artefacts, early colonial items and vintage vehicles and machinery.

At Kohi Gorge, in an isolated location inland from Waverley, there are carvings on the rock walls of a small shelter which were executed in pre-European times. Among the most important examples of Maori rock art in the North Island, the Kohi carvings include spirals and lizard and bird motifs.

AOTEA

HAWERA

The main town of southern Taranaki, Hawera, has a number of sites associated with pre-European Maori occupation of the area and with fighting between Maori and Pakeha in the later 1860s. Turuturumokai Pa is an important Maori site, the pa built there perhaps 400 years ago. Trenches, ramparts, housesites and food storage pits can be seen.

Turuturumokai also carries the history of southern Taranaki into historic times. To the north-east of the earlier pa an inscribed cairn marks the site of a European redoubt built in 1866, stormed in July 1868 by the Hau Hau, militant adherents of the new Pai Marire faith. A memorial in the domain to soldiers who died in the local campaigns stands on the site of the redoubt.

Leading the fighting in south Taranaki was the Hau Hau warrior chief, Titikowaru, whose pa was at Te Ngutu O Te Manu, west of Hawera, near the township of Kapuni. Two dramatic engagements were fought at this pa in 1868; the pa was successfully defended. Among those killed in the second attack was Gustavus von Tempsky, artist and soldier of fortune. The events at Te Ngutu O Te Manu in 1868 are recorded on a sign standing in the domain on the site. There is also a memorial near the place where von Tempsky died.

In the 1880s, at the time of the Parihaka disturbances, old redoubts in south Taranaki were reoccupied and new ones built. At Manaia there are two blockhouses erected in 1880–81 by the Armed Constabulary on the site of an old Maori pa. Between them is a concrete replica of the wooden watchtower used to keep a lookout over the Waimate Plains. Two memorials flank the Manaia band rotunda — one to New Zealanders who died in the First World War, the other to members of the Armed Constabulary, among whom von Tempsky's name is included.

Hawera and other south Taranaki towns have a number of late nineteenth and early twentieth century buildings typical of New Zealand country towns. Hawera, more unusually, has a high water tower, built in 1912–13.

Inland from Hawera and Stratford, the Matemateaonga Walkway follows, for parts of its length, old Maori trails and the line of a European road cut in the early 1900s before being abandoned. The townships of Douglas and Whangamomona, on the road to Taumarunui, each have one or two interesting buildings including, at Douglas, an old brickworks.

Between Hawera and Patea, reached from the village of Manutahi, is an important site, Manawapou. On a clifftop at the mouth of the Manawapou River was a Ngati Ruanui settlement which was the scene, in 1854, of a gathering to discuss ways of opposing the sale of land to Europeans. Historians dispute whether a 'Land League' was formed on this occasion. A great meeting house, Taiporohenui, was erected for the occasion, but destroyed by the British in 1865 after being moved to Hawera. Many food pits, house platforms and a midden remain to mark the site, although it has been partly eroded. Two redoubts were built in 1865 when the area was occupied by British troops and evidence of these is still visible by the remains of the older Maori settlement.

▲ *Watch tower and blockhouse at Manaia, erected in 1880–81.*
Alexander Turnbull Library

WANGANUI, RANGITIKEI AND MANAWATU

Between Taranaki and Wellington three great rivers flow from the central North Island into the Tasman Sea — the Wanganui, the Rangitikei and the Manawatu. The coastal lowlands near the mouths of these rivers were in pre-European times mostly under heavy bush or swamp. Comparatively few traces of the pre-European occupation of these lowlands remain. Wanganui, as an older town, is perhaps of greater historic interest than the towns or cities of the Rangitikei or Manawatu, but Marton, Palmerston North, Levin and several others all have at least one or two buildings or sites of historic note.

Interesting farmhouses and outbuildings are scattered throughout the countryside. The Wanganui Valley likewise has more places of historic interest than the upper reaches of the Rangitikei or Manawatu.

The Wanganui is one of New Zealand's most historic waterways with a number of fascinating places along its length. Both the Rangitikei and Manawatu have historic connections with transport — the Rangitikei for the building of the Main Trunk Line, the Manawatu for the building of the road and railway through its gorge.

WANGANUI

Wanganui, founded in 1841, is one of the country's oldest cities. Its site was purchased from the local Maori where the Moutoa Gardens, a historic reserve, is now situated. In these gardens are several interesting memorials and a statue of Major Kemp, who fought against the Ngati Ruanui chief, Titokowaru. Plaques attached to the base of the statue depict battles in which he took part.

There was never major fighting close to Wanganui but some skirmishing marked its early years. Several of Wanganui's historic monuments and sites relate to skirmishes of the 1840s and to efforts made in the 1860s to protect the town against attack. Queens Park was the site of the Rutland Stockade, built in 1846–47 and garrisoned until the 1870s. Nothing remains of the fortification but there is a plaque recalling the stockade.

One of Wanganui's oldest surviving buildings had military origins. The Tylee Cottage was built in 1853 for the man who headed the Commissariat of the British troops then stationed in Wanganui. The cottage has been restored.

One of the most historic places in the vicinity of Wanganui is Putiki, where there was an ancient pa with long traditions. In 1829 it was the site of a defeat inflicted on the local tribes by Te Rauparaha. In 1843 an early missionary, Richard Taylor, gathered up some bones still lying on the battlefield and buried them, calling the hill Korokota

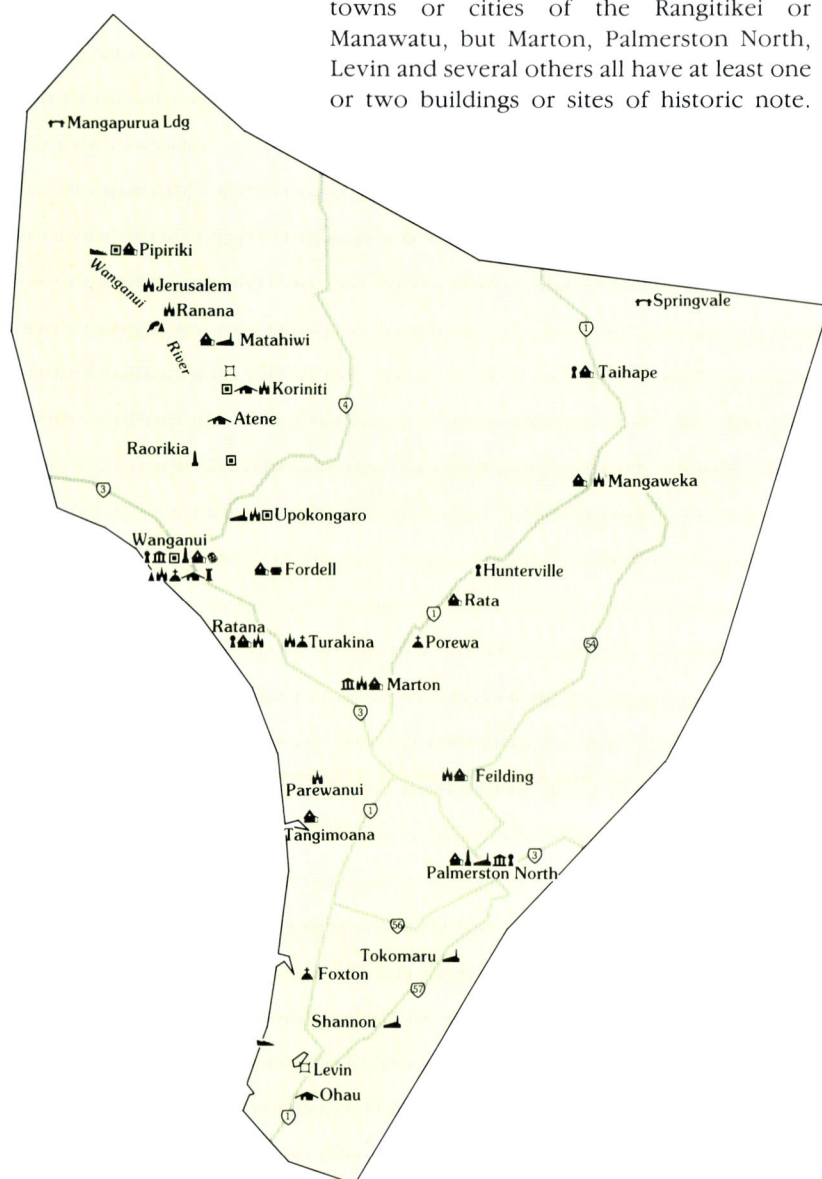

Map labels:
Mangapurua Ldg
Pipiriki
Jerusalem
Ranana
Matahiwi
Koriniti
Atene
Raorikia
Upokongaro
Wanganui
Fordell
Ratana
Turakina
Porewa
Marton
Parewanui
Tangimoana
Tokomaru
Foxton
Shannon
Levin
Ohau
Springvale
Taihape
Mangaweka
Hunterville
Rata
Feilding
Palmerston North
Wanganui River

(Golgotha). The plinth at the summit of the hill is not associated with this battle, but marks the grave of Hoani Wiremu Hipango who was killed in 1865 at the Battle of Ohoutahi.

The Anglican mission station at which Taylor served was established at Putiki in 1840 and manned until the 1880s. The present St Paul's Church dates from 1937, but it is the fifth church on the site and has long historical associations. Within the church are fine carvings, tukutuku and kowhaiwhai work. At the present Putiki Pa is a carved meeting house, Te Paku o te Rangi, which replaced an earlier house washed away in

1891. Some of the carvings may be older than the house. The pataka at the pa also dates from the 1890s.

Wanganui has a number of interesting old buildings. St Peter's Church was built as Christ Church in 1865, enlarged in the 1890s, then moved to its present site in 1921. One of Wanganui's finest old buildings is the wooden Opera House, opened in 1899. The buildings of the Wanganui Collegiate School have been declared a precinct of historic interest by the Historic Places Trust and include the Chapel, the Big School, a pavilion and the headmaster's house.

▲ *St Paul's, Putiki, is a twentieth century building, but it stands on a site occupied by several previous churches, the first of which was erected soon after a mission station was established in Putiki in 1840. Within the 1937 building is fine Maori decorative work.*

The Wanganui Regional Museum, situated in Queens Park, Wanganui, has a reproduction of a Wanganui shopping street and other displays of the city's early days. It has a Maori court which includes the canoe *Te Mata o Hoturoa* and a comprehensive collection of Maori god-sticks. In the Sarjeant Gallery are nineteenth century New Zealand paintings which help bring alive the country's past.

In the countryside around Wanganui are some attractive old farmhouses. Netherdale, near Fordell, built in the 1860s, has interesting outbuildings which complete the farmstead. The country's finest 'Hudson River Gothic' house, Oneida, also near Fordell, was built around 1869. A summerhouse, stables and a coach-house were added in 1885–86. Both Netherdale and Oneida are still privately owned. The homestead at Bushy Park, owned by the Royal Forest and Bird Protection Society, was built in 1904 and is open to the public at certain times.

Near Upokongaro, a small ruin which can be seen from the road is the remains of a brick kiln built in 1857. The earthworks of Buckthought's Redoubt, built in 1868 on the site of the Opui Pa, can still be seen.

▼ *Pipiriki Landing on the Wanganui River, 1905.* National Museum

THE WANGANUI VALLEY

Above Wanganui, the Wanganui River winds for 290 km into the heart of the North Island. It is a historic waterway, an important Maori canoe route, later used by European steamers. The settlements up the valley have associations reaching back into pre-European times, and to the 1860s, when Hau Hau adherents of the Pai Marire faith attempted to come down the river to attack Wanganui. They were defeated by other Maori at two important battles: at Moutoa Island, near Ranana, on 14 May 1864 and at Ohoutahi between Jerusalem and Pipiriki. Later the Government built redoubts at Parikino, Koriniti and Pipiriki.

The Wanganui Valley was closely settled in pre-European times and eels, caught in large numbers at weirs built in the river, were of major importance. Pa were built on defensive sites and at several places along the river the earthworks of ancient pa can still be seen. A short distance upstream from Koriniti the earthworks of the renowned fighting pa Operiki are still 3.5 m high. The

◄ *The reconstructed Kawana Mill in the lower Wanganui Valley includes the waterwheel and other equipment installed when the mill was first opened in 1854 to allow Maori farmers to mill wheat they had grown on the valley's river flats.*

Hikurangi Pa was at Galatea (Karatia) across the river from Matahiwi.

At Kauarapaoa, near Raorikia, is Kemps Pole. It takes its name from Major Kemp who, around 1880, alarmed at the continuing loss of Maori land, had the six-metre-high totara pole placed on the earthworks of an old fighting pa, Mataikai. Four poles were erected, one at each corner of an area which was to be held in trust for local tribes.

Mission villages were established up the Wanganui River in the 1840s at places like Hiruharama (Jerusalem), Ranana (London), Koriniti (Corinth) and Atene (Athens). Poplar and willow trees from these early days are often now the only sign of former villages. At some settlements rather more has survived. At Koriniti is the Pepara Church,

originally established in 1848 but rebuilt in 1920, an old mission house, a carved gateway and a meeting house and mounted canoe. The Poutama meeting house was transported to Koriniti from Karatia in 1967. Most of the important carvings from an earlier house on the Koriniti marae, Te Waiherehere, are in the Wanganui Museum. The Roman Catholic mission church at Ranana dates from the 1890s, while at Atene a small meeting house has recently been restored. Hiruharama was once a large and important kainga. A Roman Catholic mission was established at Kauaeroa in 1852, then re-established at Hiruharama in 1883. The present church and convent were built in 1890s.

In the 1850s Maori farmers had thousands of acres of river flats in the Wanganui

▶ *A leading colonial politician and artist, William Fox, had his home Westoe built in 1874 in the then fashionable Italianate style. This fine house is complemented by a splendid garden.*

Valley planted in wheat. At Matahiwi, the rebuilt Kawana mill, built in 1854, is a reminder of those days. Governor Grey assisted with the erection of this and other mills to encourage the Maori to adopt European ways of agriculture. The Kawana mill fell into ruin during the First World War, but the waterwheel and grinding stones remained, intact, allowing the mill to be rebuilt. Nearby, a miller's cottage has also been restored.

Like the Maori before them, the early Europeans used the river as a highway. The river, 'the Rhine of Maoriland', played an important part in the early development of tourism in New Zealand. The first steamer services on the Wanganui began in 1886. Some of the early improvement works undertaken by the Wanganui River Trust, established in 1903, can still be seen — training walls to direct the river's flow and the bolts for fixed cables to allow boats to be winched up through difficult rapids. The boom years of steamer services on the Wanganui were over by the 1920s. One steamer, the *Waireka*, survives in service on the tidal zone of the river. Another, the *Ongarue*, has been restored and located on land at Pipiriki.

Pipiriki House, once the most famous tourist house on the river, burned down in 1959. A colonial cottage, built around the 1880s, serves as an information centre and small museum.

Above Pipiriki there are no roads down to the Wanganui until the upper reaches at Retaruke. These unroaded sections of the valley were the scene of great attempts, between the two world wars, to develop farms on intractable hill country. Lack of knowledge of land management and the Depression doomed these latter-day pioneering activities. Remnants of former settlements — exotic trees, broken fence lines and heaps of rusting iron and chimney bricks — mark the sites of abandoned farmhouses. The most intriguing monument to these failed farming settlements is the Bridge to Nowhere, built in 1936 above the Mangapurua Landing to help, too late, with access to the valley and in anticipation of a major through road being built. The concrete arch bridge is now surrounded by bush.

RANGITIKEI

The chief town of the Rangitikei, Marton, was founded in the 1860s and grew signifi-

cantly when the building of the Main Trunk Line began in 1885. One of the town's oldest buildings is the Church of St Stephen, built 1871–73 on the site of a redoubt (built in 1868 when a Hau Hau attack was expected). The old brick courthouse, built in 1897, a fine example of late Victorian architecture, is today a restaurant. The town's old commercial buildings on Broadway, including the Bank of New Zealand and the White Hart Tavern, have been declared part of a historic precinct by the Historic Places Trust. The Captain Cook Pioneer Cottage in Marton (the town is named after Captain Cook's birthplace) is a six room cottage furnished with household items of the colonial era.

Westoe, once the home of William Fox, is about 8 km from Marton. This fine early house was built in 1874 in an Italianate style. Fox, who came to New Zealand in 1842, was four times Premier and an artist whose paintings are of historic interest as well as artistic merit. Westoe, still a private home, can be seen from the Kakariki Road a short distance from State Highway 1. Other fine Rangitikei homesteads include

Merchiston, near Rata, and Pukemarama, near Tangimoana.

Parewanui, on the north bank of the Rangitikei River below Bulls, was once an important Maori settlement. It was there that Donald McLean, in 1849, bought the Rangitikei for the Government. The Wheriko Church in Parewanui, built in the early 1860s, has recently been restored. The little cemetery is of interest.

Turakina and Ratana are both townships of historic interest. Turakina was the first European settlement between Wellington and Wanganui and contains two century-old wooden parish churches. Many early settlers are buried in the cemetery on a knoll above the town.

Ratana is the birthplace of the Ratana Church. The early years of this century were grim for many Maori and a number of religious sects emerged in this uncertain situation. In 1918 a Maori farmer, Tahupotiki Wiremu Ratana, had a vision and his resulting gift for faith-healing led to the founding, in 1925, of the Ratana Church. The most imposing building in the village is the temple with its distinctive twin towers and symbolic decoration.

The small towns up the Rangitikei Valley generally have one or two buildings or sites of interest. In Hunterville a settlers' museum in an old courthouse has early farm equipment and tools on display. Mangaweka has three older churches on the main highway, as well as some intriguing old shops and an imposing turn-of-the-century bank building, which is now a private residence.

In the Taihape Museum displays illustrate the sawmilling and building of the railway (1904) at the beginning of European settlement there.

The inland Patea route to Napier was the district's main route to the outside world until the building of the railway. At Tikitere is the site of an early water-powered mill with its headrace still well preserved. The Springvale Suspension Bridge, built 1923–25, stands on a historic reserve; it is of a type important in the history of road development of which few examples now remain. (There is another in an isolated location in the Turakina Valley.) On the river bank near the bridge is a moa-hunter

96

archaeological site, of scientific rather than popular interest.

THE MANAWATU–HOROWHENUA

Before European settlement much of the Manawatu and Horowhenua districts were covered with swamp and heavy bush. This, together with the resistance of some local Maori to land selling, meant European settlement of the Manawatu was slow. The district's main city, Palmerston North, was not founded until 1866. A reminder of the Manawatu's Maori past is a statue of Rangitane chief, Peeti Te Awe Awe (1820–84) which stands in the square, as does a neo-Gothic fountain commemorating Edward VII's coronation in 1902.

Palmerston North has a number of interesting old houses. Wharerata, now the staff common room and offices for Massey University, was built in 1901 with additions in 1931. Across the river on the edge of Hokowhitu Lagoon is Caccia Birch, a fine wooden house built in 1893 which is now being restored for use by the citizens of Palmerston North. A group of houses on Manapouri Crescent and Elmira Avenue has been declared a precinct of historic import- ance by the Historic Places Trust. Palmerston North is an industrial centre and among its older industrial structures is a Hoffman oblong continuous kiln, erected in 1916 for brick and tile making, which the Historic Places Trust is working to save.

The Manawatu Museum in Palmerston North has displays illustrating Maori life and early European settlement. In the grounds of the museum is a cottage, Totaranui, built about 1874, which gives an idea of how a middle-class family lived in the period up to about 1910. There are also reconstructions of a smithy and early general store, and an old country schoolhouse moved onto the site. Specialised museums include the New Zealand Rugby Museum and the Army Engi- neers' Collection at the Linton Camp. Fur- ther south, at Tokomaru, a steam engine museum has a magnificent collection of stationary steam engines, as well as traction engines and a working steam railway.

In Fielding is St John's Anglican Church, designed by F.deJ. Clere, and two groups of fascinating early cottages in Beattie and Goodbehere Streets.

Foxton was once the district's main centre but it lost the race with Palmerston North when, in 1886, the railway from Wellington went directly to Palmerston North, bypassing Foxton. The Ihakara Gardens in Foxton are the burial place of some early settlers and the chief Ihakara Tukumaru.

In the Tararua Ranges behind Shannon is the Mangahao power scheme, the first state hydro scheme in the North Island which was, when completed in 1924, the largest power scheme in the country. Near Shannon, at Makerua, are the ruins of the Miranui flax mill, built in 1907. The shed is derelict but important as one of the few reminders anywhere of a once thriving industry. The memorial on Mt Stewart, about 19 km west of Palmerston North, was erected in 1940 to commemorate the cen- tenary of colonisation in New Zealand.

Levin is the main town of the Horowhenua, founded as a railway town in the 1880s. In 1878, the ship *Hydrabad* was wrecked at Waitarere Beach, east of Levin. Today the hulk of the wreck can still be seen on the beach. The meeting house Kiropiri, erected in 1859 and substantially recarved in the 1920s, is in Ohau, south of Levin.

◀ *The village of Ratana has grown up on the former farm of Wiremu Tahupotiki Ratana, one of the most notable Maori religious leaders of this century. The distinctive twin-towered chapel is the most prominent building in the village.*

HAWKE'S BAY

In pre-European times Hawke's Bay was part of the extensive territory of Ngati Kahungungu and evidence of their occupation of the land can still be seen in parts of the province.

The first Europeans to settle on the Hawke's Bay coast were whalers. Missionaries followed with William Colenso founding his mission station near Port Ahuriri in 1844. He introduced fruits and grains and the few early traders were soon buying wheat and maize as well as pigs from the larger Maori population. There was little flat land in the new Hawke's Bay province, which seceded from Wellington in 1858. Much of the land was taken up in large sheep runs with a similar pastoral history to the southern Wairarapa and the South Island. Later, the large runs were broken up into smaller farms and small rural towns were established to service the fast-growing pastoral scene.

Numerous farm buildings, a legacy of those early days, remain. Small towns, many with interesting buildings, straddle quiet roads, particularly in the south.

Inland from northern Hawke's Bay is the rugged Urewera Country, important in Maori history as the homeland of the Tuhoe, and the scene of the incidents during the Te Kooti campaigns. Places associated with the New Zealand Wars are also to be found in coastal Hawke's Bay as far south as Napier.

NORTHERN HAWKE'S BAY

The sweep of Hawke's Bay begins in the north at the Mahia Peninsula. A place of extensive pre-European Maori settlement, the peninsula was a scene of early shore-based whaling.

In the 1840s the peninsula became part of the mission field which had its headquarters at Turanga (now Gisborne). Southeast of the township of Mahia, a plaque stands near a rock font which was, by tradition, used by William Williams in the early 1840s to baptise local Maori. At the tip of the peninsula, Portland Island was the location of an early lighthouse. The keepers' cottages are still on the island but the lighthouse has been shifted to Wairoa.

Wairoa attracted flax traders in the 1820s and in 1839 Captain W.B. Rhodes founded a whaling and trading station where the town is today. But as a European town, Wairoa did not really begin to develop until the mid-1860s.

Wairoa was a centre of Maori population in pre-European times and the Takitimu meeting house, dating from 1935 and with some very fine modern carvings, is the most prominent reminder of the district's long Maori history.

South of Wairoa, the township of Mohaka was the scene of the so-called 'Mohaka massacre'. In April 1869, Te Kooti laid siege to the local Maori and European inhabitants in two pa, Te Huke and Hiruharama. Te Huke eventually fell to Te Kooti. In the engagement Te Kooti's men

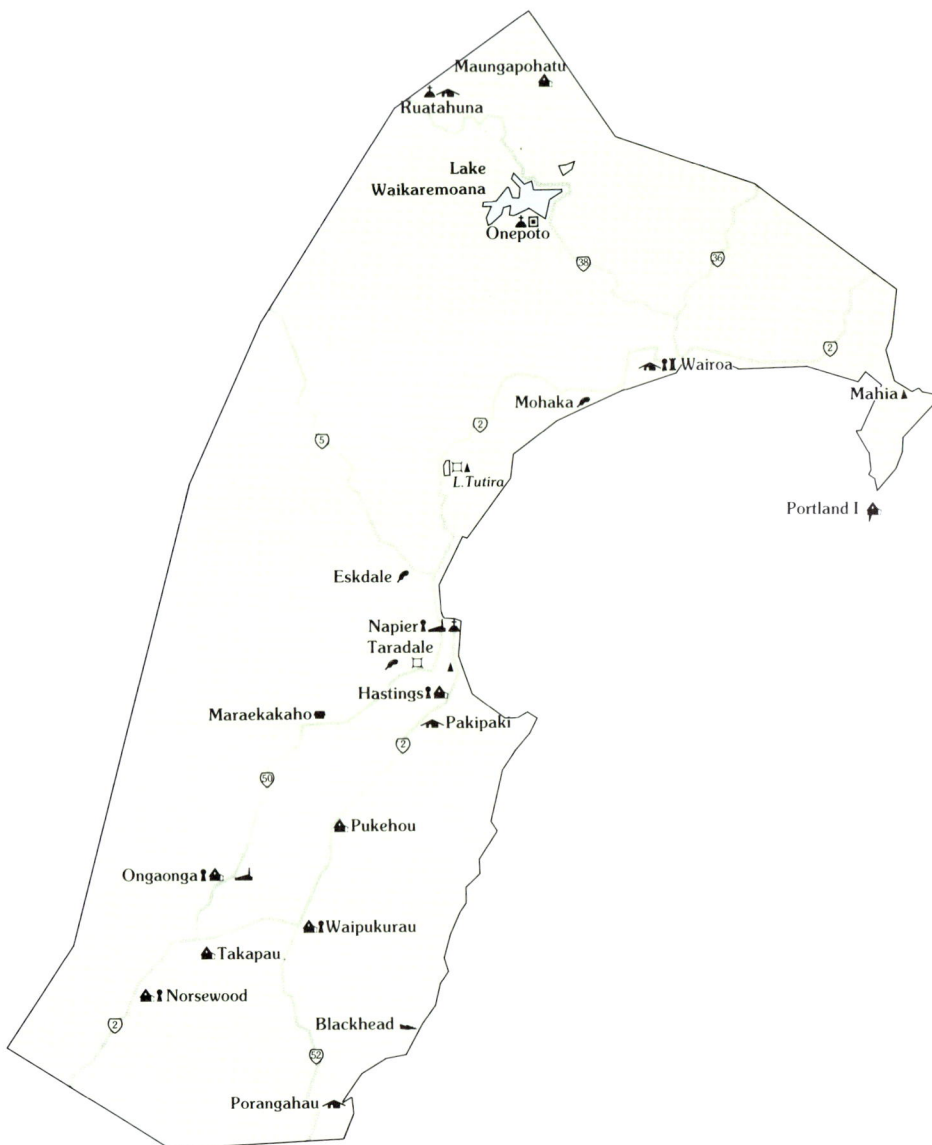

killed 60 for the loss of 10 of their own. A cairn has been erected on the grave of the Lavins family, who perished in the fighting. Inland from the township the Mohaka River is crossed by a high rail viaduct, a monument to early New Zealand engineering.

Lake Tutira, between Wairoa and Napier, was the birthplace of a New Zealand classic, *Tutira*, published in 1921, and written by the naturalist and author W.H. Guthrie-Smith who acquired the Tutira station in 1882. Before that, the lake was an important source of food to the Maori but little remains of the three recorded lakeside pa. A memorial stands on the site of one of the kainga.

THE UREWERA

Inland from Wairoa and Mohaka is the rugged Urewera country, home of the Tuhoe tribe, and at the heart of the Urewera lies Lake Waikaremoana. At Onepoto, at the southern end of the lake, is the site of an Armed Constabulary post established in 1870 during the Te Kooti campaigns. Parts of an old stone wall and military graves still exist on the site of the redoubt.

North of Lake Waikaremoana are two tiny settlements of historic interest. Maungapohatu was the home of the Maori prophet Rua Kenana who founded a Maori revivalist movement in 1905, and gathered his followers to this remote settlement. In 1916 lives were lost at Maungapohatu when Rua was arrested for offences against the licensing laws. The famous round temple was dismantled soon afterwards. A mission was founded at Maungapohatu in 1918 and some of the buildings of this period have survived, including the mission house, built of pit-sawn timber, and an old schoolroom. There is also a more recent meeting house. Maungapohatu is linked to State Highway 38 by a poor dry-weather road.

Ruatahuna is still a centre of Tuhoe life. At Mataatua, near Ruatahuna, is Te Whai a te Motu, a meeting house built between 1870 and 1888 which has important carvings with folk art elements.

NAPIER

Near Taradale is Otatara, the largest of Hawke Bay's surviving ancient pa. Although part of it has been quarried away, large terraces, storage pits and small defensive

▲ *On the site of the largest of Hawkes Bay's ancient pa, Otatara, near Napier, dwelling terraces, storage pits and defensive works are still clearly evident. Otatara is protected as an historic reserve.*

works are still obvious. Built on an easily defended site, with good access to a variety of food resources, Otatara Pa is important in the history and traditions of the Ngati Kahungunu.

At Clive, south of Napier, William Colenso established the Waitangi mission station by the Ngaruroro River, in 1844.

Napier grew after land purchases in the 1850s opened up Hawke's Bay to sheep farmers. In 1858 it became the provincial capital when Hawke's Bay broke away from Wellington.

The district saw brief activity in the later stages of the New Zealand Wars. In 1866 a band of Hau Hau marched against Napier, but the settlers made ready for them and in October repulsed the main band at the battle of Omarunui. Another smaller party of Hau Hau were intercepted near Eskdale and heavily defeated. Memorials on Omarunui Road and at Eskdale mark the sites of these two engagements.

In an old cemetery next to Napier's Botanic Gardens are the graves of leading figures in the early history of Napier, including the missionary William Colenso, Sir Donald McLean, and Major-General Sir George Whitmore, who commanded the settlers at Omarunui and later led campaigns against Te Kooti. Members of the early missionary family, the Williams, are also buried in the cemetery.

An isolated relic of Napier's earlier days is a trypot, at the Iron Pot, brought to Napier from the Tangoio whaling station.

The most famous and tragic event in Napier's history was the 1931 earthquake which levelled the city, but usefully raised much of the seabed. Some of the damage is still visible in the twisted wharf pilings at the Iron Pot. Another relic of the earthquake is the bell, on Marine Parade, of HMS *Veronica* which was in port when the earthquake struck and whose crew helped to rescue victims of the disaster.

As a result of the earthquake most of Napier's interesting buildings are comparatively recent. Those with an interest in architectural history will find in Napier a world class concentration of buildings in the art deco style of the 1930s. The Waiapu Cathedral stands on the site of the 1886 cathedral which collapsed in the earthquake. The original foundation stone is preserved in the new building. A group of industrial buildings at West Quay, including wool stores, offices and factories, has been classified as a precinct of historic interest by the Historic Places Trust.

Hastings was also levelled by the 1931 earthquake. The nearby winery at Greenmeadows, 'The Mission', is the country's oldest, founded last century. On the Te Mata Estate the original cellars of the country's oldest commercial vineyard are still used.

SOUTHERN HAWKE'S BAY

South of Hastings are two places of importance in the Maori history of Hawke's Bay. The settlement of Pakipaki has a 1916 carved meeting house, Houngara, standing opposite an attractive stone church. Te Aute College, at Pukehou about 30 km south of Hastings, was founded in 1872 and has had a continuous history since. Among its famous old boys are Sir Maui Pomare, Sir Apirana Ngata and Sir Peter Buck.

Most of the buildings of the college date from the fire which, in 1918–19, destroyed most of the original buildings. The simple chapel dates from 1900 although it was extended later. A stained glass window in the chapel is a memorial to Archdeacon and Mrs Williams. Possessions and mementoes of Buck and Pomare are displayed in the foyer of the main building.

Much of Hawke's Bay south of Napier and Hastings was first taken up as large sheep stations, which were broken up in the late nineteenth and early twentieth century into today's smaller farms. Several homesteads and farm buildings remain from those early days, some of which can be viewed from the road and a few visited. Sheep farming has a long history in Hawke's Bay. A noticeboard at the coastal township of Pourerere records that the first sheep run in Hawke's Bay was established there at the beginning of 1849 with a flock driven up from the Wairarapa. At Maraekakaho, west of Hastings, there is a wooden woolshed built in the 1880s on part of Sir Donald McLean's estate.

Mt Vernon station, near Waipukurau, has a homestead, still a private home, which was built in 1882–83 and has been substantially restored from the late 1950s on. It stands on land which has remained in the hands of the same family since it was first taken up in 1853, although much of the estate was bought by the Crown for closer settlement in 1905.

Near Takapau is an imposing, two-storeyed Italianate homestead, Oruawharo, which was built in the late 1870s, and added to in 1899. The homestead is now a guesthouse and restaurant. It has around it old stables, a coach-house and an implement shed, from the days when it was at the centre of a large estate.

Some towns of southern Hawke's Bay, like Waipawa and Waipukurau, came into existence to service the estates, then grew as the estates were broken up into smaller farms. From Norsewood and Dannevirke, down into the Wairarapa, many of the towns originated as the bush settlements of Scandinavian migrants.

At the village of Ongaonga there are several old buildings, notably the Coles Joinery Factory, the original parts of which were probably there by 1880. The firm closed about 1953. Much of the equipment and machinery has survived and the factory is thought to be the only remaining example of a small town/rural joinery and construction workshop.

At Puketitiri is a private collection of colonial antiques, early agricultural machinery and vintage cars. The Waipukurau museum has early settler furniture and historic photographs on display in an original settler's home. Ongaonga's museum is in an old schoolhouse and features a classroom furnished in the period of 1875–86. At Norsewood, the Pioneer Museum, housed in an 1888 cottage, illustrates the lives of the Scandinavians who settled the area.

At Porangahau is the Poho o Kahungunu carved meeting house, built in 1910–12 and incorporating some older carvings.

◀ *The former butcher's shop in the tiny Hawke's Bay farming settlement of Onga Onga is being preserved as one of the most elegant small-town buildings in New Zealand.*

WAIRARAPA

Once heavily bushed in the north, with more open grassland in the south, the Wairarapa, which is part of Ngati Kahungunu territory, includes today a few ancient Maori sites and places associated with Maori history in the nineteenth and twentieth centuries. The European history of the Wairarapa is essentially that of farming.

The southern Wairarapa was one of the earliest parts of the North Island to be settled by Europeans. Much of it was without bush or covered only in light scrub which the first graziers were swift to penetrate and utilise. Vast areas were subdivided into large stations, some of which have remained to the present day. West of the plain, along the foothills of the Rimutaka Range, was the scene of the country's first small-farming bush settlements. Further

north, Scandinavian settlers broke in country where the dense bush cover had restrained previous settlement. Even today, the north has retained the distinctive character of its early days.

Although no dramatic events ever broke the even tenor of Wairarapa life, much of the story of European settlement in New Zealand can be read from its rural landscape, its old farmhouses and farm buildings, and the old buildings of its towns.

EARLY WAIRARAPA

In pre-European times, the Wairarapa was part of the territory of the Ngati Kahungunu. One of their important marae is Papawai, near Greytown, which became, in the 1890s, a focal point of the Kotahitanga or Maori Parliament movement. In 1898 the Premier, Seddon, came to Papawai to meet the Maori King, Mahuta, and other tribal delegations. Two houses on the marae were destroyed by wind in 1934 but Papawai still has impressive carved figures around its perimeter and a house, Hikurangi, built in 1888.

There is another important Wairarapa marae at Te Ore Ore, on the outskirts of Masterton, with a house, Nga Tau e Waru, and another restored monument. Across the road from the marae is a tiny but delightful early church.

European settlement of the southern Wairarapa began in the 1840s with the grazing of sheep on the area's grasslands. A sign on the road to Lake Ferry from Martinborough marks the site of New Zealand's first sheep station, established in 1844, when flocks were driven from the Hutt Valley and set to graze on land leased from the Maori. This land became the stations Wharekaka and Pihautea. From these southern Wairarapa stations sheep were taken in 1847 to Flaxbourne in Marlborough to establish the beginnings of South Island pastoralism.

A legacy of those days of large sheep runs is the imposing homestead, privately owned, at Whangaimoana on the road to Cape Palliser. White Rock, on the other side of Cape Palliser, has an interesting group of station buildings and a memorial to an early runholder. The homestead of the privately owned Brancepeth Station, 22 km east of Masterton, dates from the 1880s.

The Wairarapa also has an important place in the history of New Zealand farming as the scene of early efforts to encourage small farmers to take up land. The oldest Wairarapa towns were born in the mid-1850s when the Wairarapa Small Farms Association negotiated with the local Maori to buy land. The land was then sold to settlers who walked over the Rimutaka Range, from the Hutt Valley. These were the earliest subdivisions on heavily forested land and thus the first chapter in the 60-year story of North Island bush settlement. In later decades the heavily bushed country north of Masterton was cleared by Scandinavian settlers. The northern Wairarapa merges into southern Hawke's Bay, with which it shares an early history of Scandinavian bush settlements.

NORTHERN WAIRARAPA

The railway junction town of Woodville, strictly in Hawke's Bay, has a small pioneer museum, an imposing wooden school building and, on Atkinson Street, a row of early railway houses. At Mangatainoka, an old brewery building will interest those keen on New Zealand's industrial history.

At Pahiatua there is an interesting old Anglican church, an old courthouse and a district pioneering museum housed in a 90 year old cottage. A memorial on State Highway 2 south of Pahiatua, unveiled in 1975, marks the site of a camp set up during the Second World War to accommodate Polish children made homeless by the German and Russian invasions of their country.

Eketahuna was founded by Scandinavians in the early 1870s in the Seventy Mile Bush, which has long since disappeared. The prominent St Cuthbert's church was built in 1898. Eketahuna also has three smaller old wooden churches. There is a district museum in a school building erected in 1884, of interest in its own right. Between Eketahuna and Masterton, on State Highway 2, is an unusual war memorial — an Anzac bridge built in 1922 over the Makakahi Stream, unfortunately in poor condition.

The Scandinavian church on a knoll above a side road at Mauriceville North has a delightful tapering spire. In the churchyard of the simpler church at Mauriceville West is the grave of a local Scandinavian rhymster, Lars Andersen Schow. Near this church a roadside cairn, built in 1973, commemorates 100 years of Scandinavian settlement in the district.

▲ Train on the Rimutaka Incline, which crossed the Rimutaka Range from the upper Hutt Valley to the Wairarapa.
Alexander Turnbull Library

103

▶ Papawai, near Greytown, an ancient marae of Ngati Kahungunu, was of great importance around the turn of the century as a centre of the Kotahitanga or Maori Parliament Movement. Carved guardian figures protect the perimeter of the marae.

A plaque at Kopuaranga marks the site of the Scandinavian Camp where the settlers lived in slab huts between 1872 and 1874, building roads while they waited for their sections to be surveyed. The Kopuaranga church dates from 1884, the school from 1885 and the hall from 1897.

MASTERTON TO GREYTOWN

Masterton was founded when the Small Farms Association settlers took up bush sections in the area. A noticeboard on the bypass west of the town tells the story of early land purchase and settlement. Its buildings include a historic courthouse, recently restored borough council offices, a Bank of New Zealand, an Anglican vicarage and many houses and cottages as well as a number of churches. On the way to Tauweru is a fine house, Otahuao, and at Tauweru is an historic church.

Carterton was founded in 1857 by the Wellington Provincial Government. Among the older buildings of interest are the public library, an imposing 1881 wooden building, a lovely cast-iron band rotunda and St Mark's Church.

Greytown's older buildings include an old Bank of New Zealand, what is now the Electric Power Board office and a relocated former lodge, now a library. In the Cobblestones Museum are examples of old household, farming and transport equipment displayed in an 1850s cottage, an 1870s hospital and other relocated buildings. Stables on the site date back to the 1850s.

SOUTHERN WAIRARAPA

Featherston was surveyed in 1857, but grew little until construction of the railway over the Rimutaka Range. It has two old churches, a courthouse and a library, all wooden and all in close proximity.

Between the lower Wairarapa and the Hutt Valley lies the Rimutaka Range. A plaque at the road summit records the first European crossing of the range in 1841. The railway crossing of this range is an interesting chapter in New Zealand's transport history. The Rimutaka incline was completed in 1878, the Fell engine system being used only 15 years after it had been patented. The incline remained in use until the mid-

1950s when the Rimutaka tunnel was completed. One of the historic Fell engines is housed in a shed in an historic precinct.

The site of the Featherston military camp, from which 30,000 men were sent to the First World War, and where many died in the flu epidemic that followed the war, is marked by a monument. During the 1939–45 war the Featherston military camp from the First World War was re-opened to house Japanese prisoners of war. In February 1943 the prisoners rioted, 50 prisoners and a guard being killed. A plaque records this tragic incident. In Featherston itself, the Anzac Hall, built in 1915 as a venue for entertaining the troops stationed at the camp, now houses paintings and

photographs of historic interest.

Martinborough's street plan reproduces the Union Jack with eight streets radiating from a central square. It was subdivided in the 1870s by Sir John Martin, a patriotic man. The old post office, opened in 1896, has been restored for new uses. The Bank of New Zealand was built in 1909. Nineteenth century churches also remain. A small museum is housed in an old wooden building on the main square.

TOWARDS THE COAST

A large area of hill country lies between the Wairarapa Valley and the coast. Tinui was the scene, in 1916, of the country's first Anzac Day ceremony, when a cross was erected on a large rock outcrop. The plane which completed the country's first commercial top-dressing flight took off from the Tinui sports ground. The Wairarapa coast has two old lighthouses, both magnificently situated. The older, on Cape Palliser, was erected in 1897. The lighthouse at Castlepoint was built in 1913. Near Castlepoint, Wharepouri's Mark is a stone cairn erected on the site of a sandstone pillar, raised last century by the Te Atiawa chief, Te Wharepouri, who went to Castlepoint to make peace with the Ngati Kahungunu living there. This ended a tribal feud which had flared up in the early nineteenth century.

► *Brancepeth Homestead, part of which dates from 1886, with additions in 1905, is the centre of one of the most historic of the Wairarapa's great sheep runs. The homestead stands by an important group of farm buildings, some of which are well over a century old.*

WELLINGTON

The Wellington area has a long pre-European history associated with several different tribes. The locations of nineteenth century cultivations and settlements, including three pa in what is now downtown Wellington, are known. Today's Ngati Poneke marae stands on the site of the Pipitea Pa. Much earlier, about 925 AD, according to tradition, Kupe visited Wellington Harbour, camped where Seatoun is now, then sailed round to Porirua. Several coastal features are associated with Kupe.

The traditional date for the arrival in the harbour of Tara and Tautoki, sons of the explorer, Whatonga, is 1100 AD. Tara gave his name to what is now known as Port Nicholson or Wellington Harbour — Whanganui a Tara — the great harbour of Tara. The first British ship recorded as entering the harbour was the *Rosanna*, of Captain Herd, in 1827. Not long after that, whalers began using Oriental Bay to boil down their catches, but nothing remains of this early European activity.

Wellington's colonisation by Europeans began in September 1839, when the New Zealand Company vessel *Tory* arrived. Not long afterwards, in the first three months of 1840, emigrant ships of the Company discharged their passengers on the foreshore of Petone. A Hutt River flood and the exposed anchorage persuaded the settlers that a better site for the new town was Thorndon, and on the beach front there, now Lambton Quay, today's city had its beginnings.

WELLINGTON'S OLD BUILDINGS

In spite of the recent intensive development which has transformed downtown Wellington, the city still has a number of historic buildings. Three houses on Boulcott Street are of particular interest. No. 12, built in 1902, now resited at the Willis Street corner, is an imposing, elaborately decorated wooden townhouse. This house was designed by Thomas Turnbull and Son as was No. 63, Antrim House, built in 1904–05 for a wealthy shoe manufacturer. Antrim House is another fine example of the way wood was used to imposing effect. It is now the headquarters of the New Zealand Historic Places Trust. The house is occupied by Trust offices, but the grounds are open to the public.

Plimmer House, the third house on Boulcott Street, is older and smaller. It was built about 1873 and was for some time the home of descendants of an early merchant, John Plimmer. Now hemmed in by tower blocks, Plimmer House, with its decorated gables and small tower, retains its original character.

Two historic houses have survived near the Beehive. On Bowen Street is the brick townhouse Alexander Turnbull had built in 1916 to house his collections which, bequeathed to the nation, became the basis of the Alexander Turnbull Library. The Library has outgrown the house, which is now used for meetings and exhibitions. No.

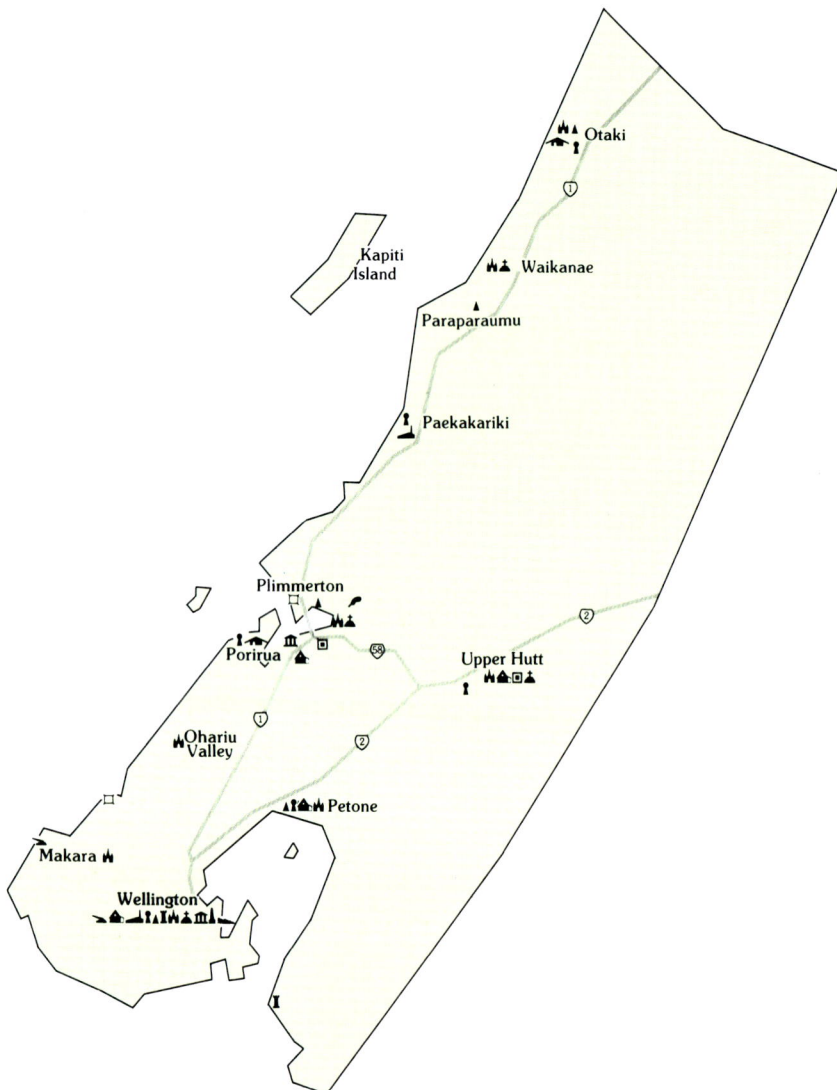

Otaki

Kapiti Island

Waikanae

Paraparaumu

Paekakariki

Plimmerton

Porirua

Upper Hutt

Ohariu Valley

Petone

Makara

Wellington

▲ *A carefully restored mid nineteenth century cottage on Nairn Street, Wellington, has been furnished as a small museum.*

22 The Terrace, built in 1866, is an example of a professional man's residence in Wellington's early days, the last remaining building of its age and type in the city proper. It now houses the New Zealand Crafts Council gallery which is open to the public.

Nearby, on Bolton Street, is the small Sexton's Cottage of the Bolton Street cemetery, built in 1857 and added to in 1885. In the same general area, the Custodian's House in the Botanic Gardens, slightly grander than the Sexton's Cottage, is also a typical early residence. It dates from the 1860s. Most of the northern end of The Terrace is now lined by tall office blocks, but south, towards Boulcott Street and beyond, a number of old houses have survived. Just above St John's Church on the corner of Willis and Dixon Streets is Spinks Cottage, built between 1854 and 1863, a typical larger cottage. It has been restored. Beyond the southern end of Willis Street, on steeply

rising Nairn Street, is a charming little square cottage, with two small dormers, built as an artisan's home around 1858–59. This cottage has been preserved as a museum, with furniture and household articles which illustrate life in colonial Wellington.

Returning north, the inner suburb of Thorndon, around and behind Parliament Buildings, is one of the best places in Wellington to search out old houses. Some are the humble cottages of workmen and artisans, dating from the 1870s and 1880s, like those on Ascot and Glenbervie Terraces. Others are grander, like the imposing house with three-storeyed tower which is part of Queen Margaret College. Also in Thorndon is the former Bishopscourt, next to Old St Paul's Church in Mulgrave Street, which was built of totara in 1879.

In Thorndon, too, is an old house of added interest as the birthplace of one of New Zealand's greatest writers. Katherine

Mansfield was born in 25 Tinakori Road, on 14 October 1888, and lived there for the first five years of her life. It is one of New Zealand's few 'literary shrines' and is being carefully restored by a preservation society. It is open to the public. The site of another of Katherine Mansfield's childhood homes on Fitzherbert Terrace is occupied by the American Embassy. On the same street is the Katherine Mansfield Memorial Park.

Among the old houses in the suburbs are Chews Cottage, Ottawa Road, Ngaio, and the Wilton Farmhouse, 116 Wilton Road, Newtown, Berhampore, and the Aro Valley have large numbers of nineteenth century houses, many of them workers' cottages.

Many of Wellington's older commercial buildings have succumbed to development, though some have survived. Two are old wooden pubs. The Thistle Inn, the second oldest New Zealand hotel still occupying its original site, was built in 1866 when its predecessor burned down. The Shamrock Tavern, resited in Tinakori Road, was built in 1869 and rebuilt in 1893.

The elaborate former Public Trust Office on Lambton Quay, built early this century, tells the perceptive observer much about Edwardian New Zealand. The St James Theatre, Courtenay Place, built in 1912, has a fine facade and magnificent auditorium. Another old theatre, the State Opera House, is nearby. Two turn-of-the-century brick buildings occupy prominent sites. The Hunter Building of Victoria University was built in 1904–06 in an institutional Gothic style. Now surrounded by newer buildings, the Hunter Building, the University's first permanent home, is being upgraded and enlarged, the additions being compatible with the Gothic original. On the opposite side of the city, the Church of St Gerard's Monastery, on the slopes of Mt Victoria, is a simple Gothic building dating from 1903. The larger monastery itself was completed in 1932.

The appealing little brick Dominion Observatory on the ridge above the Botanic Gardens was built in 1907, but beneath it are cellars dug at the time of the first Russian scare in the late 1870s.

WELLINGTON MISCELLANY

All cities have appealing historical curiosities. At the Karori Reservoir a caretaker's store and a watertower built over

the main intake illustrate the Victorian love of whimsy.

In central Wellington are two cemeteries. The Bolton Street cemetery was set aside in 1840 and closed in 1892. Now divided by the motorway, the two parts of what is now the Bolton Street Memorial Park are of great interest. They contain the graves of many early settlers, including that of Edward Gibbon Wakefield. At the head of the cemetery is an imposing memorial to Richard John Seddon. Along The Terrace, adjoining the University, is the tiny Mount Street cemetery, consecrated in 1841 and in use until 1891. Here are the graves of early

▲ *Though severed in two and partly destroyed by motorway construction, Central Wellington's Bolton Street Cemetery still has a number of notable early graves and pleasant, peaceful corners.*

Catholics, including the grave of Wellington's first resident priest.

In the Karori Cemetery, fascinating hours can be spent learning history from gravestones. The cemetery has an attractive wooden chapel. Such chapels were once common in larger New Zealand cemeteries, but are now quite rare.

On the top of Mt Victoria is a monument to the American explorer, Richard Byrd, who pioneered the use of aircraft in Antarctica, using New Zealand as a base for his expeditions. Also on Mt Victoria are an old cannon, once used as a time signal, and the 1940 Centennial Memorial. The remains of fortifications and observation posts, part of Wellington's coastal defences during World War II, can be seen on Beacon Hill above Miramar, on Wright's Hill above Karori and on Point Halswell above the Massey Memorial. The latter commemorates W.F. Massey, an MP for 31 years and Prime Minister from 1912–25. Point Gordon was first fortified during the Russian scare of the 1880s.

The National Museum has a rich Maori collection including the fine meeting house, Te Hau ki Turanga, carved in the 1840s in the Poverty Bay region. Relics of Cook's visit include a cannon he jettisoned on the Great Barrier Reef during his first voyage and the figurehead of the *Resolution* in which he made his second and third voyages to New Zealand. One of de Surville's anchors, recovered from Doubtless Bay in the 1970s, is on display. Some of the museum's items from the days of early European settlement are displayed in an early Wellington house exhibit. The Alexander Turnbull Library, which is now part of the National Library complex opposite Parliament Buildings in Molesworth Street, has books, manuscripts, maps, photographs and art works which illuminate New Zealand's history.

PARLIAMENT

Wellington became the country's capital in 1865 but it was not until 1897 that the first of Parliament's three existing buildings was built. The General Assembly Library is a masterpiece of Victorian Gothic design, containing hundreds of historic documents and items, many of which are on display. Between the Library and the Beehive is a truncated, pillared building, completed in 1922, which is all that was erected of a

more grandiose plan. The Chambers inside, for the House of Representatives and the now-abolished Legislative Council, were modelled exactly on the British Houses of Parliament.

In the grounds of Parliament are statues of two leaders of the Liberal Party which, in 1890, inaugurated a period of significant change in New Zealand life. They are John Ballance, Prime Minister from 1890 to his death in 1893, and his successor, Richard John Seddon, Prime Minister from 1893 to his death in 1906. Close to the Beehive is the Cenotaph, erected as Wellington's memorial to the dead of the First World War. It also commemorates the Second World War.

Across Lambton Quay from Parliament Buildings is the wooden Government Buildings, built in 1876 to house the country's civil service. It is one of the largest wooden buildings in the world. Nearby is the classical High Court building, Wellington's first stone public building, erected in 1879–80.

◄ *One of Wellington's finest Edwardian Baroque buildings, the former Public Trust Office on Lambton Quay was built in 1908.*

▼ *Perhaps New Zealand's best known former politician is Richard John Seddon, who died in office in 1906. He is commemorated by a statue, unveiled in 1915, which stands in front of Wellington's Parliament Buildings.*

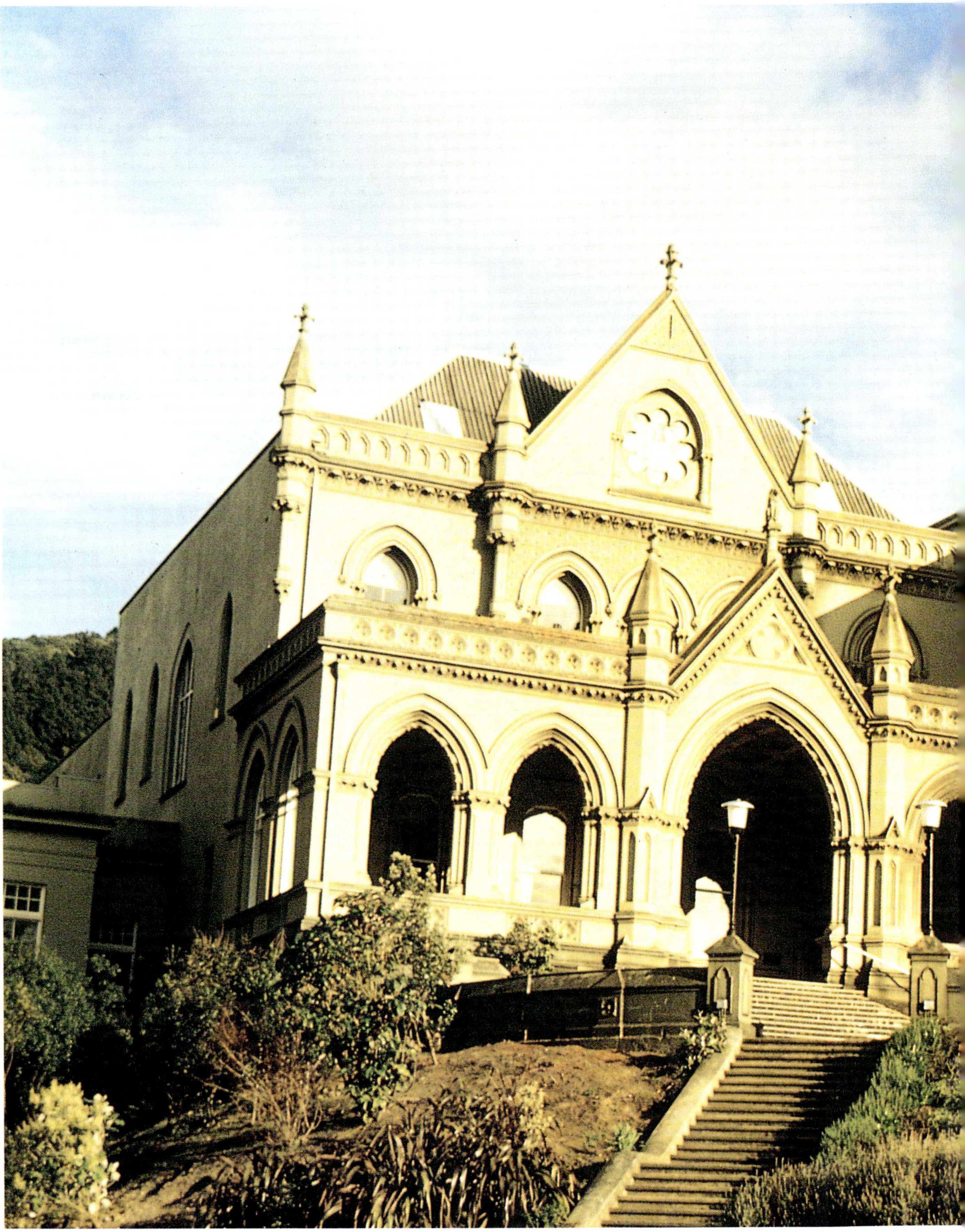

◀ *Designed by*
Thomas Turnbull in
1898 in Gothic Revival
style, the General
Assembly Library is the
oldest of the three
linked buildings that
house New Zealand's
Parliament.

THE WATERFRONT

The port of Wellington has always been a busy one. The Thorndon container terminal has made redundant several wharf sheds which are of historic interest and architectural merit. The sheds were built over a period of 30 years from the mid-1880s to 1920 in a variety of styles, and those remaining are important as reminders of how exports and imports were handled. The Harbour Board's handsome Head Office and Bond Store building, among the wharf sheds, was erected in 1891. Also on the waterfront are some smaller wooden buildings of interest. The Eastbourne Ferry ticket office recalls the ferries which crossed the harbour from 1889 to 1948, a service recently renewed. The Star Boating Club building was built in 1885, and the Wellington Rowing Club building in 1894, originally for the Naval Artillery Volunteers. In the Maritime Museum on Queen's Wharf are displays which illustrate all aspects of shipping. The new Lambton Harbour development means that, while some historic buildings will be preserved and some resited, the future of others is uncertain.

Most of these harbourside buildings, and parts of downtown Wellington, were built on reclaimed land. People walking around the city today, from Thorndon to Oriental Bay, encounter distinctive Shoreline 1840 plaques, set into the footpath, which mark where the shoreline was when the settlers arrived.

One of the major monuments of Wellington's maritime history is the Pencarrow Lighthouse, the country's first. It was prefabricated in England and erected on Pencarrow Head in 1859. In use until 1935, it is now in the care of the Historic Places Trust. Although generally accessible only on foot from Eastbourne, the lighthouse can be seen from the road around Palmer Head, on the opposite side of the harbour entrance.

In a carpark below Palmer Head is a screw from Wahine, the inter-island steamer ferry which was wrecked on Barrett Reef in 1968, one of New Zealand's worst disasters. A plaque describes the wreck.

WELLINGTON'S CHURCHES

The oldest of Wellington's churches is Old St Paul's. The first parts, consecrated in 1866, were designed by Frederick Thatcher and in later years the church was extended. It is today a triumph of Gothic architecture adapted to wood and to New Zealand's colonial conditions. In 1966 the church was bought by the Government and is now administered by the Historic Places Trust.

Three notable old churches are located on Willis Street. Overlooking the corner where Willis, Boulcott and Manners Streets join is the Gothic St Mary of the Angels, designed by Frederick Clere in 1919 and built of concrete and brick in 1922. It has the aspect of a mediaeval cathedral, crowded in by city buildings but dominating its site. Further up Willis Street are two imposing wooden churches with high spires, both designed by Thomas Turnbull. St Peter's was built in 1879 and St John's in 1885. Both are free adaptations of Gothic style and both stand on the sites of earlier churches.

The Wesley Methodist Church on Taranaki Street, built in 1880 and also designed by Turnbull, is Wellington's other important inner-city, early wooden church, Norman or Romanesque, rather than Gothic in appearance. The Basilica, near Parliament, was opened in 1901. It was designed in a classical style by the South Island architect, F.W. Petre, and built in brick. Shorn of its towers, it is still a handsome building. St Andrew's on the Terrace was built in 1922, its design following in stone that of the building's wooden predecessor.

Beyond Johnsonville, in the rural Ohariu Valley, is the tiny Holy Trinity Church, built in 1879 of pit-sawn timber.

HUTT VALLEY

The settlers who founded Wellington in 1840 first landed on the Petone foreshore, before most retreated to the more sheltered shores of Lambton Harbour. There on the foreshore is the Wellington Provincial Centennial Memorial, which houses a small settler's museum. Close by is an Iona cross, erected in 1940, which marks where, on 23 February 1840, a Presbyterian minister conducted public worship. This event is taken to mark the beginnings of the Presbyterian Church in New Zealand. Not far away, in a private cemetery, is the grave of Te Puni, the Te Atiawa chief who befriended the Europeans on their arrival and helped protect the infant settlement against attack by other Maori.

▲ *A relic of the fighting between Maori and Pakeha over land in the mid nineteenth century, the wooden blockhouse at Upper Hutt was built in 1860. Though occupied by militia in 1861, the building never saw any fighting.*

On Britannia Street, Petone, not far from the Provincial Centennial Memorial, are two old wooden churches, St Augustine's and St David's. St David's, a rather typical wooden Gothic New Zealand church, was built in 1899. Britannia was the settlers' first name for Petone. Patrick Street, Petone, on which stand the first houses erected under the Workers Dwellings Act 1905, is an historic precinct.

In the 1840s tension grew in the Wellington area between Maori and Pakeha over land sales. In 1845 some Ngati Toa, led by Te Rangihaeata, attempted to drive the settlers out of the Hutt Valley. A memorial stone at High Street and Military Road and headstones in St James' churchyard recall an engagement in May 1846 at a stockade erected on Boulcott's farm. A cannon used at Pauatahanui in the campaign against Te Rangihaeata and now mounted at the Trentham Military Camp is another relic.

The Upper Hutt blockhouse, built in 1860, dates from a later period of tension between Maori and Pakeha. Though occupied by militia from December 1860 to May 1861 it never saw hostilities. It now sits in a park off Fergusson Drive.

The oldest building in the Hutt Valley is the tiny but charming Christ Church, Taita, built in 1853–54 but badly damaged by fire and under restoration in 1990. The little Gothic building, of pit-sawn totara, once stood on its own in a bush clearing. Old headstones in the graveyard add to the interest.

The railway line, which reached Upper Hutt in 1876, has long played an important part in Hutt Valley life. The Lower Hutt station is an interesting example of early railway architecture. Further up the valley, on a bypassed stretch of line at Silverstream, is a steam railway museum. At the head of the Hutt Valley, above Upper Hutt, there are tunnels in the Te Marua reserve along the line the railway followed over the Rimutaka incline before the Rimutaka tunnel was opened. The old railway formation can be followed along a walkway.

THE PORIRUA BASIN

Separated by hills from both Wellington and the Hutt Valley, the Porirua Basin has long Maori associations. Mana Island, off the coast at the mouth of the Porirua Harbour, is, by tradition, where Kupe left his wife and daughter while exploring the Cook Strait area. The Takapuwahia Marae in Porirua is one of the present headquarters of the Ngati Toa tribe and has a carved meeting house.

Ngati Toa, Ngati Raukawa and Te Atiawa were relative latecomers to the Wellington area. In the 1820s Te Rauparaha established Ngati Toa on Kapiti Island and the adjacent coast. Plimmerton is the site of Taupo, the pa where he was captured on 23 July 1846.

The first Europeans to settle in the Porirua area were whalers who established shore stations on Kapiti and Mana Islands and the adjacent coast in the 1820s. One of the first recorded shipments of wool from New Zealand left Mana in 1835.

Near the head of the Pauatahanui Inlet is the site of one of Te Rangihaeata's pa, now occupied by St Alban's Church, built in 1895. Most of the fighting at Pauatahanui in 1846 occurred not at this pa but further up the Horokiri Valley. Battle Hill was the site of the main engagement and below the hill are the graves of some of those who died in the fighting.

At the mouth of the Pauatahanui Inlet is

another survivor from the fighting of the mid-1840s. In 1846–47 stone barracks were built at Paremata as a base for miliary operations against Te Rangihaeata. The four-square barracks were damaged in an earthquake in 1848 and abandoned four years later, but the ruined stone walls remain in the Ngati Toa Domain.

The Porirua Basin also has a place in the history of New Zealand letters; one of the leading scholars of Maori culture, Elsdon Best, was born in Tawa in 1856 and his ashes were buried there on his death.

Much of Porirua's growth is recent but a few historic buildings remain in Porirua itself. Two houses have survived from earlier days. Soon after 1882, James Gear, a butcher and freezing works owner, built himself a stately house above Porirua Harbour. The Gear homestead is now used as a community and functions centre and its woolshed for cultural activities. Another old house, Papakowhai, can be seen nearby.

A small collection illustrating the Maori and Pakeha history of the area is held at the Porirua Museum near Takapuwahia Marae. At the Police Training School is a museum of police history in New Zealand.

On the coast south of Porirua is Ohariu Bay where, in the 1840s, the local Maori had extensive cultivations from which they supplied Wellington with wheat and potatoes. The Makara Walkway passes some still visible earthworks of the Wharehou Pa. Further along the walkway are the remains of a Second World War coastal battery.

THE KAPITI COAST

In the early nineteenth century, shore whaling stations were established on Kapiti. The opportunity for trading offered by these stations was one of the island's attractions to Te Rauparaha who made his headquarters on Kapiti after leading his tribe from Kawhia and defeating the local tribes. There are still traces of Ngati Toa pa and the whaling stations but they are not easily accessible.

In 1840 Octavius Hadfield founded a mission station at Otaki. The Rangiatea Church at Otaki (1849) is the most important survivor from the days of Hadfield's mission and one of the finest Maori churches in the country. Tapu soil, said to have been brought from Hawaiki on the *Tainui* canoe, was placed under the altar. Opposite the church is a memorial over Te

Rauparaha's grave — though his remains possibly lie in an unknown location on Kapiti. At the Roman Catholic mission, established at Otaki in 1844, stands an early church, built about 1857, and other buildings which date from about 1900.

The important Otaki meeting house Raukawa was rebuilt in the early 1930s on the site of an earlier meeting house. Other meeting houses can be seen on marae in the Otaki area. The Otaki museum is housed in the old Bank of New Zealand building, itself of historic interest.

St Luke's Anglican Church, Waikanae, dates from 1877. It is a pit-sawn timber building with an historic graveyard.

On Otaihanga Road in Paraparaumu, a plaque marks the point at which the Wellington and Manawatu railway line — the only major line built by a private company — was opened in November 1886. Three museums in the district cater for those with an interest in New Zealand's transport history. At Paraparaumu, the Southward Car Museum displays cars from the last century and other vehicles. The Engine Shed at Paekakariki features steam locomotives and other aspects of New Zealand's rail history. The Tramway Museum at Queen Elizabeth Park has old trams in working order.

▲ *The Wellington Provincial Centennial Memorial was built on the Petone foreshore, close to the spot where Wellington's first European settlers stepped ashore in 1840. The distinctive building now houses a small settlers museum.*

NELSON

The first recorded encounter between Maori and European occurred in 1642 when Abel Tasman, seeing signs of human habitation, anchored off the coast of what is now the Abel Tasman National Park. Nelson's two great bays, Tasman and Golden, have long histories of Maori occupation but although traces of some pa can still be seen in different parts of the province, none are major features of the landscape. The fertile Waimea Plains were the scene of extensive Maori kumara gardens in pre-European times, the Maori modifying the soils by adding sand and gravel to give better crops. Most traces of these early Maori gardens have been obliterated by modern agriculture but some can still be seen. From the hills around Nelson the Maori quarried stone for tools and there are some ancient though hard-to-find quarrying sites.

Nelson was founded in 1842 as one of Edward Gibbon Wakefield's New Zealand Company settlements. The site of the first landing after the European discovery of Nelson Haven in 1841 is marked by a plaque on Haven Road. A stone on the foreshore marks where Captain Arthur Wakefield stepped ashore in November 1841. At the end of that year Captain Wakefield raised the Union Jack on Britannia Heights, where today the site is marked by a noticeboard. A redwood was planted there in 1900 in memory of Captain Wakefield, killed on 17 June 1843 during the Wairau Incident.

NELSON'S OLD HOUSES

Nelson is well endowed with old houses. Those on Richmond Avenue and South Street have been declared precincts of historic interest by the Historic Places Trust. Melrose, a grand Italianate house of the 1880s, is now owned by the city and has been restored. Fairfield, another old wooden house, built between 1872 and 1883, has been restored and can be viewed by the public. The Cawthron Institute owns and leases a wooden house with a sturdy verandah and Gothic detailing built in the late 1860s.

Two of Nelson's most notable old houses which the public are invited to visit are in Stoke. Isel House in Isel Park is an attractive stone house built between 1880 and 1905. The Nelson Provincial Museum, which has Maori and pioneer artefacts on display, is situated behind the house. Broadgreen, one of the country's largest and finest earth-built houses, was built in the 1850s. It has been restored and furnished as an example of a colonial gentleman's residence.

The countryside around Nelson is good territory for spotting interesting old farmhouses. Along the Waimea West Road is an old house, The Gables, built in brick in the mid-1860s as a store and accommodation house and almost unaltered. Stafford Place, off State Highway 60, built in 1866, was the home of the Redwood family. Both these houses are privately owned but can be seen from the road.

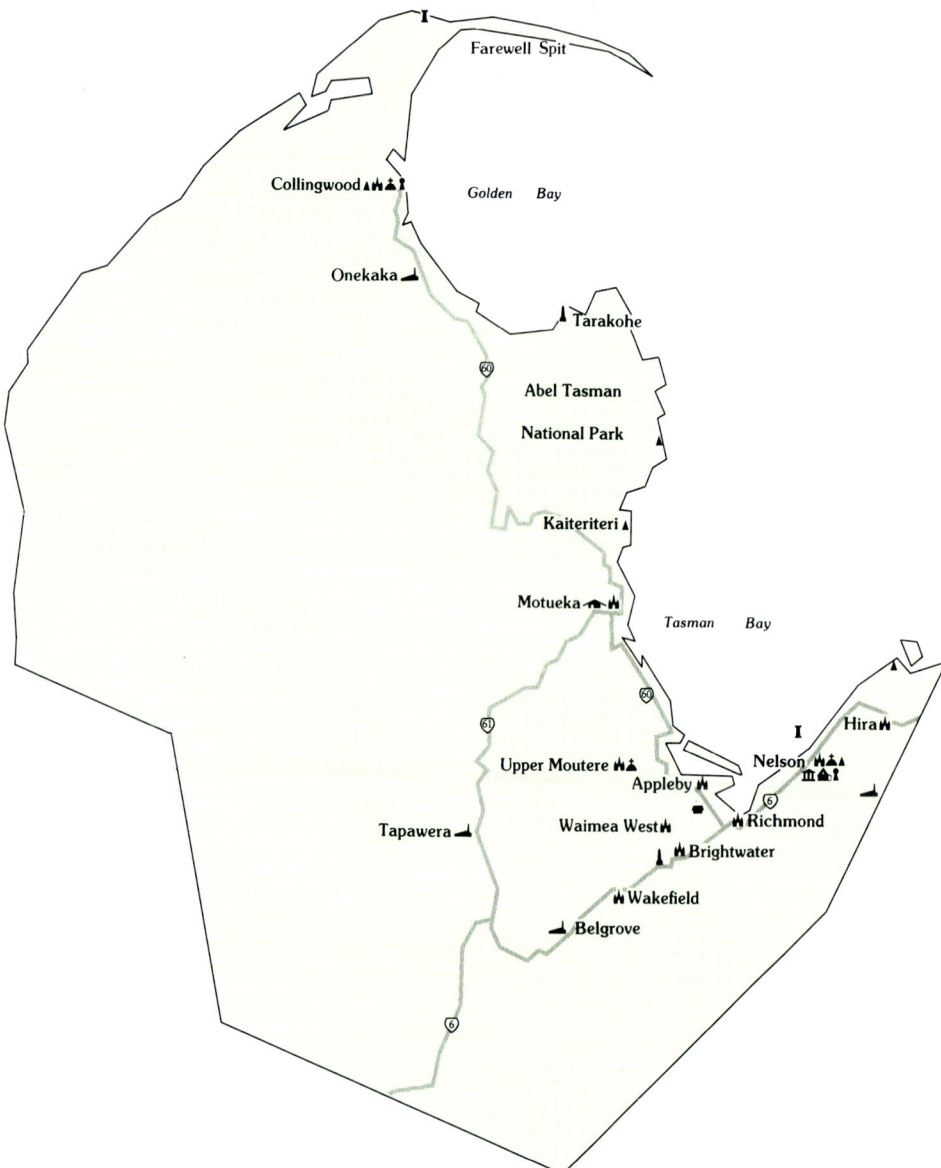

NELSON'S CHURCHES

Nelson's churches are among its most interesting historic buildings. The present cathedral, built over a period of 40 years from 1925, is the third church to occupy the Church Hill site overlooking the central city. In pre-European times a pa occupied the site but the hill has been associated with Christian worship from the earliest days of European settlement. The first church was built on the site in 1851 and the second construction was consecrated as Christ Church Cathedral in 1887.

In Nelson city are a number of historic wooden churches. Near each other, and built in the same decade, are Trinity Presbyterian Church, 1891, the Baptist Church, 1897, and St John's Methodist Church, 1899. St Mary's Catholic Church, 1882, is noted for its fine wooden shingled spire. All Saints, built in a Byzantine style, was begun in 1868 and completed in 1890, the style marking a departure from the Gothic traditions of Nelson's other early churches. The Chapel of the Holy Evangelists at Bishopdale, residence of the Bishop of Nelson, was built in 1876–77. It has a slate roof and vertical timbering and stands in a peaceful setting in the grounds of Bishopdale. It is open to the public.

In the countryside near Nelson some of the South Island's most historic and pictur-esque churches can be found. The simple wooden St John's Church, Wakefield, was built in 1846 and is the oldest surviving church in the South Island. In the church-yard are the graves of many pioneer settlers. St Paul's Anglican Church, Brightwater, was completed in 1857 and enlarged in 1895. Holy Trinity, Richmond, consecrated in 1872, was one of New Zealand's loveliest country churches until alterations in the late 1980s. St Michael's at Waimea West, designed by the explorer Thomas Brunner and opened in 1867, has the general appear-ance and setting of an English village church. St Paul's Lutheran Church at Upper Moutere replaced an earlier church in 1905. Headstones in its graveyard inscribed in German provide a link with the German set-tlers who arrived in Nelson in the 1840s.

The first stone church in the Nelson province, St Barnabas, built in the 1860s, but added to in the early 1970s, stands at the entrance to Isel Park, Stoke. The graves of some of Nelson's original settlers can be found in its churchyard. The Wakapuaka Cemetery includes the graves of the victims of the notorious 1866 Maungatapu murders.

The charming Bishop's School has strong ecclesiastical associations. Opened in 1844 as an Anglican elementary school, it was a church school for boys from 1860 to 1895. The school was substantially rebuilt

▲ *Tasman's ships at the site of the incident in Murderers (Golden) Bay in 1642.* Alexander Turnbull Library

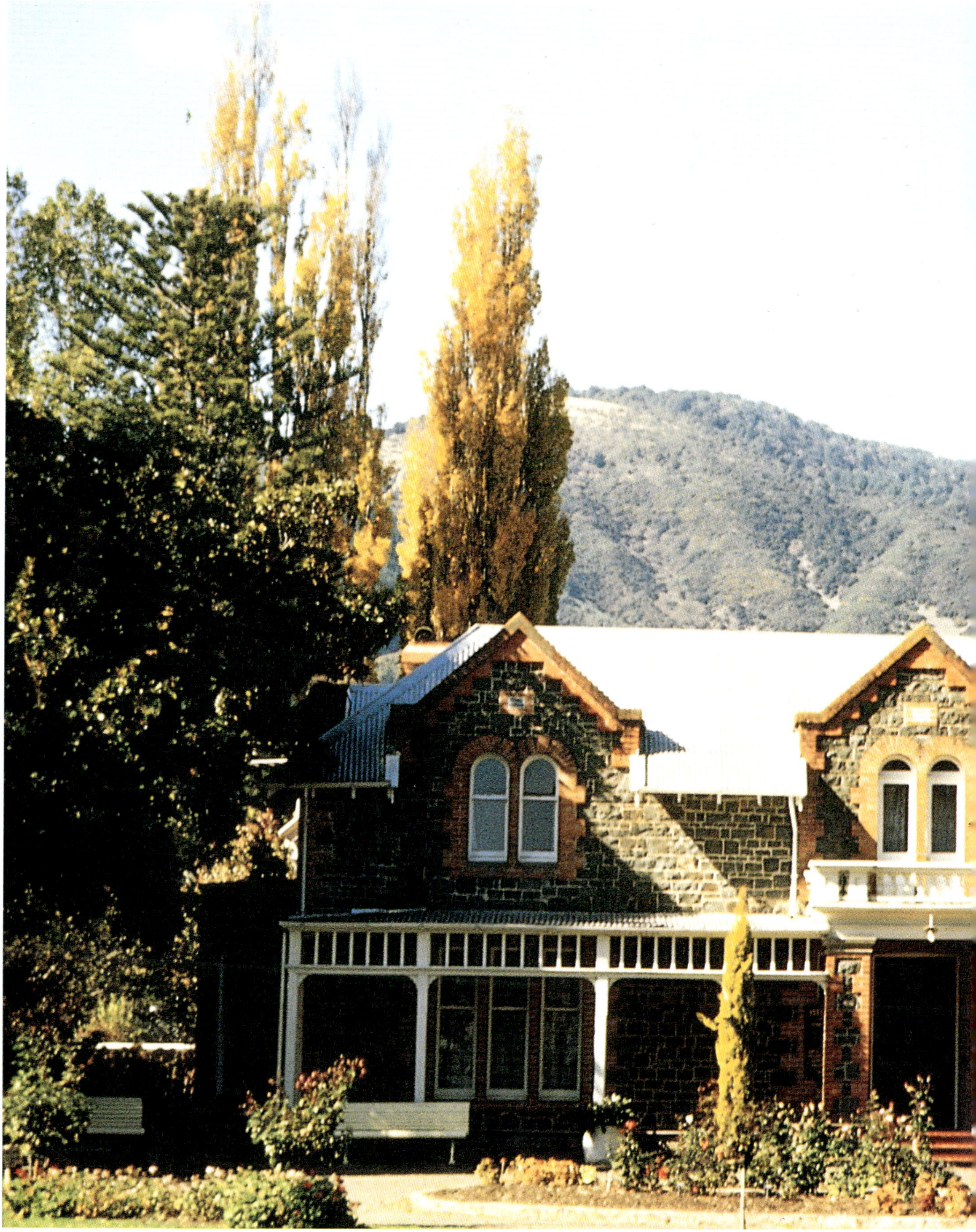

◀ *Isel House at Stoke, near Nelson, was built in stages between 1880 and 1905, with red brick facings contrasting attractively with the grey stone used for the walls. The Nelson Provincial Museum is situated behind the house.*

▲ *This row of humble working class cottages near the centre of Nelson dates from last century. They stand in interesting contrast with the city's grander old homes like Isel House and Broadgreen.*

in 1881, but some brickwork remains from the original structure. The Gothic-flavoured building has been restored by the Historic Places Trust as an educational museum and is open to the public. Also of interest is the 1866 Engine House, built to house the Government fire engine. Located behind the Suter Art Gallery, it is all that survives of the Nelson Provincial Council buildings.

A LIGHTHOUSE AND RAILWAYS

Nelson has some fascinating reminders of early transport in New Zealand. The British-made cast-iron lighthouse on the Boulder Bank, erected in 1861–62, is New Zealand's second oldest. Only Wellington's Pencarrow Light has stood longer.

But Nelson's main claim to a place in the history of transport is based on its being the site of New Zealand's first 'railway', although some dispute whether a horse-drawn tramway can properly be called a railway. The Dun Mountain Railway was opened in 1862 to bring chrome ore from a deposit on the Dun Mountain 21 km to the port of Nelson. The line ceased operating in 1866. A plaque on Upper Brook Street marks where the railway opened and it is possible to walk along parts of the old formation. Another curiosity at Belgrove is one of the country's only two surviving 'railway windmills', built to pump water into trackside tanks to replenish the boilers of steam locomotives. The Nelson to Glenhope railway, which this windmill served, was closed in the 1950s. Traces of the line can be seen as far south as Kawatiri, in the form of embankments, old bridge piers and tunnels.

Near Belgrove there are several nineteenth century hop kilns, and at Tapawera an old flour mill which opened in 1871. Ask for directions locally to reach this building, as it is not easy to find.

NELSON PROVINCE

Nelson's most famous native son was Lord Rutherford and a monument at Brightwater has been erected to mark his birthplace.

North of Nelson is Cable Bay where the first trans-Tasman telegraphic cable came ashore in 1876. A plaque marks the site of the cable station.

West of Nelson lie the districts of Motueka and Riwaka and, beyond the Takaka Hill, Golden Bay. At Motueka is one of the South Island's few Maori churches, Te Ahurewa, built in 1897. Just beyond Motueka, towards Kaiteriteri, is a cairn of old millstones, erected to the memory of Captain Arthur Wakefield and to commemorate the coming of the first settlers to the Riwaka district.

Tasman Bay is separated from Golden Bay by hills which jut into the sea and form the Abel Tasman National Park. The visit of the Dutch navigator to Golden Bay in 1642 is commemorated by an imposing monument on a headland just past Tarakohe. The monument looks out over the water on which four men of Tasman's crew were killed by local Maori, prompting him to call it Murderers Bay. French navigator Dumont d'Urville anchored at the east corner of the Park, at the Astrolabe Roadstead in 1827.

Collingwood was the scene of a small gold rush up the Aorere River in 1857, the first discovery of payable gold in the South Island. A roadside plaque about 6 km from the township records the discovery in Lightband's Gully, 3 km to the west. The museum at Collingwood has goldmining relics on display. At Onekaka is evidence of other mineral deposits in the area — the remains of an old iron works and wharf. The first lighthouse was erected on Farewell Spit in 1869–70, and the present structure in 1897. A walking route of historic interest, the Heaphy Track, connects Collingwood with Karamea on the West Coast. The line of the track was an old Maori route, first traversed by Europeans in the 1850s and cleared and formed in 1888.

▲ *One of the country's largest and grandest houses made of earth, Broadgreen was built in the 1850s. It has been restored and is open to the public as an example of a substantial Victorian dwelling.*

MARLBOROUGH

In the northern part of Marlborough are the long inlets and deep bays of the Marlborough Sounds. The Sounds were favourable to Maori ways of life and sites of pre-European settlements can be visited. In 1770 Captain Cook found one of his favourite anchorages near the entrance to Queen Charlotte Sound. From the 1820s the outer Sounds attracted whalers and later farming settlers. At Tuamarina, on the landward fringe of the Sounds, a hostile encounter between Maori and Pakeha in the South Island occurred in 1843.

The valleys to the south of the Sounds — the Wairau and the Awatere — and the hill country surrounding them saw the birth of the South Island pastoral industry in the 1840s and today old station and farm buildings are among the province's interesting historic places. Picton and Blenheim, early rivals for the title of Marlborough's main town, both contain relics and buildings that will interest visitors. Kaikoura, in the southern part of Marlborough, is a picturesque fishing settlement with a fascinating Maori history and relics of its European whaling origins very much in evidence.

THE SOUNDS

Many travellers approach Marlborough through the maritime gateway of Tory Channel and Queen Charlotte Sound. The Sounds were well populated in pre-European times and there are many old pa throughout, some now quite inaccessible. One old pa is on Moioio Island in Tory Channel and at Karaka Point, beyond Waikawa, is an ancient peninsula pa which fell to Te Rauparaha in the 1820s. This last site has road access, but the pa has recently been damaged. In Pelorus Sound there are Maori food storage pits cut into soft rock on a historic reserve at Crail Bay. Mahakipawa, also in Pelorus Sound, is the terraced site of another ancient Maori settlement.

Inside the northern entrance of Queen Charlotte Sound and accessible only by boat or on foot is Ship Cove, Captain Cook's New Zealand base which he used first in January 1770 and on four other occasions on subsequent voyages. The monument on the foreshore can be reached along the Endeavour-Resolution Walkway. It was from the lookout above Umuwheki Bay, Arapawa Island, that Cook first saw the strait that bears his name. On Motuara Island, 3 km east of Ship Cove, a cairn and tablet mark the spot where Cook took possession of what he termed 'the mainland' in the name of George III, naming the sound after the monarch's wife.

The Sounds are also associated with early French exploration of the New Zealand coast. At Elmslie Bay, a roadside plaque records the discovery, in 1827 by Dumont d'Urville, of French Pass, the treacherous channel which separates d'Urville Island from the mainland. The Pass was later used regularly by ferries between Nelson and Wellington.

The Cook Strait side of the Sounds has an important place in whaling history. In the late 1820s John Guard set up the South

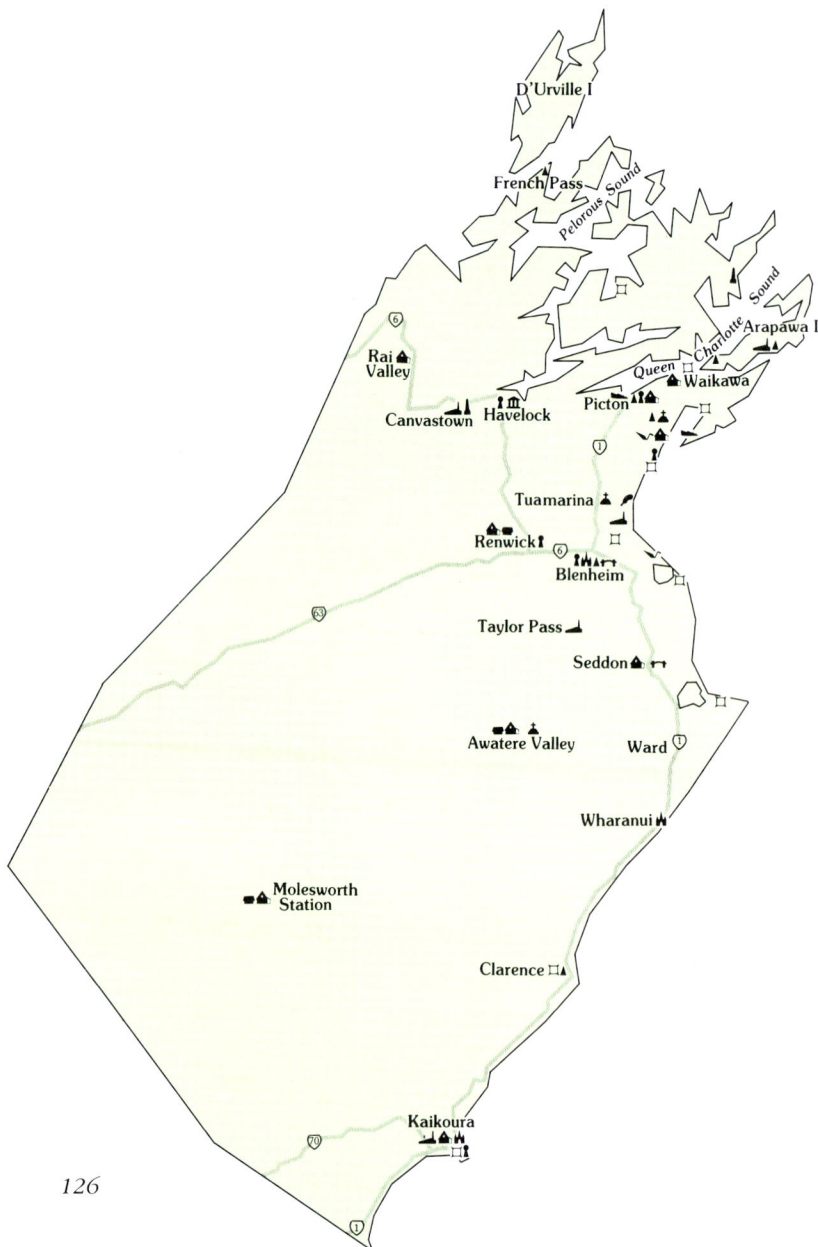

Havelock PBA 2915

Island's first shore whaling station at Te Awaiti in Tory Channel, and later moved to Kakapo Bay in Port Underwood. Whaling was continued from Tory Channel until 1964. The old tin factory sheds and wharves at Whekenui can be seen from the ferries just inside the Cook Strait entrance to Tory Channel. A plaque and four whaling trypots mark the site.

PICTON

Picton, at the head of Queen Charlotte Sound, was the first capital of Marlborough, from 1859 to 1865. A plaque on the police station marks the site of the Provincial Government buildings, opened in 1861.

Two old vessels are among Picton's interesting historic relics. The scow *Echo*, built in 1905, had an adventuresome 65 years as a trading ship and was used by the United States Navy in 1943 as an escort vessel in the Bougainville campaign. It now rests on the Picton foreshore and is used as a clubroom. Moored close to the ferry wharf is the hulk of an older vessel, the *Edwin Fox*, a fully rigged ship built of teak in Bengal in 1853. After service with the British Navy conveying troops to the Crimean War, it became an immigrant clip-

per, bringing hundreds of new settlers to New Zealand in the 1870s. Pensioned off, it became a floating refrigerated store and was eventually sold by the freezing company to a preservation society. After years of uncertainty, the preservation and partial restoration of this important maritime relic are now going ahead.

The Smith Memorial Museum on the Picton foreshore has relics of the whaling industry and exhibits from the *Edwin Fox*. Picton's interesting older buildings include the old Smith homestead on Oxford Street, built in 1875. A cottage on Devon Street may have been built in 1872. These are private homes and can be viewed only from the street.

PORT UNDERWOOD

The first cable beneath Cook Strait was a telegraph cable laid in 1866, which came ashore at Whites Bay, along the road to Port Underwood from Cloudy Bay. Between 1867 and 1873 a full telegraph station was maintained at Whites Bay and an operator-linesman remained on duty there until 1895. The original cable station building now houses a small telegraphic museum. On the spur between Whites Bay and

▶ *Havelock gained this distinctive post office in 1875. It has changed little since the days when coaches passed down the town's main street.*

Rarangi the old earthworks of Pukatea Pa can be seen, as can many other archaeological sites around the shores of Port Underwood.

Port Underwood also reveals reminders of its earliest European settlers. At Robin Hood Bay is a cottage, notable for its method of construction (cob and rickers), which may be the oldest dwelling still standing in the South Island. Port Underwood was an early haunt of whalers, the first shore whaling station being established at Kakapo Bay by John Guard.

At Ngakuta Bay, the Rev. Samuel Ironside landed in 1840 to found the second mission station in the South Island. The station failed after the Wairau incident of 1843. Mounds indicate where the chimneys of the homestead once stood and there is a solitary grave of an early settler.

On Horahora Kakahu Island, beyond the end of the road on the eastern shore of Port Underwood, is a plaque on a historic reserve marking the spot on which the Union Jack was raised on 17 June 1840, when British sovereignty was proclaimed over the South Island by Major Bunbury, sent south by Governor Hobson to obtain the signatures of South Island Maori chiefs to the Treaty of Waitangi. The island was previously the site of an ancient pa. Beyond the island, in Cutters Bay, are wrecks of two old ships.

HAVELOCK

Havelock, at the head of Pelorus Sound, owed its early importance to the discovery of gold on the small but rich Wakamarina goldfield, in 1864. It later became a sawmilling town when the fine stands of native timber in the area were cut out, a woodburning locomotive bringing timber from Carluke to Blackball, just west of Havelock.

New Zealand's notable expatriate scientist, Lord Rutherford, received his early schooling in Havelock; his old school is now a youth hostel. The old Havelock Post Office, built in 1875, is a fine example of a small-town, wooden public building. The Havelock Museum is housed in a former Methodist church, the exhibits featuring gold and timber and a mill locomotive of the 1890s.

Outside Havelock are traces of the gold rush of the mid-1860s. The site of Cullensville, a flourishing goldmining township from the late 1880s until the second

half of the 1890s, is marked today by only a few heaps of stones and some derelict equipment. In Canvastown, an obelisk marks the site of the 1865 gold discovery and there are relics of mining days in front of the hotel.

In the pastoral Rai Valley, a short distance off State Highway 6 on the road to Tennyson Inlet, is a cottage built in 1881 by Charles Turner. He and his wife were the district's first pioneers, who cleared the virgin bush for their home. The cottage was built of materials to hand — totara slabs for walls, shingles for the roof and river stones for the fireplace. Restored in 1969, the interior of the cottage, furnished in pioneer style, can be viewed through glass panels.

BLENHEIM

East of Blenheim, at the mouth of the Wairau River, is one of the country's most important archaeological sites. Excavations carried out since the 1930s reveal a site of extensive settlement in the early years of Polynesian occupation, associated with the capture of moa. Burials there contained the richest grave goods yet discovered in New Zealand. The site is difficult of access and there is little evidence to enable the casual visitor, not accompanied by an archaeologist, to appreciate its scientific importance. Well presented displays based on investigations of the site can be seen in the Canterbury Museum in Christchurch.

The 8 km Boulder Bank extends from the Wairau Bar to an ancient Maori pa, Hautaki, near the White Bluffs. Most of Marlborough's wool, until the mid-1870s,

▼ *The slab-walled, shingle-roofed cottage at Carluke in the Rai Valley was the first home, built in 1881, of pioneers in the district who cleared bush to create farmland. Restored in 1969, the cottage is furnished in pioneer style.*

was hauled along the Boulder Bank then barged from the Wairau Bar to the province's deep sea port at Port Underwood. A memorial on the Wairau Pa side of the river mouth (reached by road from Spring Creek) salutes those pioneer settlers.

The road into Blenheim from the north crosses the Opawa River over a bridge built between 1911 and 1917, one of New Zealand's earliest concrete bridges. Blenheim was founded in 1850 and the site on which the first store was opened in that year is marked by a plaque. In 1865 the town became the provincial capital of Marlborough. In the Blenheim area are several old cob buildings, the best presented of which is the restored cottage at Riverlands, south of the town. The cottage was built about 1860 for a local farmer and still has colonial furniture and fittings.

The aerodrome at Woodbourne, just west of Blenheim, has a plate set in the ground to commemorate the flight of Charles Kingsford Smith in the *Southern Cross* for the first east-to-west crossing of the Tasman Sea on 13 October 1928.

Marlborough was a leading pastoral province in the nineteenth century and the Langley Dale station at Renwick has an old homestead and interesting outbuildings. The station is still privately owned and the buildings can be viewed only with the owner's permission.

The once important flax-milling industry which processed native flax into fibre for use in rope and twine has left little to remind later generations of its importance. At Marshlands, near Blenheim, is a surviving flax mill, with some structures and machinery dating from the rebuilding of the mill in the late 1880s. The mill, unused since 1963, is now undergoing restoration.

The Brayshaw Museum Park in Blenheim has displays of vintage machinery, particularly farm implements and agricultural machinery. In the park's Beavertown (as Blenheim was first known), ten replica shops are set up as they were in the nineteenth century. In the Renwick museum just beyond Woodbourne, more relics of early European settlement are on display, some housed in a reconstruction of an early tavern.

TUAMARINA

The Wairau Incident, 17 June 1843, is recorded as an early clash between Maori and Pakeha over land. A dispute over the ownership of the Wairau Valley, which the New Zealand Company claimed to have bought, erupted in June 1843 into a bloody confrontation in which 22 Europeans and about six Maori were killed. The fighting broke out at Tuamarina when Te Rauparaha and Te Rangihaeata attempted to stop a survey of the disputed land. The fray did not lead to a general outbreak.

The place on the river bank where the event occurred is marked, and an old titoki tree stands at the point where the parties crossed the river during the parleying which preceded the incident. In the Tuamarina cemetery, on a hillock above the town, is a monument erected in 1863 to those killed in the fighting twenty years earlier. A carronade which figured in the events leading up to the incident stands on the corner of High and Seymour Streets in Blenheim.

About 3 km towards Blenheim from Tuamarina is the site of Henry Redwood's water-driven flour mill, established in 1865. Redwood imported thoroughbred horses into New Zealand and became known as the 'father of the New Zealand turf'.

SEDDON AND WARD

There are traces of early Maori occupation of Marlborough at Marfells Beach near Seddon. The road into Seddon from the north crosses a feature fast disappearing from New Zealand — the combined road and rail bridge. This one has the road on a lower deck and the rail on an upper.

The hill country around Seddon and Ward, and up the Awatere Valley, saw the beginnings of large-scale pastoral farming in the South Island. The Flaxbourne run, the first in the South Island, was established in 1847 on land leased from the local chief. Like other great sheep stations, Flaxbourne was eventually subdivided into smaller farms. On the privately owned Langridge Station up the Awatere Valley is a cob cottage, an old stable and stone enclosures which date from the early days of pastoral farming. There is another old cob cottage, the Burtigill cottage, and an early cottage on the Mount Gladstone station, also up the Awatere Valley. The cemetery at the old Awatere township is worth exploring.

Far up the Wairau Valley are the remains of the Rainbow Accommodation House, built in the 1890s. The original cob homestead still stands on the Molesworth Station alongside the Awatere River.

South of Ward, along the east coast road, the picturesque stone church of St Oswald's at Wharanui was built in 1927 as a family memorial. Further south again, at Clarence Bridge, are traces of early Maori occupation in the form of faint lines on a hillside marking old kumara gardens. A plaque on the river bank under the southern bridge approach marks the height of the great flood of 1868.

KAIKOURA

The Kaikoura Peninsula has an important place in the Maori history of the South Island. Archaeological excavations have shown that there have been Maori settlements in the area since the moa-hunter period, but the visible traces of Maori occupation are of more recent origin. The earthworks of several pa can be seen; Takahanga and Nga Niho are on the town side of the peninsula and others can be identified at South Bay. South of Kaikoura earthworks can still be discerned at Puketa and Omihi.

In the late 1820s the pa at Kaikoura itself were the scene of fighting during Te Rauparaha's expeditions against the tribes of the South Island. In 1828 the pa were captured by Te Rauparaha but southern Ngai Tahu chiefs prevented Te Rauparaha's Ngati Toa from occupying the area. Both Takahanga and Nga Niho can be visited along the route of the Kaikoura Walkway.

Kaikoura's European history began in 1842 when Robert Fyffe established a shore whaling station on the north side of the peninsula. Standing near the site of this shore station is Fyffe House, built about 1860 by Robert Fyffe's cousin, George. The house, at 62 Avoca Street, rests partly on whale vertebrae piles. It has changed little since the early 1860s and is a typical colonial cottage, in a superb setting. It is now owned by the Historic Places Trust and is open to visitors.

The old wharf near the Fyffe House dates from 1882. Other reminders of Kaikoura's whaling origins include old whale jawbones in the Garden of Memories and two trypots by the Memorial Hall. Whaling continued from a shore station at South Bay until well into the twentieth century. The Kaikoura Museum covers the full span of Kaikoura's history.

When European settlement began in Canterbury in the 1840s, there were probably fewer than 500 Maori inhabitants. A few decades earlier the number had been substantially greater but intra-tribal wars and the raids by North Island warriors wreaked havoc on the local Ngai Tahu people. Traces remain, however, of the Maori presence in North Canterbury — from very early rock drawings to the earthworks of pa which featured prominently in the tribal fighting. The Europeans have also left their mark and grand homesteads, fine churches and the evidence of early industry are a testament to their skill and labour.

NORTH CANTERBURY

North Canterbury is sheep country and many of its historic places are connected with the great runs of the nineteenth century. Two of the most valuable runs were Glenmark and Cheviot Hills, the latter covering more than 34,000 hectares. Its sale to the Government in 1892–93 was hailed as the first triumph in 'busting up the big estates'.

A memorial to Sir John McKenzie, the Minister for Lands who subdivided the estate for closer settlement, stands opposite the Cheviot Post Office. The homestead of the estate burned down in the 1930s and only its concrete foundations remain, but the manager's house is still standing and can be seen from the road to Gore Bay, just south of the Cheviot Domain. At Gore Bay stands a two-storeyed cottage built in 1867.

Glenmark, north of Waipara, covered at its peak about 31,000 hectares and was the most valuable single run in nineteenth century Canterbury. The lavish homestead built in 1881–88 burned down in 1890. What survive are a Gothic gatehouse, the manager's house and huge stables, built of concrete in 1881. (Visits to the privately owned Glenmark buildings should not be made without prior arrangement.) St Paul's Church, Glenmark, was built early this century as a memorial to runholder George Moore.

At Waipara, State Highway 7 leaves the main highway and passes several places of historic interest. The Weka Pass Railway is based at Waipara itself and runs excursions using vintage engines and rolling stock from the old relocated Mina railway station along a picturesque stretch of the former Waiau branch line. A side road just south of Waikari leads past the Timpendean homestead to the Weka Pass Historic Reserve where visitors can see prehistoric drawings, in charcoal and red ochre, on the limestone face of an overhanging rock. This natural shelter was used by the Maori probably about 500 years ago.

In Waikari and Hawarden are some interesting older buildings and at Hurunui is a gem of early New Zealand architecture — a hotel built of local limestone blocks in 1869, when the river nearby was first being bridged. The hotel, which has one of the country's longest continuous licences, has been restored by local enthusiasts.

Throughout parts of inland North Canterbury are many charming old homesteads. One such place is Leslie Hills, near Culverden. The house, built in 1900, is still in the hands of the Rutherford family and

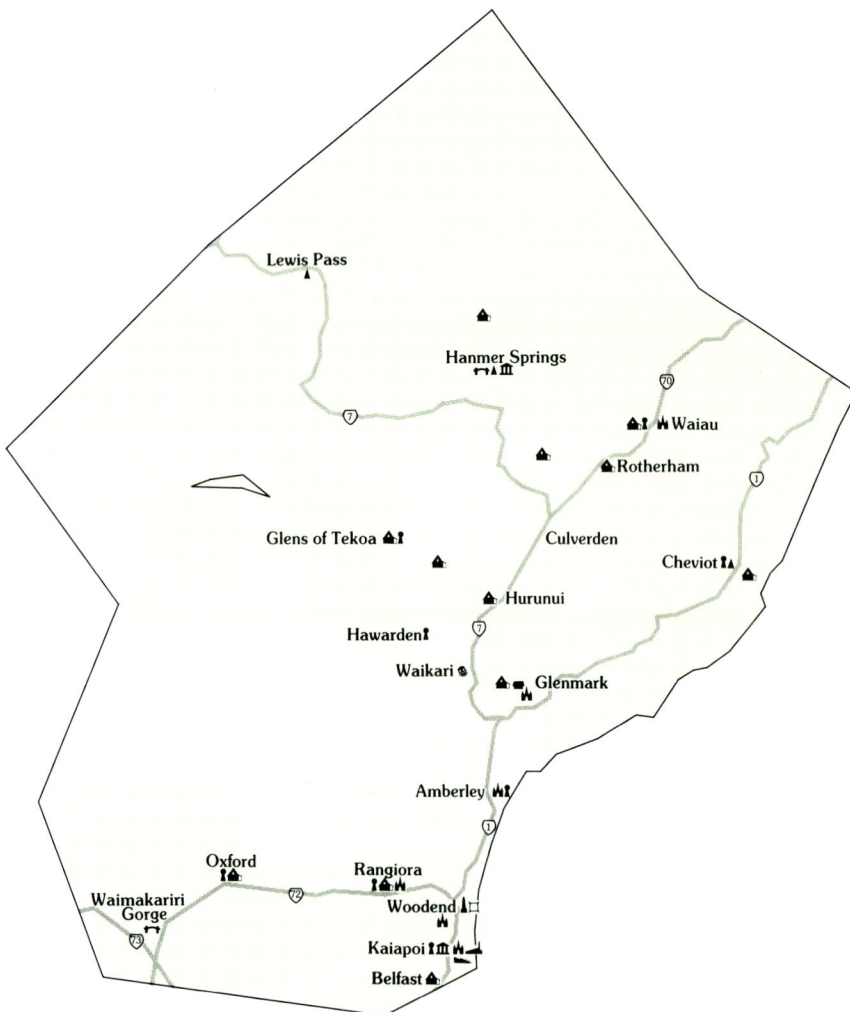

can be seen from the Leslie Hills Road which branches off the Lewis Pass highway near Montrose. At Glens of Tekoa there is an early cottage, built about 1861–62, which houses the family museum of the McRaes, who have held the land since it was first taken up as a run. The cottage is near the present homestead (1865) and can be visited by prior arrangement.

Waiau, the oldest Amuri township, has several nineteenth century buildings, including the Presbyterian Church, built in 1888, and behind it an earlier church building of 1877. Another Amuri township, Rotherham, was founded in 1877. Its old buildings include a century-old cob cottage visible from the main road.

The road into Hanmer Springs crosses the Waiau River on the historic Waiau Ferry Bridge, constructed in 1886–87 and one of Canterbury's most remarkable nineteenth century engineering achievements. Hanmer Springs grew up as a spa around its popular thermal springs. Few buildings survive from the town's early days but the wooden post office, erected in 1901, is one of them.

Beyond Hanmer, mountain passes lead into the remote back country. On the Jollies Pass road a noticeboard records that the first flock of sheep driven south from the Wairau Plains was brought over the pass in March 1852. Many of the founding flocks of

the Amuri and Canterbury came over this route. Over Jacks Pass, about 27 km from Hanmer (just beyond a locked gate), is the old Acheron Accommodation House, a cob building erected in 1862–63. It served travellers on horseback or on foot using what was then a main route between Canterbury and Nelson. The building gives an idea of travelling conditions in the nineteenth century.

The route over Lewis Pass was surveyed in the 1880s but the road between Glynn Wye and Springs Junction was not built until 1929–36, largely by relief workers during the Depression. Below the pass, Cannibal Gorge on the Maruia River was an important route in pre-European times. Today the St James Walkway traverses this old Maori route.

TOWARDS CHRISTCHURCH

South of Waipara, the main road town of Amberley has two charming historic churches. The Church of the Most Holy Passion was built in 1866 on the Brackenfield run, and shifted into Amberley nearly 90 years later. The Church of the Holy Innocents was built in 1877. At Saltwater Creek, 'Harleston', the remains of

▲ *The Mansion House on the Cheviot Hills Run in 1893. Only the foundations remain.*
Alexander Turnbull Library

133

▲ *The pleasing simplicity of colonial architecture is evident in the lines of the Hurunui Hotel, built of local limestone in 1869 and still functioning as a hotel on one of the country's longest continuously held licences.*

a port used until the early 1870s is marked by a plaque. North of Saltwater Creek, a house built of limestone in the 1860s by an early waggoner stands by the highway.

Down a side road just south of Woodend a tall monument erected in 1898 marks one of Canterbury's most historic sites. The great pa Kaiapohia, one of the most important Ngai Tahu pa, was built on a peninsula projecting into a swampy lagoon. In the late 1820s and early 1830s it was the scene of stirring episodes in the conflict between the Ngai Tahu and the Ngati Toa led by Te Rauparaha. The Ngati Toa captured the pa after a siege.

In the 1850s many Ngai Tahu were living nearby at Tuahiwi. A mission station was established there in that decade and a lovely little Maori church, St Stephen's, built in 1865, still stands in the settlement.

Rangiora has a number of interesting older buildings, including the remodelled Red Lion Hotel (1874) and the handsome Church of St John the Baptist, begun in 1858 but extended later. An 1869 cob cottage is part of the local historical museum. There are several interesting old farmhouses in the countryside around Rangiora. One of the grandest is Ohoka, built of brick in the 1870s. More typical of North Canterbury's farmhouses is Brooklands, a smaller wooden house of the 1870s which can be seen from the road near Rangiora.

Kaiapoi, like Rangiora, has some inviting older buildings, in particular St Bartholomew's Church, which dates from

1855. On the river is the *Tuhoe*, a coastal trading vessel built in Auckland in 1919, a reminder of Kaiapoi's earlier importance as a river port. The vessel makes regular weekend sailings from the wharf at Kaiapoi down the river. For 100 years, from the late 1870s, Kaiapoi was the site of a woollen mill which made the town's name well known throughout the country. The mill building and the old Bank of New Zealand building still stand.

Oxford began life as a saw milling settlement and boasts a good complement of early buildings. The road between Oxford and Sheffield crosses the Waimakariri Gorge on a bridge built in the late 1870s which carried rail and road traffic. This bridge is of great importance in

New Zealand's engineering history as are the Waiau Ferry Bridge to the north and the Rakaia Gorge bridges to the south.

Local historical museums can be found in Waiau (a furnished cottage), in Hawarden (displays in an Edwardian Methodist church), in Cheviot (a collection emphasising regional artefacts), in Amberley (a rebuilt cob cottage), in Rangiora (local historical displays housed in an old wooden building), in Oxford (exhibits of local life in a new building) and in Kaiapoi (displays in an old courthouse).

Belfast's most interesting old building is a schoolhouse built in 1878, a typical early cottage which has been restored for community use. It stands on the Kapuatohe Historic Reserve.

▲ *Near Woodend, this tall obelisk, erected in 1898, stands on the site of the major Ngai Tahu pa in North Canterbury, Kaiapohia. Its economy based on the working of greenstone brought from the West Coast through the Southern Alps, Kaiapohia was sacked by Te Rauparaha in 1831.*

▶ *The Oboka Homestead was built substantially of brick in the domestic Gothic style favoured for early Canterbury farmhouses in the 1870s. Its grandeur is an indication of the prosperity of Canterbury's large landowners in the nineteenth century.*

MID-CANTERBURY

▶ *The attractive Dutch-style facades of Ivey Hall, the original building of Lincoln College, were retained in a recent development which saw a new library built within the old walls. Designed by Frederick Strouts, Ivey Hall was first erected in 1878.*

The plains that surround Ashburton and the hill country at the foot of the Southern Alps were first taken up as leasehold runs. Some of the larger runs were freeholded but the smaller farm eventually won over most of the plains, especially as water supply systems spread. The region's historic places are mainly old buildings, for few events of drama or note broke the story of Canterbury's farming development. In the west, beyond the sheep country, the main historical interest stems from the exploration and the opening up of routes across the Alps.

ELLESMERE DISTRICT

The Ellesmere District, bordering on Lake Ellesmere, was divided into small farms soon after the founding of Canterbury. Along the district's back roads and in sev-

eral country towns are many interesting old farmhouses, cottages and churches.

All Saints' Church, Prebbleton, was built in 1907 as a copy of an 1872 building which burned down in 1906. In Lincoln, the re-located Liffey Cottage stands next to the handsome Presbyterian church. Both are nineteenth century buildings. The original building at Lincoln College, now known as Ivey Hall, is an attractive Dutch-gabled brick structure, the oldest part of which was erected in the 1870s. Its facades have been retained and restored in an imaginative scheme to provide the college with a new library.

In the Burnham military camp stands another All Saints' Church, dedicated in 1864 as 'the First Church on the Plains'. It was moved at the beginning of the century to the Burnham Industrial School, established in the 1870s. It became the chapel of the army camp when the Defence Department took over the site in 1918. Other buildings from the Industrial School days survive within the camp. There is also a medical corps museum there which can be visited by arrangement.

Taumutu, at the southern end of Lake Ellesmere, is one of Canterbury's oldest sites. Lake Ellesmere was a major source of food for the Maori, especially eels, and Taumutu was the site of a large settlement in pre-European times. The earthworks of two fortified pa are still obvious as high banks with ditches. A 100 year old Maori church stands on the site of one of these pa. Behind trees is a homestead built in the early 1880s by the Maori Member of Parliament, H.K. Taiaroa, which is still owned by his descendants.

WEST OF CHRISTCHURCH

West of the Main South Road, the plains meet the foothills of the Southern Alps. Providing water for stock was a major problem when the plains were first occupied by European farmers and at Kirwee, on the Main West Road, there is a memorial to Colonel de Renzy Brett, one of the initiators of the water-races which brought stock water onto the plains.

The hill country was taken up in runs beginning in the 1850s. One of Canter-

▶ *The striking Romanesque Church of the Holy Name, completed in 1931, and its companion Presbytery, built in 1907, are among the finest of Ashburton's many brick buildings.*

bury's pioneer families, the Deans, established Homebush, which became a very large estate with a number of ancillary industries nearby, especially a large brick and tile works at Glentunnel. There are many interesting farm buildings at Homebush, which remains in the Deans family and is private property. The imposing Homebush woolshed, built of brick, can be seen from State Highway 72 a short distance south of its junction with Highway 73.

In Hororata is a substantial stone church, St John's, erected in 1910 as a memorial to the wife of Sir John Hall, a noted politician who owned the nearby Terrace Station. An earlier timber church, mid-1870s, is now used as a hall. Coton's Cottage is a rebuilt cob cottage housing part of the local historical society collection. It is opened to the public on Sunday afternoons and on request.

The road across Arthur's Pass was built in haste in 1865–66 to provide a route between the newly discovered West Coast goldfields and Christchurch. Where the modern road deviates from the old road — at the bottom of Porters Pass, around Parapet Rock in the Castle Hill basin and in the lower Bealey Valley — it is possible to walk along the old coach road. Old milestones can be seen at a few places along the road.

The small, remote township of Arthur's Pass began life as a construction village for the Otira tunnel but has become something of a holiday centre in recent years. The museum in the National Park headquarters includes several displays about exploration, goldmining and transportation across the Alps. Stage coaches crossed Arthur's Pass until 1923, when the Otira tunnel was opened, and an old coach is one of the museum's major exhibits. The tunnel, built between 1908 and 1923, was for many years New Zealand's longest. Its portal can be seen across the river from the station. A stone monument to Arthur Dudley Dobson, European discoverer of the pass, stands at the summit. This route was one of those used by the Maori on their greenstone expeditions to and from the West Coast.

On the north bank of the Rakaia River is the Lake Coleridge power station (built 1911–14). It was the country's first state hydro-electric scheme, the forerunner of much larger schemes throughout the land. The station still generates power for the national grid. At Rakaia Gorge, Highway 72 crosses the river on two bridges, one of which dates back to the last century. This is a Bollman truss bridge, one of only two to have survived anywhere in the world.

THE CENTRAL PLAINS

Mid-Canterbury is a broad stretch of plain between the Rakaia and Rangitata Rivers. The plains looked inhospitable when Europeans first arrived in Canterbury but moa-hunter camp sites have been located, generally at the river mouths or on the edge of the foothills, which confirm that there was some Maori habitation.

At the centre of these plains is the town of Ashburton. Settlement at the river crossing began in the 1850s and the first accommodation house was opened in 1858 on the corner of East and South Streets. Ashburton's oldest buildings date mostly from the early years of the century. The 1917 wooden Railway Station is a fine example of this type of building. The town's old Technical School, one of Ashburton's many interesting brick buildings, now houses the local historical museum. It has displays featuring early European settlement of the area and the construction of irrigation schemes in Mid-Canterbury.

The Church of the Holy Name and the brick presbytery next to it, together with the former Presbyterian church and old houses in Havelock and Winter Streets, form a precinct of historical and architectural importance. There are other old houses of interest elsewhere in Ashburton and also other nineteenth century churches. Ashburton has some fine old farming-related industrial buildings and structures, including an early concrete mill shed built in 1873.

On the Springfield Estate, near Methven, stands an imposing homestead. The district's first water-race system was developed nearby. At Tinwald, the Plains Village operates a vintage railway, the prize exhibit being a restored K-88 locomotive which pulled the first express train between Christchurch and Dunedin, in 1878. Two other steam locomotives also work the line. A collection of old buildings is being assembled on the site: an engine shed, a station, a church and an early tractor shed. Tinwald is also the home of the Ashburton Vintage Car Museum.

On the south bank of the Rakaia River, between Rakaia and Methven, is New Zealand's own 'deserted village', Barrhill. The village was subdivided by a local land-owner, John Cathcart Wason, to encourage the settlement of farm labourers in the area. Wason returned to his native Scotland in 1900. The lodge (1877) of Wason's house, Corwar, survives as a small museum, but only the foundations are left of the house itself. At Barrhill, where a community of artisans and labourers lived for 30 years, there are now only St John's Church (1877) and the old school and schoolhouse.

The town of Methven has a fine library building (1883) and a historical society museum. The church of All Saints was built in 1879 at Sherwood and shifted to Methven in 1884. In the hills above Staveley are nineteenth century lime kilns which can be reached only by walking across private land. Permission and directions to visit them must be sought locally. Just south of Staveley, Mt Somers has worked small coalmines and quarries for many years and there are interesting sites in the hills for the venturesome to visit. There is an excellent local museum in the old Springburn School.

Longbeach, south-east of Ashburton, is one of the most famous of Canterbury's great runs. The present homestead was built in 1937 but many of the farm buildings date from the 1860s and 1870s when John Grigg made Longbeach the principal centre of farming innovation in New Zealand. He built his own brick and tile works and flour mill there. The farm buildings include a cookshop and dining hall, meat store, stables, grain mill, blacksmiths shop and woolshed. Longbeach is privately owned. Most of the buildings can be viewed from the public road which ends at the entrance to Longbeach. Visitors must not venture onto the private property.

CHRISTCHURCH

Banks Peninsula, thickly populated by the Maori, was the scene of earliest European interest in Canterbury. It drew flax traders in the 1820s, whalers in the 1830s and a party of French settlers in 1840. The Peninsula has many sites and buildings of historic interest. A few settlers established themselves on the Canterbury Plains in the 1840s but the beginning of the great age of Canterbury pastoralism was delayed until the 1850s, after the founding of the Canterbury settlement and its main town, Christchurch.

Christchurch was originally laid out in a grid pattern bounded by four great avenues, a large open square being left in the centre for the Anglican cathedral. The city grew quickly with generous provision being made for church, educational and other amenities such as the large tracts of parkland of which Christchurch is justly proud. The planned English flavour is reflected not only in its parks but in the fine public buildings of the city, its statuary and interesting Victorian houses of the inner suburbs.

EARLY CHRISTCHURCH

The site of Christchurch in pre-European times was swampy, partially drained by two small rivers. Small Maori settlements dotted the area, for example at South Brighton where the remains of old eeling traps made of manuka stakes survived in the Avon until European times. An earlier Maori site is the Moa Bone cave at Redcliffs, on the road to Sumner. The cave was used as shelter 500 or 600 years ago and excavations of its floor have thrown light on the way of life of the area's earliest inhabitants, when moa and shellfish were the main food sources.

Christchurch was founded in December 1850 when a body of Canterbury Association settlers arrived in the first four of many immigrant ships. A plaque in Hagley Park, across the river from the children's playground, marks the site of early whare and 'V-huts'. Another stands nearby, marking the place where settlers farewelled John Robert Godley, agent of the Canterbury Association, on his return to Britain in 1852. Christchurch grew up as a market town serving the sheep runs and then the smaller farms which gradually spread over the plains.

The Port Hills which separate Lyttelton from Christchurch were a major barrier to these earlier settlers. The road over Evans Pass through Sumner was not completed by the time they arrived, so a bridle track was hurriedly cut over a steeper route to Heathcote and this still provides a walk of historic interest. At the summit is a small stone shelter, a memorial to the women pioneers. Above Sumner, on the opposite side of the valley and visible from the present Evans Pass Road, is a track which follows the line of the original road cut in 1850. Within two decades of Christchurch being founded, the enterprise of the early settlers resulted in the hills being pierced by a railway tunnel, opened in 1867. This tunnel is the most impressive achievement of early Canterbury engineering. The stone-faced portals of the tunnel at Heathcote and Lyttelton are worth viewing.

When the settlers first arrived there were only two substantial areas of bush in the Christchurch area, at Papanui and Riccarton. A noticeboard on Sawyers Arms Road marks the site of the Papanui Bush which supplied early Christchurch with building timber and firewood until it was cut out by about 1857. At Riccarton a patch of the original bush survives and near it is Christchurch's oldest surviving building. In

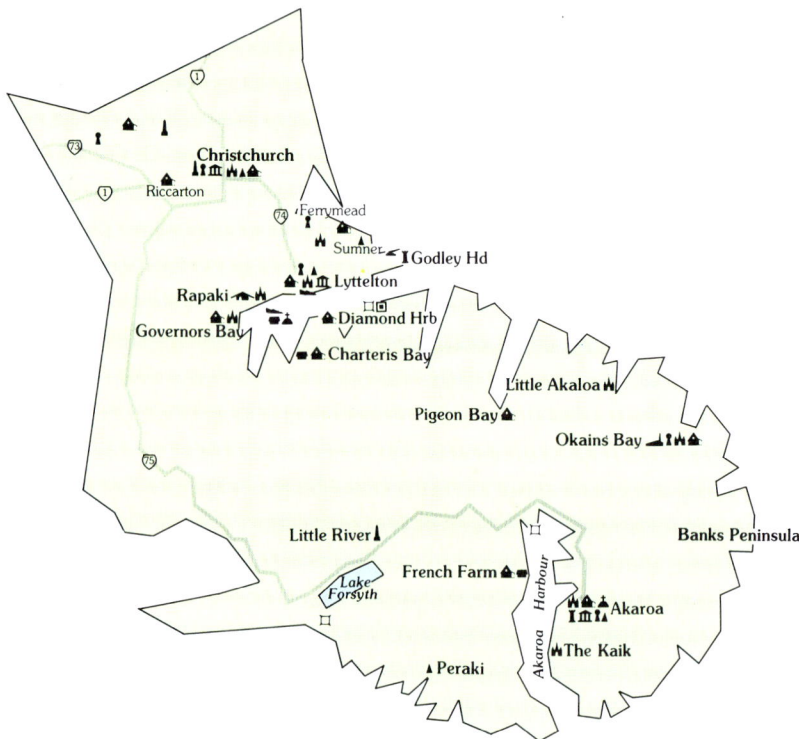

1843 members of the Deans family established a farm at Riccarton and the cottage they built in 1844 still stands. It is a simple colonial cottage which has been carefully restored. Near the cottage is Riccarton House, a homestead which was begun in 1856. It is now publicly owned and used for receptions and similar functions. These two houses, side by side, give an impression of Christchurch growing from a township of small wooden cottages to a city of many grand houses.

The other important early cottage in Christchurch is Tiptree, on Savills Road, west of the airport. This three-storey cob and wooden cottage was built about 1864 and is one of the most impressive survivors of the hundreds of cob cottages built in early Canterbury. Tiptree is now a private museum. Nearby, close to the Riccarton Racecourse, is Chokebore Lodge, a restored cob house which has had long associations with the racing industry and is now in public ownership.

Christchurch has many other older houses, some built in its earliest years. On Oxford Terrace, near the hospital, is a cottage built in 1852, added to ten years later and then substantially rebuilt in 1989. At the foot of the Cashmere Hills, near the Princess Margaret Hospital, is Cracroft House, built of cob in 1854. It is now owned by the Girl Guides Association. Nearby is the three-gabled Old Stone House, built in 1870 for the Indian workers of the Cashmere Estate. It is now a community centre.

Other early houses include the brick Englefield (1857) on Fitzgerald Avenue, and several smaller wooden houses along Avonside Drive.

A number of large nineteenth century wooden houses have survived in Christchurch. Among them is Risingholme, now a community centre in Opawa, which was the boyhood home of William Pember Reeves, a prominent intellectual and cabinet minister of the 1890s. Strowan House on

▲ *Many of Canterbury's earliest European settlers built their first homes of earth. Tiptree Cottage, near Christchurch Airport, is a survivor from this period of Canterbury's history. It now houses a private museum.*

▶ *Finest of all Christchurch's stone nineteenth century buildings are the Provincial Government Buildings. A cluster of buildings (the earliest of wood) in the Gothic style was put up between 1858 and 1865 to house the Canterbury Provincial Government. The interior of the Council Chamber is the finest High Victorian interior in New Zealand.*

Papanui Road is now part of St Andrew's College. Rangi Ruru, another school, has grown around what was Te Koraha, a centre of social life in the late nineteenth and early twentieth centuries.

Important large houses of the turn of the century include the palatial McLeans Mansions, on Manchester Street. It is in a unique style for New Zealand and has a superb stair hallway. It now houses the Christchurch Academy, an educational institution. Mona Vale, off Fendalton Road, is publicly owned and can be visited.

Some early wooden buildings, besides houses, have survived. A tiny commercial building of the 1850s, known as Shands Emporium, still stands as a charming anachronism on Hereford Street. The Christchurch Club, on Latimer Square, was built in 1862 and once had the author Samuel Butler as a member. The Canterbury Club, built on Cambridge Terrace in 1873, has a hitching post and gas lamp. Other survivors include the Marist cricket pavilion in Hagley Park (1863) and the Antigua Boat Sheds (1882), the last of several sheds which once housed craft for pleasure boating on the Avon.

STONE BUILDINGS

Earliest Christchurch was wooden, but the city is renowned today for its nineteenth century stone Gothic buildings, particularly the stone portions of the Provincial Government Buildings. These are a fascinating melange of wood and stone, designed by Christchurch's most notable early architect, Benjamin Mountfort. The oldest parts are the wooden sections (1858–61) with stone towers breaking the vertical weatherboard and Gothic detailing of the wooden wings. The original council chamber is a superb miniature of Gothic form and a stone-flagged corridor has a distinctly mediaeval air about it. The climax of the whole group is the stone Provincial Council Chamber, built in 1865. It is a magnificent example of High Victorian Gothic with its soaring roof and intricate decoration. New Zealand was governed as a group of provinces from the early 1850s until 1876 and these buildings are the only provincial government buildings to survive intact, with the humble exception of the premises in Invercargill of the shortlived Southland Province.

The other group of stone Gothic buildings in Christchurch is the Arts Centre,

▶ *To design the centrepiece of their new town, the Anglican Cathedral, Canterbury's European pioneers employed the most notable British ecclesiastical architect of the day, George Gilbert Scott. Begun in the 1860s, the Cathedral was not consecrated until 1904.*

formerly the University of Canterbury. The original clock tower block was built in 1877, followed in 1882 by the fine Great Hall. Building in stone continued on the site until well into this century, resulting in a cluster of buildings grouped around two quadrangles, one of them cloistered. Today they house a variety of well-used theatres, shops, restaurants and club rooms. In one corner of the North Quadrangle is a 'den' in which the famous scientist Lord Rutherford carried out experiments in the early 1890s. The public are free to wander around the buildings of the Arts Centre and through many of them.

Across the road from the old University's Great Hall is the original building of the Canterbury Museum, erected in 1870. The building itself is of historic interest, apart from the displays inside it. A short distance along Rolleston Avenue are the buildings of Christ's College, another superb group of mostly stone buildings. The big school (1863) is the oldest educational building still in use in New Zealand. Rolleston Avenue, on which stand the College, Museum and former University, is where Christchurch comes closest to the ideal of some of its founders of a transplanted English town.

On Cranmer Square, the stone Gothic building of the old Normal School, built in 1876 and long under threat, has been converted to luxury apartments and a restaurant, with the important street facades carefully restored. Near the old Normal School, now known as Cranmer Courts, is another, later, Gothic stone building, the former Teachers Training College. This is now the Peterborough Centre, run in conjunction with the Arts Centre, and includes the regional office of the Historic Places Trust. On the other side of Cranmer Square, the former Girls High School is a good example of nineteenth century brick Gothic architecture. A humbler building than those of the city centre, is the old stone Malthouse on Colombo Street South, built in 1867. It is one of the city's oldest surviving industrial buildings and now houses a children's theatre.

CHURCHES OF CHRISTCHURCH

Christchurch has several stone churches among its historic buildings. The foundation stone of the Anglican Cathedral, designed by the prominent English architect Sir George Gilbert Scott, was laid in 1864 but the finished building, in whose design Mountfort played a part, was not consecrated until 1904. Two other early central city stone churches are the unassuming St John's Latimer Square, built 1864–65, and the forthright Durham Street Methodist Church, 1864. A decade later, in 1874, the Trinity Congregational Church, now converted to a concert hall, was built on Worcester Street behind the cathedral.

In the same decade Holy Trinity on Avonside Drive was begun but was not to be completed until the mid-twentieth century. Several notable settlers are buried beneath the noble trees of the churchyard. St Peter's, on a prominent corner in Upper Riccarton, was also built in stages over several decades, beginning in the 1870s.

Churches were built of stone in Christchurch well into the twentieth century. The most important twentieth century church is the grand Roman Catholic Cathedral of the Blessed Sacrament, designed by F.W. Petre and opened in 1904. It is one of New Zealand's finest classical buildings and has a superb interior.

Not all Christchurch's historic churches are stone: many are wooden and a few brick. Notable among the wooden churches is St Michael's, on Oxford Terrace, built in 1872 in Gothic style. Its separate bell tower is older than the church itself. Parts of the present St Andrew's Presbyterian Church, which once stood near the hospital, date from 1857, but the building assumed its present form when it was substantially enlarged in 1891–92. In the 1980s the church was moved to Rangi Ruru School, where it is now visible from Merivale Lane.

In the suburbs, St Mary's Addington was begun in 1867. Its exterior has been stuccoed, but its interior remains one of the loveliest in Christchurch. Next to St Mary's a bell tower commemorates Richard John Seddon, whose son-in-law was vicar of the parish. St Paul's Papanui, built in 1877, is one of the finest of Benjamin Mountfort's wooden churches. It has some interesting old graves in its churchyard.

St Paul's Presbyterian Church, built in the early 1870s of plastered brick, marked an important break from Christchurch's predominantly Gothic traditions of church architecture. The Gothic brick Church of the Good Shepherd (another Mountfort church), built in 1884 in what is now the

▲ *Canterbury's long association with the exploration of Antarctica is commemorated in the statue of Robert Falcon Scott, whose last, fatal, expedition sailed from Lyttelton. Sculpted by Scott's widow, Kathleen Lady Kennett, the statue was unveiled in 1917.*

are the former Public Library buildings, a group of nineteenth and early twentieth century brick Gothic buildings. Just south of the Square the small brick Fishers Building, built in the early 1880s, occupies a prominent corner site.

Behind the Anglican Cathedral are two brick buildings typical of early twentieth century commercial buildings. The Gothic Press building (1907) contrasts with the solid Italianate style of the Government Buildings (1911–12). Both are of brick with stone facings. The Theatre Royal (1909) on Gloucester Street, with its elaborate interior, is one of the country's best older theatres. It is being preserved and restored by a local trust.

The cast-iron bridges which span the Avon in the central city date from the nineteenth century, the oldest being the Victoria Bridge by the Town Hall. The city's other notable example of Victorian ironwork is a clock tower on Victoria Street.

Christchurch has a number of memorials of interest and several Victorian cemeteries. The city's oldest cemetery, in Barbadoes Street, was opened in 1852 and contains the graves of many early settlers. The central city has two war memorials. One, a group of classical figures, stands beside the cathedral in the square. The other, the Bridge of Remembrance built in 1923–24, crosses the Avon at Cashel Street, where men marching from King Edward Barracks (1905) to the battlefields of the First World War crossed on an older bridge.

The statuary of Christchurch is also worth inspecting. The oldest statue is of John Robert Godley, cast in bronze in England and unveiled in 1867. Along Rolleston Avenue are the statues of three superintendents of the Canterbury Province. In Victoria Square, the town's original market place, stands a statue of Queen Victoria, with sculptured panels around its base depicting scenes of early settlement. Near her is a 1932 statue of James Cook.

The statue of the Antarctic explorer Robert Falcon Scott, which stands on the river bank west of the Square, was sculpted by Scott's widow and unveiled in 1917. This is the most obvious of several reminders in and near Christchurch of the connection between New Zealand and the exploration of Antarctica. A plaque at Lyttelton records that it was a port of departure for several early Antarctic expeditions including Scott's 1901 *Discovery* expe-

industrial area of Phillipstown, is another historic inner-city church.

CHRISTCHURCH MISCELLANY

The heart of Christchurch has several interesting nineteenth and early twentieth century public and commercial buildings. The Italianate Chief Post Office on Cathedral Square was built in 1877. Next to the Post Office the Four Ships Court commemorates the arrival of the first main body of Christchurch's early settlers. Not far away, on Oxford Terrace, is an attractive brick building, designed by S. Hurst Seager and built in 1887 as municipal offices. It houses a tourist information office. Diagonally across the river bank from this building dition, Shackleton's 1908 *Nimrod* expedition and Scott's last 1910 *Terra Nova* expedition. Since the 1950s, the Christchurch Airport has been the main base for American operations in the Antarctic. A totem pole from Oregon was erected at the airport as a gesture of thanks for its hospitality to the first Deep Freeze expeditions.

New Zealand's connection with Antarctica is also recalled by the important Antarctic collection at the Canterbury Museum. On display are relics from early Antarctic expeditions as well as material illustrating recent activities on the continent. Other displays of historical interest at the Museum are the hall of Maori history, a reconstructed Christchurch street of the 1860s, a rural village and a costume gallery.

Christchurch's other major museum at Ferrymead stands on a historic site where New Zealand's first steam locomotive was assembled and steamed in the 1860s. The country's first true railway line linked the Ferrymead wharf with Christchurch. Trains are still prominent at Ferrymead; a working steam railway runs for part of its length along the line of the original railway embankment. There is also a working electric tramway, with restored trams, which runs for part of its length along a replica street of about 1910. The Hall of Flame is devoted to the history of firefighting in New Zealand. Other museums emphasising machinery and transportation are the Yaldhurst Museum, west of the city, and the McLeans Island Steam Museum to the north.

LYTTELTON

Lyttelton is more than the port of neighbouring Christchurch — it is a town of considerable historic interest in its own right. It is slightly older than Christchurch and its lack of growth since the late nineteenth century has helped a fine array of old buildings to survive.

Plaques mark the sites of historic events and demolished buildings. One, at the landing place of the Canterbury Association settlers, is rather lost among railway buildings behind the old post office; another marks the site of the house built in 1850 for John Robert Godley who arrived in Lyttelton in April 1850. Yet another indicates the site of the immigrant barracks in which the settlers were first housed.

Canterbury's main jail was at Lyttelton from 1851 to 1919. On its Oxford Street site

today are massive concrete walls and a few remaining cells. A memorial clock to a local doctor relieves the otherwise forbidding atmosphere of the place where seven murderers were executed. The jail warden's house stands across the street. Another waterfront plaque records Lyttelton's association with early expeditions which set out from the port to explore the Antarctic.

Three early stone churches stand on Winchester Street, the oldest being the Anglican Holy Trinity built in 1859 of a warm red volcanic stone. Almost opposite is the Catholic St Joseph's, built in 1866, and a short distance west is the Presbyterian St John's, 1864. They form the port's most interesting group of historic buildings. With its many nineteenth century houses and cottages, Lyttelton is one of the best places in Canterbury to learn about the region's early domestic architecture.

The castle-like Timeball Station, on a superb site above the town, was completed in 1876, although added to later. The station signalled the time to ships in the harbour by dropping the ball down the mast on top of the tower. This fascinating Victorian mechanism has been restored to working order, one of only a handful of working timeball stations in the world. The building is owned by the Historic Places Trust and is open to the public.

▲ *One of only a handful of timeball stations in the world still in working order, Lyttelton's castle-like building is a landmark above the town. It was built in 1876 to send a time signal to ships in port. In 1978 it was reopened to the public after restoration.*

On the other side of the inner harbour is the graving dock. It was opened in 1883 and is a good example of nineteenth century marine engineering. Another structure of interest in the history of transport is the Lyttelton portal of the railway tunnel, opened in 1867.

A trip on the harbour can be enjoyed on summer weekends aboard the steam tug *Lyttelton* which was built in Glasgow and arrived in Lyttelton in 1907. Its working life lasted until 1971. Now the oldest tug in New Zealand, it is in the care of a local preservation society. The Lyttelton museum has displays illustrating its nautical history and the port's connections with the Antarctic.

At Godley Head, reached from the top of Evans Pass or by a walkway from Taylors Mistake past Sumner, is a lighthouse, built in 1864–65 but rebuilt in 1939 on a new site. There are also Second World War coastal defence fortifications, including gun sites, underground magazines and a tunnel which gave access to searchlight stations at sea level.

The road around the head of the harbour passes a short distance west of Lyttelton, the Maori settlement of Rapaki, one of the original reserves set aside at the time Canterbury was purchased from the Ngai Tahu. A small church opened in 1869 still stands.

Governors Bay also has a historic church, St Cuthbert's, constructed of cob faced with stone in 1860–62. Nearby is the privately owned Ohinetahi, a fine homestead built in 1867, its blend of stone and timber giving it an Australian air. Trees planted by T.H. Potts, the pioneer botanist for whom the house was built, are still a feature of the district. In the Orton Bradley Park at Charteris Bay there is a stone hut built probably in the 1840s and other old buildings including a stable, smithy, dairy, cottage, millhouse and school. The historic farm centre is being developed as one of the park's attractions.

At Diamond Harbour the simple Stoddarts Cottage (1862) and the grander Godley House (1880) survive, the latter as a tearooms. At Purau is a privately owned reddish volcanic stone homestead dating from 1853.

Ripa Island, at the point beyond Purau, was once the site of a pa and was converted into a fort in the late 1880s during a Russian invasion scare. The fortifications include the remains of huge 'disappearing' guns.

During the First World War, the German seaman Count Felix von Luckner was held prisoner here for some months. Quail Island, in the centre of Lyttelton Harbour, now a reserve, has some interesting traces of its varied history. The island was first taken up for farming in 1850 and tumbledown rock walls mark the site of the original cottage. The island served as a quarantine station from the 1870s and a barracks built in 1874 still stands on the shoreline. For some years up to 1925 the island was a leper colony; the graves of two lepers, foundations and a stone wall built by convicts mark the colony's site. Eleven ships were scuttled west of the island between 1902 and 1951 and the ribs of some of them still lie offshore. The development of Quail Island as a reserve, with walkways, has opened up these historic places to the public.

BANKS PENINSULA AND AKAROA

Banks Peninsula has been occupied by the Maori for 700–800 years and has a longer European history than the rest of Canterbury; it is justly regarded as the region's most historic area.

Reminders of Banks Peninsula's Maori past can still be seen in a number of places. Most of the bays show evidence of Maori settlement and the sites of at least sixteen pa are known. Two accessible pa sites are at Oruaka and Onawe. Near the outlet of Lake Forsyth the faint defence lines and dwelling terraces of Oruaka, now a historic reserve, can be observed from the main highway on a low hill across the lake. The site can be visited via the Te Oka Road or more simply by walking across the shingle bank at the outlet of the lake.

Onawe Peninsula, at the head of Akaroa Harbour, was fortified by the Ngai Tahu as a place of refuge at the time of Te Rauparaha's raids in the early 1830s. The pa was taken by Ngati Toa and their allies, probably early in 1832. Onawe Peninsula is now a reserve and some of the earthworks can still be seen.

Beyond Akaroa is a small Maori settlement, the Kaik, where a Maori church, opened in 1878, stands in an incomparable coastal setting. At Little River there is another marae on which stands a statue of the Ngai Tahu chief, Tangatahara, who led the unsuccessful defence of Onawe.

The first Europeans to frequent the bays and harbours of Banks Peninsula were flax traders, whalers, timber cutters and boat builders. Canterbury's first permanent settlers were whalers who established shore stations in some of the southern bays in the late 1830s. A few relics remain from whaling days: relocated trypots on the foreshore at Akaroa, a memorial at Peraki where the first shore station was established in 1837, and a few fast-disappearing traces at Oashore, Ikoraki and Island Bay.

Akaroa, one of the South Island's most historic towns, was settled by French emigrants in August 1840, ten years before the Canterbury Association settlers founded Christchurch. There is a memorial on the foreshore near where the French landed. Many of the early settlers lie in the old French cemetery where there is a monument inscribed with the names of the pioneers buried there. Another picturesque cemetery is at the other end of the town. On Greens Point, the Britomart memorial marks the place where British sovereignty was demonstrated in 1840, a few days before the French settlers arrived.

One of Akaroa's most prized buildings, the Langlois-Eteveneaux cottage, was the home of an early French settler. It has an unmistakeably Gallic flavour and is now part of the Akaroa museum, furnished in French settler style. Displays in the museum behind the cottage include Maori artefacts, further French settlement items, whaling relics, and equipment and photographs of the old cocksfoot seed industry.

Another early building is the simple Customs House by Dalys Wharf, built in 1852 of pit-sawn totara. It is now a small museum. Beyond the main wharf, on Cemetery Point, stands the Akaroa lighthouse. Originally erected on Akaroa North Head, it was first lit in January 1880 and remained in use there for a hundred years. When it was superseded by an automatic light it was removed to the town to ensure its preservation, thus becoming one of the most accessible of New Zealand's nineteenth century wooden lighthouses. A few traces, including the foundations of the tower, remain at the historic reserve at the heads.

The old Criterion Hotel (now a store), built in 1863, the Courthouse (1878), a bank building and some venerable shops, all close to the Langlois-Eteveneaux cottage, are also of historic interest. So is the Coronation Library (most of it dating from 1875),

the Church Street shipping office (1875), and the Britomart gun, by the main wharf. Akaroa has two attractive old churches. St Patrick's Roman Catholic, with its coxcomb inverted bargeboards, was built in 1864, with the little tower added in 1893. St Peter's Anglican was first erected in 1863 but substantially enlarged in 1877.

One of the delights of Akaroa is to wander along its picturesque streets observing the many gems of colonial architecture, some dating back to the 1850s. All are privately owned but most owners do not object to visitors peering over gates or through hedges. The most substantial private homes to survive from pioneering times are Oinako, near the main wharf, and Blythcliff, off Rue Balguerie.

Old cottages and houses can also be seen in many of the bays and valleys of the peninsula. Pigeon Bay was first settled permanently by Europeans in 1843. Some old Pigeon Bay houses include Tanglewood, Brookshaw and Annandale, with verandahs and gables typical of early New Zealand farmhouses. Splendid scenery adds to the enjoyment of searching for old buildings in places like Pigeon Bay, Port Levy, Little Akaloa and Le Bons Bay. One of the most individual peninsula churches is St Luke's, Little Akaloa, with a paua-decorated exterior and superb wood carvings within.

The Okains Bay Maori and Colonial Museum spans the history of Banks Peninsula from Maori times into the early years of European settlement. It has an extensive collection of Maori artefacts and canoes and a modern carved meeting house. The colonial displays include a totara slab cottage and an outside bread oven built at Lavericks Bay in 1878. Okains Bay has an early church, St John the Evangelist, and at the French Farm en route to Wainui are some original houses and farm buildings.

▲ *Part of Akaroa's excellent local museum is housed in a cottage, the Langlois-Etevenaux House, which dates back to the early years of French settlement of the town, although its Gallic air today may stem from alterations later in the nineteenth century.*

SOUTH CANTERBURY

outh Canterbury also has a runholding past, with small farms gradually taking the place of large runs, except in the dry inland basin of the Mackenzie Country.

Settlement stopped short of the foothills until John Acland and Charles Tripp proved in 1856 that it was possible to over-winter sheep in the high country. The move into the alpine basins and river valleys began with vast tracts of land being fired first. Lush grass quickly covered the ashes. The practice was continued annually which greatly contributed to the later problems of erosion. The introduction of deer, thar and chamois for sport hastened the deterioration, and today's sheep population is well below that of the late nineteenth century.

Old farmhouses and outbuildings are among the historic places of rural South Canterbury. Timaru began to grow significantly in the 1860s and a number of interesting old buildings have survived, as they have in smaller towns like Geraldine, Temuka and Waimate. South Canterbury has retained strong Maori associations and has more places of historic Maori interest than the less hospitable plains of mid-Canterbury.

EARLY DAYS

For centuries before the Mackenzie Basin of inland South Canterbury became sheep country, groups of Maori from the coast camped in the area in summer to forage. Sadly, no traces of their camps remain.

The most intriguing evidence of early Maori occupation of South Canterbury are the drawings on the walls of limestone rock shelters throughout the region, executed largely with charcoal and red ochre. The drawings are very old and many are difficult to decipher and interpret. Drawings of birds, lizards, fish, birdmen and other mythical forms can be seen on a historic reserve at Raincliff, on the Middle Valley Road, and elsewhere throughout South Canterbury. At Frenchman's Gully and Craigmore, 20 km west of Timaru, are private historic reserves with rock drawings. There are also drawings at the base of a large limestone block near Cave, indistinct where they have not been retouched in modern times. Retouching at many rock art sites is not always faithful to the original drawings.

South Canterbury remained an area of Maori settlement into the classic period of Maori culture. On the coast east of Temuka is the site of the Waiateruaiti Pa, the principal settlement of the local Ngai Tahu. At Arowhenua, the Maori presence in South Canterbury in modern times is made evident by a Maori church, an early twentieth century meeting house and a memorial, unveiled in 1935, to South Island Maori soldiers who served in the First World War.

South Canterbury is a region with a strong sense of being distinct from the rest of Canterbury. The European pastoral history of South Canterbury began with the taking up of sheep runs in the 1850s. In the northern part of South Canterbury, at Mt Peel, is a fine brick homestead built in 1865–66 which has been lived in by four generations of the Acland family. The homestead is still a private home but the

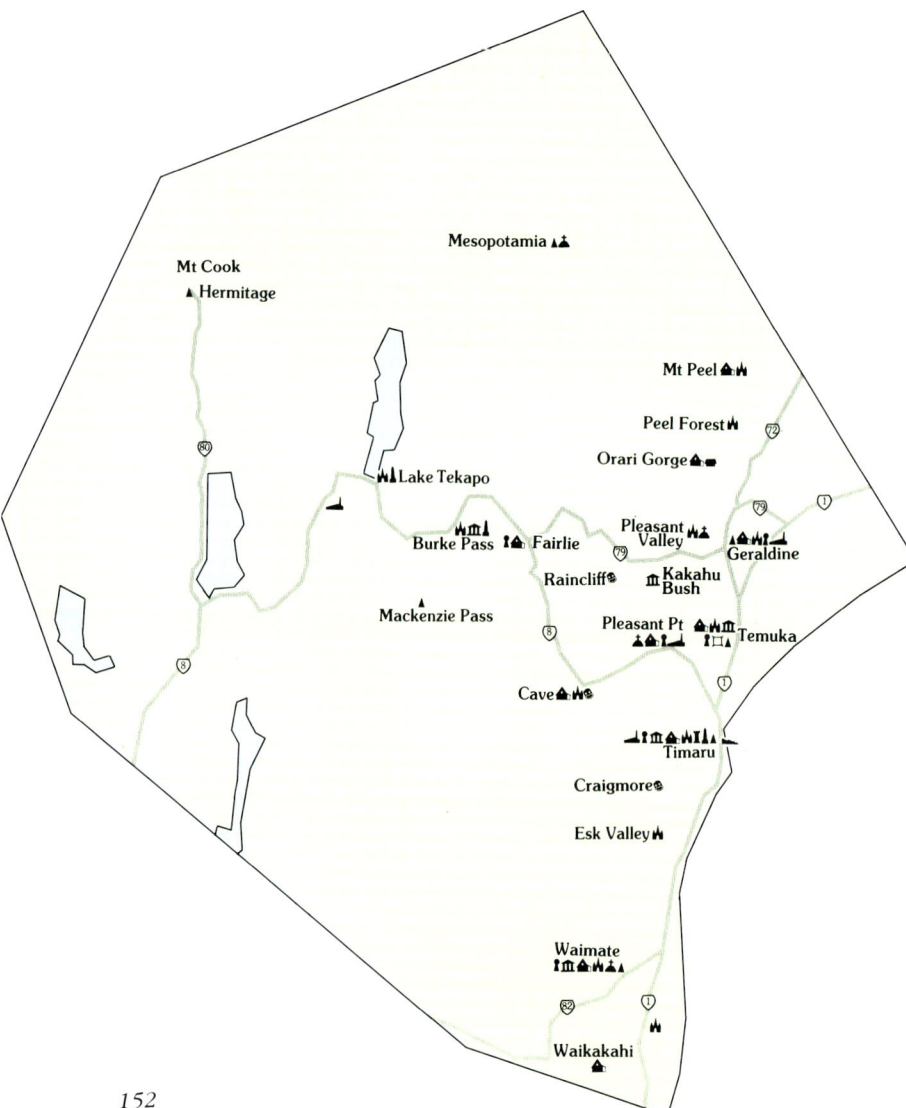

Mesopotamia
Mt Cook
Hermitage
Mt Peel
Peel Forest
Orari Gorge
Lake Tekapo
Pleasant Valley
Burke Pass   Fairlie
Geraldine
Raincliff   Kakahu Bush
Mackenzie Pass
Pleasant Pt   Temuka
Cave
Timaru
Craigmore
Esk Valley
Waimate
Waikakahi

public may visit the nearby stone Church of the Holy Innocents, built in 1868–69, beautifully decorated with stone carvings.

The Mesopotamia run in the high country at the head of the Rangitata River was taken up in the 1860s by a notable figure in English literary history, Samuel Butler. The opening chapters of *Erewhon* are a superb description of the high country in the early days. Butler lived in a V-hut he built at Forest Creek, then moved to a house at Mesopotamia. Both are marked by plaques. Butler returned to England after four years in Canterbury, his fortune doubled.

The farm buildings at the Orari Gorge Station, on the Tripp Settlement Road, date from the 1850s to 1860s. They include a cadet building, a blacksmith's shop, stables and a storehouse. An 1859 totara slab cottage has also survived.

St Stephen's Church, Peel Forest, was built in 1885 to replace an 1868 church blown down in 1884.

GERALDINE

Geraldine nestles between the plains and the hill country in the northern part of South Canterbury. A commemorative plaque in Talbot Street marks the site of the first totara bark hut built by an early surveyor. The Waitui homestead, built in 1861 by a pioneer runholder, and an original 1854 cottage stand on the outskirts of the town. St Mary's Church was built in stone in 1882 to replace an earlier wooden structure. Another stone building of about the same age is a cheese factory, built in 1884 of basalt with limestone dressings: it stands on the Pleasant Valley Road, just off Highway 79. This is now New Zealand's oldest remaining cheese factory building.

Geraldine supports two museums. The County Historical Society Museum is housed in the former Geraldine Town Council offices. The Vintage Car and Machinery Museum has old cars, tractors, an aeroplane and agricultural machinery on display.

▲ *South Canterbury abounds in attractive rural churches. The stone Church of the Holy Innocents, Mount Peel, was built in 1868-69 by the Acland family, whose large brick homestead stands nearby. The church was named after infants buried in the churchyard.*

In Pleasant Valley, St Anne's Church, built in 1863 of pit-sawn timber with cob packed between the studs, is South Canterbury's oldest surviving church. It was restored in the early 1960s.

Down a side road off Highway 79, between Geraldine and Fairlie, is a well preserved pot-style lime kiln, built about the 1870s. Wood, coal and limestone were tipped in at the top of the kiln which was then lit from the bottom. Burnt lime, used for building, was extracted from the bottom when the burning was completed. There are the remains of four more kilns in the vicinity.

At Kakahu Bush, the original school building erected in 1884 is now a public hall. It has historic links with New Zealand poet Jessie Mackay. The downlands and valleys inland from Timaru between Geraldine and Waimate contain some of the loveliest farmland in New Zealand. Along the back roads are many stone, cob and wooden farm buildings and homesteads, some now well over 100 years old.

TEMUKA

Temuka can boast some delightful old buildings, notably its 1904 brick Courthouse, now a museum, which is one of the finest small-town Edwardian public buildings in the country. The Courthouse is on a side road just off the main road. The Temuka Post Office, built in 1902, is another good example of the same sort of building. Old commercial buildings, shops, a hotel, the post office and library make up a precinct which creates an impression of how smaller New Zealand centres looked at the turn of the century. The large homestead of a pioneer settler on Milford Road is now a children's home. St Peter's Anglican Church was built in 1899, its predecessor the victim of fire.

At Milford, towards the coast, a plaque marks the site of the boiling-down works established in 1870 in an effort to get something of value (tallow) from surplus sheep before the development of refrigeration.

At Waitohi, a roadside memorial commemorates the pioneer aviator Richard Pearse who achieved powered flight some time in 1903–04, about the time the Wright Brothers were engaged in similar experiments in the United States. The memorial is a replica of Pearse's craft and was erected in 1979.

WASHDYKE TO FAIRLIE

The Levels run, the first taken up in South Canterbury, once covered a vast tract of country between the Opihi and Pareora Rivers. One building remains from its early days, a totara slab, thatched cottage, built in the early 1850s. George Rhodes, one of the brothers who held the lease, lived in it with his wife in the mid-1850s. The cottage was restored by the Rhodes family in 1951 and is now a private historic reserve close to a modern farmhouse. It lies just off State Highway 8, a short distance north of Washdyke.

A lone chimney stands forlornly in Pioneer Park, Raincliff, all that remains of the home of the pioneer runholder Michael Burke, whose name was given to Burkes Pass. (The Park is close to the Raincliff Historic Reserve which protects the Maori rock drawings.)

The railway station at Pleasant Point is now the centre of a fine local museum. On a stretch of line remaining from the old Fairlie branch line (which closed in 1968), runs a 1922 steam locomotive; one of the carriages it pulls is a rare 1895 birdcage carriage. Other railway relics, including an old signal box, are also on display. The museum has an antique printing press, a vintage radio station, an old manual telephone exchange and a general store arranged as in the 1920s. Pleasant Point has the usual complement of old buildings for a country town and a beautifully situated old cemetery. On Mill Road, near Pleasant Point, is the restored Parr's Mill waterwheel. It stands on private land and permission to visit it must be sought locally.

In the hills near Cave is St David's Church, a rugged stone building put up in 1930 by the Burnett family as a memorial to Andrew and Catherine Burnett who pioneered the Mt Cook Station in the Mackenzie Country. Much of South Canterbury sheep farming history is told in the plaques and memorial tablets on the walls of the church. On each side of Cave, at Sutherlands on State Highway 8, and at Monavale on a side road to the west, are old country schools.

At Albury just off the road to Fairlie is an accommodation house, the second on its site, built probably in 1867 and providing a link back to coaching and riding days.

Fairlie, founded in the 1860s, was served by trains from 1884 until 1968. It has a museum housed in a century-old cottage, furnished in the style of the early 1900s. A stone county chambers, built in 1876, was used by the Mount Cook Road Board, forerunner of the Mackenzie County Council. It stands opposite the hotel, parts of which date from 1861. At Burke's Pass is a small 1870s church.

THE MACKENZIE COUNTRY

Roads lead over two passes into the high basin of the Mackenzie Country, each with a monument. State Highway 8 crosses Burkes Pass, where a monument records that Michael Joseph Burke, who took up the Raincliff Station in 1854, entered the Mackenzie Country through the pass about 1857. The memorial on Mackenzie Pass, crossed by a rougher road, recalls the romantic figure whose name now belongs to the pass and the Mackenzie Country itself. It was erected by a local runholder, T.D. Burnett, on the probable spot where the alleged sheep stealer James McKenzie was caught with about 1000 sheep from The Levels station in March 1855. Sentenced to five years hard labour he made spirited efforts to escape from the Lyttelton Jail. His sentence was remitted and he was released in January 1856, whereupon he disappeared from the pages of history, but became firmly established in legend. The inscription on the monument is in Maori, English and Gaelic, for many Scottish shepherds in the area still spoke Gaelic when it was erected.

Once the potential of the high tussock grassland was appreciated, the Mackenzie Country was quickly occupied by runholders. The Mt Cook Station has been held by members of the Burnett family since it was taken up. T.D. Burnett, who died in 1941, has one of the most spectacular graves in New Zealand, looking up to Mt Cook from Rock Etam.

At Lake Tekapo, the sturdy Church of the Good Shepherd was built in 1935 as a memorial to the pioneer runholders. Nearby is a statue of a sheep dog, recalling the animal's services to the runholders and shepherds.

In recent years the Mackenzie Country has been transformed by the Upper Waitaki power scheme. The area's hydro-electric potential was first recognised as long ago as 1904, although the first power station at Lake Tekapo was only completed in the 1950s. At Irishman Creek, the runholder

and inventor Bill Hamilton (later Sir William) first developed and tested the jetboat. The powerhouse, workshop and dam make up a precinct important in New Zealand's engineering heritage.

The Hermitage at Mt Cook has played an important part in the history of mountaineering and tourism in New Zealand. The first alpine reserves were set aside at Mt Cook in 1881 and the first Hermitage built in 1884, beneath White Horse Hill. It was damaged by a flood early this century but a few remains can be seen. On the track to the Hooker Swing Bridges, near the old Hermitage site, is a memorial to three climbers who were killed in the area's first major mountaineering accident in 1914. In the National Park headquarters at Mt Cook are displays of early climbing equipment and photographs of the first ascent of Mount Cook in 1894.

TIMARU

Timaru had a broken early life. A whaling station was established there in the late 1830s (a trypot can be seen at one of the entrances to Caroline Bay) but abandoned by the early 1840s. Huts were built near the shore when the Rhodes Brothers took up The Levels run in 1851. The town began to grow significantly when the *Strathallan* settlers arrived in 1859. A plaque marks the site of the Government Landing Service, used before the harbour was built when ships anchored at the open roadstead to be unloaded by small boats. The bluestone Landing Service building near the railway station is a relic of the days before Timaru had a proper port. It was built of locally quarried stone in the 1860s to serve as a boatshed and warehouse. It is one of Timaru's oldest surviving buildings.

The port's breakwaters were built in the 1870s and 1880s. The old quarries and the remains of the railway line used to bring the rocks down to the shore can be seen along the Centennial Park Walkway. One of the dramatic incidents in Timaru's history was the 1882 wreck of the *Benvenue* and the *City of Perth*. Some of the wreckage has been seen at very low tides at the foot of the Benvenue Cliffs and there is a monument near the post office to those who lost their lives. The Timaru lighthouse, which was built in 1878, is a typical early wooden tower; it was moved in 1980 to a site in Maori Park.

Timaru has a number of interesting old buildings. At one end of the Centennial Park Walkway is the small stone Gleniti School. The town's notable older churches are St Mary's, a magnificent Gothic building built in the 1880s, Sacred Heart, built 1910–11 to a design of F.W. Petre, and Chalmers Presbyterian. One of Timaru's finest public buildings is the 1902 Custom House. City Council Offices were built in 1912.

Timaru's industries have been based largely on the produce of South Canterbury's farmlands. Three nineteenth century mill buildings are of note. The Belford Steam Flour Mill, opened in 1875, is now a cabaret. The six-storey brick building of the Timaru Milling Company was built in 1882 as the first complete roller mills in New Zealand. The Evans Flour Mill was built in 1888, with additions in 1897. These three mill buildings and the Landing Service building comprise a precinct of historic importance.

There are several fine houses among Timaru's historic buildings. Some now house institutions, among them the Aigantighe Art Gallery which occupies a 1905 brick and stone house. Some of the city's larger houses are built of local bluestone. The Pioneer Museum displays domestic appliances and furniture of the town's early settlers and traces the history of the development of Timaru's harbour.

In the downlands south of Timaru are many old farmhouses, outbuildings and country churches, in particular St Mary's, Esk Valley, built of Albury limestone and consecrated in 1880. On the Pareora River, 3 km west of Holme Station Corner, are the remains of two early lime kilns. The Pareora River was tapped early for Timaru's water supply. In 1875 a dam was built and a race constructed to a reservoir at Gleniti. These early waterworks can now be reached on a walkway. At Adair a water supply tunnel, a tower which supported a flume and a raceman's cob cottage date from the time works were undertaken in the 1880s to improve Timaru's water supply.

A cairn on Lower Hook Beach records a meeting in January 1844 between Bishop Selwyn, on his first South Island journey, and Edward Shortland, Sub-protector of the Aborigines, who was undertaking a census of South Island Maori.

WAIMATE

Waimate, with a sawmilling past, is now a farming and horticultural centre. A prominent feature is the figure of a Clydesdale horse on a hillside above the town, commemorating the role of draught horses in the agricultural development of New Zealand. A walkway gives access to the figure and a cairn.

In a Maori cemetery on Point Bush Road is the grave of the local chief Te Huruhuru who died in 1861. He had one of his principal pa at Waimate at the time of European settlement. A memorial at the corner of Queen Street and Gorge Road marks the place where Te Huruhuru and Micheal Studholme are said to have met in 1854. A prominent memorial is the statue in Seddon Square of Dr Margaret Cruickshank, one of New Zealand's earliest women doctors.

Waimate's museum is housed in a handsome nineteenth century courthouse, built in 1879. The museum has Maori artefacts, pioneer household implements and farm machinery on display. Waimate also has two churches of note. The wooden St Augustine's was built in 1872 and enlarged in 1880. The memorial lych gate and bell tower were built early this century. The Roman Catholic Church was built of brick and stone in 1906–07.

The Te Waimate Station was taken up in 1854 by Michael Studholme and is still farmed by his descendants. Its oldest building is The Cuddy, a totara slab and lath-and-daub cottage with a thatched roof, built in 1854, which served as the station homestead until 1860. It has been kept in good repair by the family and the Historic Places Trust. As a private historic reserve it can be visited with permission. Other interesting old farm buildings on the station include a woolshed, cookhouse, grainstore and raised storehouse.

The Otaio Run, a little north and towards the coast from Waimate, was taken up in 1855 by an intrepid Scot, Jeanie Collier, on behalf of her orphaned nephews. When she died in 1861 she was buried at a spot she had chosen. In 1955 a stone was placed on the grave which has since become a historic reserve.

Another major station in the area was Waikakahi, owned by Allan McLean who built McLeans Mansion in Christchurch. His homestead, The Valley, a large wooden house built about 1874, is now a private farmhouse which can only be viewed with permission. Te Kiteroa, built by McLean's housekeeper, is now a bed and breakfast place and restaurant. It has attractive gardens and views. St Matthews Church, Morven, was built in 1903 to serve settlers who took up farms after the breakup of the McLean property.

From the road through the Waihao Gorge beyond Waimate can be seen old formations of the railway line which once ran to Waihao Downs. This road, Highway 82, eventually reaches the north bank of the Waitaki River. Beside the highway, towards Hakataramea, is a cob cottage believed to have been built by James Paterson about 1880. It may have been used to accommodate stock drovers and other travellers using the route to and from Hakataramea. It has been reroofed with wooden shingles and now houses a craft shop.

◀ *This large brick building was erected in the early 1880s to house the Royal Flouring Mills. It is one of an important group of early mill buildings in Timaru, of historical significance because it was built to house the first roller mills imported into New Zealand.*

NORTH OTAGO

When Europeans reached the Otago coast in some numbers in the early nineteenth century, there were scattered Maori settlements at places along the coast, including a major settlement at Otakou just inside the Otago Heads. There are also traces inland of the Maori occupation of the southern half of the South Island. The earliest European settlers were whalers, many of whom married into the local Maori communities. In the early 1840s, at Matanaka, Johnny Jones supervised the shift from whaling to a true farming settlement. Later in that decade the founding of the Otago settlement brought settlers in greater numbers. Otago prospered on the basis of Central Otago gold in the nineteenth century and throughout the region, but especially in Dunedin and Oamaru, are many fine old buildings, reminders of the province's years of affluence. The farming history too is well recalled by its old farmhouses and farm buildings.

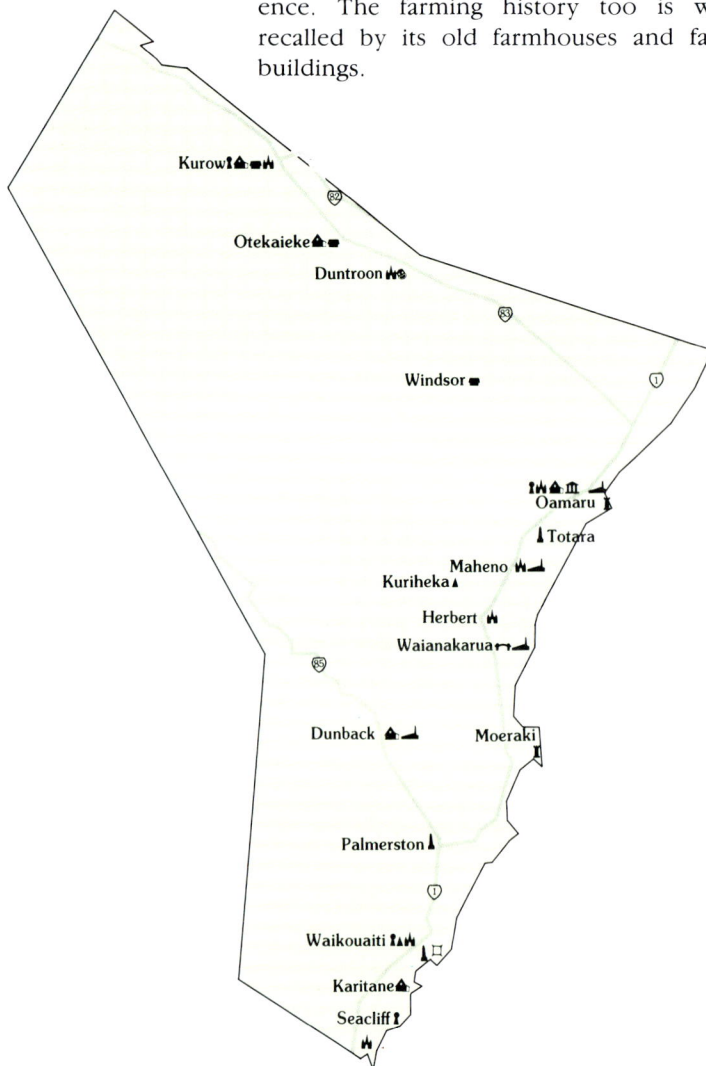

Kurow
Otekaieke
Duntroon
Windsor
Oamaru
Totara
Maheno
Kuriheka
Herbert
Waianakarua
Dunback
Moeraki
Palmerston
Waikouaiti
Karitane
Seacliff

LOWER WAITAKI VALLEY

Like South Canterbury, North Otago shows evidence of early Maori occupation of the area in the form of rock shelter drawings. Two of these shelters are near Duntroon. The Takiroa rock shelter is signposted beside Highway 83 and the Maerewhenua shelter is just beyond the town up the Danseys Pass Road. In both places the drawings are executed in red ochre and charcoal, under limestone overhangs which the early Maori used for shelter. Unfortunately some drawings were removed to museums many years ago.

The Otago side of the Lower Waitaki Valley also has places of European historic interest. At Otekaieke, between Duntroon and Kurow, is the huge baronial homestead built by the early runholder Robert Campbell. It is evidence of the wealth that could be made from sheep farming in the nineteenth century. From 1908 to 1987 the homestead was a residential school for boys. The property is now privately owned but visible from the road. Near the homestead is a stone cottage built in the late 1850s and interesting old farm buildings — a woolshed, cookshop, men's quarters and implement shed.

The Campbells were responsible for other buildings in the area. A bequest by Mrs Campbell provided for the building in Kurow of a large vicarage with a chapel attached and a stable block behind. The imposing house, built in 1896, is easily visible from the highway. In Duntroon the large St Martin's Church was built in 1901 under the same legacy.

A pioneer museum at Kurow displays vehicles and other material relating to the early history of the area. About 5 km above Kurow is the first hydro-electric station on the Waitaki River, built between 1928 and 1934. Lake Waitaki Village, with its Staff Hostel and nine houses, historic trees and streetscape, is one of New Zealand's early examples of State housing.

OAMARU

Known as 'The White Stone City', Oamaru has a large number of old buildings of white Oamaru stone which has been used throughout New Zealand for many notable buildings. The town, founded in the 1850s, boasts many fine nineteenth century buildings which give it a distinctive character.

The old post office, still standing, was built in 1864. Of the handsome jail, built in the same decade, only the stables remain. Near the 'old' post office is the 'new' post office, built in 1884, with a handsome tower. Two bank buildings make an imposing pair. The National Bank (formerly Bank of Otago) dates from 1870–71 and the former Bank of New South Wales (now the Forrester Gallery) from 1884. The Waitaki County Council Chambers date from 1881 and the Courthouse from 1883. The other dominant civic building is the Municipal Chamber and Town Hall, built in 1906.

Three Oamaru churches are worth seeing. St Luke's Anglican was begun in 1865 but not completed until this century. St Paul's Presbyterian was built in 1876 and St Patrick's Basilica completed in 1918. The parish hall and vicarage at St Luke's, with the church itself, make up a historic precinct.

One Oamaru school, St Kevin's College, occupies the Redcastle Homestead, 1903, the old stables now housing the school tuckshop. Waitaki Boys High still occupies its original 1883 building. The school's Hall of Memories, with many historical items on display, can be visited by arrangement. Notable 1860s houses are the Homestead (now used for receptions) and Casa Nova.

A precinct near the port is New Zealand's only nineteenth century central business district which remains intact. Known as 'Historic Oamaru', the town's Victorian character is recalled in the stunning concentration of more than thirty limestone buildings which are being carefully restored by the community. They include the massive wool and grain warehouse and date mostly from 1870 to 1890 when Oamaru was for a time the ninth largest town in New Zealand.

North Otago, once a great grain-growing district, has several historic flour mills. Now all closed, three can be seen within a few minutes of each other in Oamaru. The Red Lion mill is in Harbour Street and Meeks Mill, built 1878, by the Oamaru Creek between Severn and Thames Streets. Meeks elevator building, with its massive storage capacity of 20,000 sacks, was built for 10,000 pounds in 1883 and stands at the end of Itchen Street. At the Phoenix flour mill site is a huge waterwheel, 10.3 metres

in diameter, which came into use in 1878. A complete circuit of the town on foot, taking in almost all its historic buildings, takes 1½ to 2 hours.

The North Otago Museum is housed in the Athenaeum building of 1882. Adjoining the Museum and Library is the North Otago Archive, newly built but in architectural harmony with its historic neighbours. It has an excellent collection of newspapers and civic, church and community records.

OAMARU TO DUNEDIN

South of Oamaru are two places important in New Zealand's agricultural and industrial heritage. Sheep killed on the Totara Estate were railed south to Port Chalmers and frozen aboard the *Dunedin* for despatch, in February 1882, to England. This first successful shipment of frozen meat from New Zealand laid the foundation for the freezing industry, and for the country-wide pros-

▲ *The Forrester Gallery in Oamaru is North Otago's Art Gallery and Cultural Centre. It is housed in the former Bank of New South Wales building, one of the finest of the town's remarkable collection of nineteenth century Oamaru stone buildings. The Gallery offers guided tours of historic Oamaru.*

▲ *The limetone farm buildings on the Totara Estate, just south of Oamaru, are of special historic interest because it was there that the sheep were slaughtered whose carcasses became the first consignment of frozen meat sent from New Zealand to Britain in 1882.*

perity of small farmers raising sheep for meat as well as wool. A number of limestone farm buildings on the estate, built in the late 1860s, have survived and form an attractive group. They were restored by the Historic Places Trust for the centenary of the frozen meat industry.

A few kilometres south of Totara, just north of Maheno, is Clark's Mill, where flour was produced from 1867 until 1977. This limestone building has been restored by the Historic Places Trust and is open to the public for tours by arrangement.

At Kuriheka, near Maheno, is an unusual

war memorial with field guns from the 1914–18 war mounted around it. There are also palatial stone farm buildings on a nearby privately owned farm. Two churches in the area warrant visits. The Church of St Andrew in Maheno (1938) is an architectural gem and as a family memorial has local historical interest. In Herbert is the older Presbyterian church, built in 1866.

Waianakarua's most notable historic structure is a lovely stone arched bridge (1874) across the north branch of the Waianakarua River by the main highway bridge. The old mill house in Waianakarua, built in 1879, is now a restaurant and motel.

At Moeraki, a shore whaling station was established in 1836–37, but nothing remains in the settlement from this chapter of its history. The plain but historic Kotahitanga Church, built in 1862 and moved to its present site and renovated in 1961, is a reminder of the very long Maori presence in the district. The Moeraki Lighthouse is an early wooden tower built in 1877. The coastline around Moeraki has an important place in Maori traditional history, associated with the voyage of the *Arai-te-uru* canoe, which by tradition was wrecked in the vicinity. (The geological curiosities, the Moeraki boulders, are held in Maori tradition to be the petrified food baskets washed ashore when the canoe was wrecked.) At the mouth of the Shag River is a moa-hunter campsite and also an old coalmine.

In gold rush days Palmerston was the setting-off point for the Central Otago goldfields over the 'Pig Root'. Some interesting older buildings remain in the town which has lost some of its earlier importance. On the crest of the hill above the town is a monument to Sir John McKenzie, who rose from shepherd on the Shag Valley run to Minister of Lands in the Liberal Government of the 1890s. He was a passionate advocate of the small farmer and worked to break up the great estates.

A short distance up the Pig Root (Highway 85) at the Makaraeo Lime Works near Dunback is an important group of early lime kilns, three of which are well-type kilns. The other is freestanding. There is an old coaching inn on the outskirts of Dunback.

Waikouaiti is one of Otago's oldest towns. There was extensive Maori settlement in the area in pre-European times and pa and other sites can be seen on the coastline from Waikouaiti south of Otago Harbour. In 1838 the Sydney-based trader and shipowner Johnny Jones established a whaling station on the coast near Waikouaiti. Two years later, in 1840, settlers sent out by Jones arrived and established a permanent farming settlement near the coast.

The transition from shore-based whaling to farming is illustrated by the Matanaka farm buildings, probably the oldest surviving farm buildings in the South Island. The farm on Cornish Head, above the beach settlement, was begun in 1843 and some of the farm buildings date from about this time. The dramatically situated buildings

include a stable, small storehouse, granary, schoolhouse and three-seater 'loo'.

The presence of Maori, whalers and then settlers prompted the interest of missionaries in Waikouaiti. The first Methodist missionary, James Watkin, arrived in 1840. A plaque in a Maori burial ground overlooking the estuary records that Watkin preached the first Christian sermon in Otago in May 1840. Two old churches have survived, St John's Anglican and the Presbyterian church which now serves as a Sunday School hall. An Early Settlers Museum contains a fascinating collection of pioneer relics.

The Huriawa Peninsula, near Karitane, was the site of a pa from at least the early eighteenth century, and probably for much longer. Some of its earthworks are still visible. The homestead of Sir Truby King, founder of the Plunket Society, still stands at Karitane. In Warrington is a lovely little church, St Barnabas's, built in the 1870s. At Seacliff is Dunedin's Museum of Transport and Technology, on the site of an old psychiatric hospital. Trams and cable-cars are among the items on display. More Maori sites lie around Blueskin Bay. Near Kaikai Beach is the site of one of New Zealand's earliest Polynesian settlements.

▲ *In a fine setting on a headland overlooking the Pacific Ocean, the farm buildings at Matanaka, near Waikouaiti, date from the 1840s and are probably the South Island's oldest surviving buildings.*

DUNEDIN AND
THE TAIERI

The city of Dunedin had its origins in organised settlements. In Scotland in the 1840s, leading members of the Free Church of Scotland planned a new settlement in New Zealand's South Island. Determined to found a society based on solid principles of religion, education and industry, 344 colonists arrived in 1848 aboard two small sailing ships and Dunedin was born. The infant settlement struggled for a time but the discovery of gold in Central Otago provided the impetus for growth which, by the 1880s, made Dunedin the largest, most industrialised and the most important commercial centre in the land. Numerous buildings reflect that preeminence, even today. They are not confined to the city, either, for the Otago Peninsula and the Taieri Plains to the south are also well endowed with grand homesteads, industrial buildings and farm buildings that recall the early years of colonisation.

FROM SCOTTISH BEGINNINGS

Dunedin has been described as 'the most perfectly preserved Victorian city on earth' and its old buildings make it a fine place to observe Victorian architecture. Dunedin was founded in 1848 when the first immigrant ships of a Free Church of Scotland settlement arrived at Port Chalmers. The settlers were led by William Cargill and Thomas Burns. Cargill is commemorated by a prominent Gothic monument. A link with Burns is provided by the nineteenth century statue in the Octagon of Robert Burns, who was Thomas Burns' uncle. The discovery of gold in Central Otago in the early 1860s made Dunedin for a time the most important city in New Zealand and many of its fine buildings reflect this early pre-eminence.

The city's prominent First Church is a triumph of Victorian Gothic design. It was completed in 1873. Its architect, R.A. Lawson, also designed the city's other two notable early Presbyterian churches. Knox was built in 1876. St Andrew's, 1870, has added historic interest as the building in which Rutherford Waddell, in 1888, preached the influential sermon 'The Sin of Cheapness'. The Trinity Methodist Church, another Lawson church, now the Fortune Theatre, was built in 1869. Dunedin's oldest surviving church, which was once Congregational and is now Seventh Day Adventist, was built in 1864.

Dunedin has impressive Roman Catholic church buildings too, four of which were designed by the architect F.W. Petre. St Joseph's Cathedral, a huge, still incomplete Gothic building, was built between 1879 and 1886. Next to it stands St Dominic's Priory, 1877, an early concrete building of great architectural distinction. St Patrick's Basilica, in a different style, was completed in 1894. The Sacred Heart was built two years earlier, in 1892.

Scottish respect for education is evident in Dunedin's old educational buildings. The University of Otago, New Zealand's oldest university, founded in 1869, is centred on its stone Clocktower Block, erected in 1878–79. Nearby are brick professorial houses built about the same time. The cren-

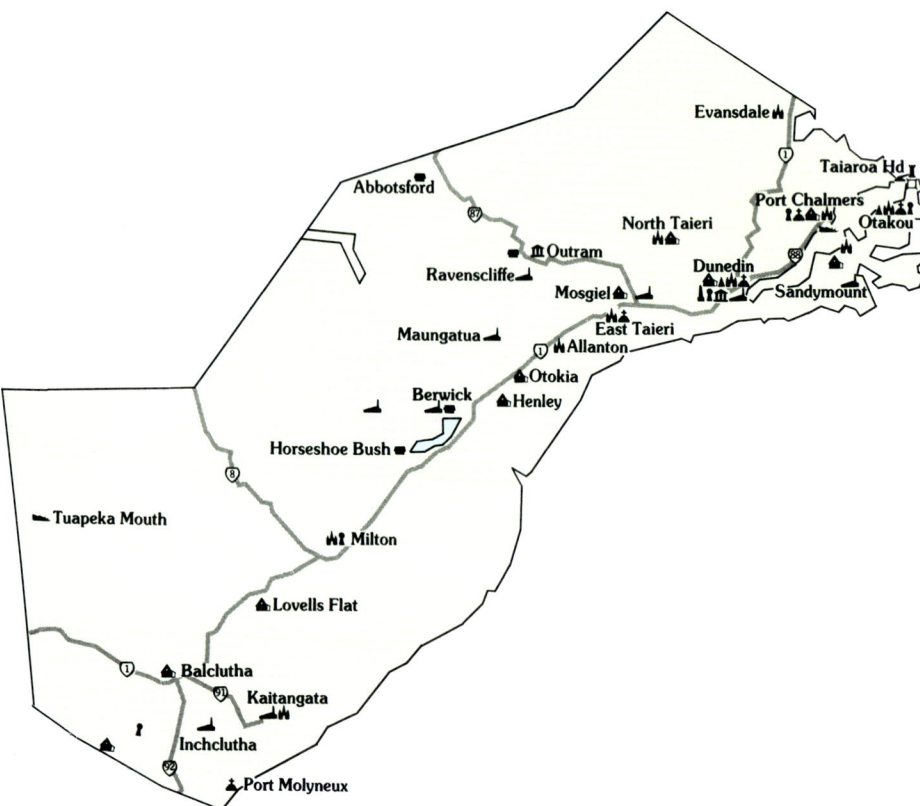

Evansdale
Taiaroa Hd
Abbotsford
Port Chalmers
North Taieri
Otakou
Outram
Ravenscliffe
Dunedin
Mosgiel
Sandymount
Maungatua
East Taieri
Allanton
Otokia
Berwick
Henley
Horseshoe Bush
Tuapeka Mouth
Milton
Lovells Flat
Balclutha
Kaitangata
Inchclutha
Port Molyneux

ellated towers of Otago Boys' High School date from 1884–85. The substantial brick Presbyterian theological hall, Knox College, was constructed in 1907–09.

Dunedin's railway station, opened in 1906, is the country's most imposing monument to the heyday of travel by train. Some of the lavish internal appointments of the station have been restored, making it as interesting inside as out. Nearby are the police station (a brick building erected in 1895), the Law Courts (a stone battlemented building of 1902) and, head-high over the Octagon, the restored Municipal Chambers built in 1880.

Dunedin's pre-eminent position in nineteenth century New Zealand is also reflected in many surviving commercial buildings. Perhaps the most important is the 1874 ANZ Bank building, recently restored. Other surviving commercial buildings of the same decade include the former Hallenstein's warehouse (1874), the Sew Hoy warehouse (1878) and Wains Hotel (1878). The Southern Cross Hotel, with some original internal fittings, dates from 1883. The Mutual Fund Building, put up in 1908–10, was Dunedin's first 'skyscraper'.

Dunedin was also an important early industrial centre. The stone building of the Willowbank Brewery, begun in the 1860s, is still in use and there is a small stone malthouse on the banks of the Water of Leith. The Crown Roller Mills, a fine brick industrial building with stone facings, was begun in 1867 and assumed its present form about 1890. Other early industries included the Hillside Railway Workshops, opened in 1875, the country's first commercial paper mills at Woodhaugh, which began operation in 1876, and an early freezing works at Burnside. South of Dunedin, at the former woollen mills in Mosgiel, the building in which Otago's first woollen mill was established in 1871 is still standing.

The best known of Dunedin's old houses is Olveston, a Jacobean style mansion, designed by the British architect Sir Ernest George for a wealthy local family, the Theomins. It was built of brick faced with Oamaru stone and Moeraki gravel in 1904–06. Bequeathed to the Dunedin City Council in the 1960s, it is now open to the public and houses a large collection of the fine and decorative arts. It is less an art gallery than a superb lesson in how a family of wealth and taste lived in Edwardian times and later.

A fine house built of bluestone in 1878, Marinoto, is now the home of the Sisters of

▲ *The Cargill Monument and Stuart Street, Dunedin.*
Alexander Turnbull Library

Mercy. The house now occupied by the Fernhill Club was the home of Johnny Jones, who became, after his early start at Waikouaiti, a leading businessman of early Dunedin. Columba College, on Highgate, occupies the original nineteenth century Bishopscourt. Lisburn House in Caversham (1864–65) is a gabled building with striking decorative patterns in its brickwork. At Chingford Park the stables, built in the 1880s, have survived.

Not all Dunedin's interesting old houses are grand mansions. The Cable House of Cumberland Street although entirely rebuilt, is with its verandah, high gables and dormers, like many ordinary homes of the 1860s, but unusual in being semi-detached. Ferntree House at Halfway Bush, Dunedin's oldest house, built before 1852, is the only pioneer ponga (tree-fern) house still standing anywhere in New Zealand. Queen Street and George Street both have fine old houses from the time they were fashionable streets for professional and business families. Dunedin has no peer in New Zealand for Victorian terraced housing, especially along Victoria Terrace, Dundas Street, Stuart Street, Royal Terrace and other inner city streets.

Sports enthusiasts will find historic interest in Carisbrook, where there have been playing fields since the 1870s (the main stand dates from 1913). At the Oval, cricket has been played since the 1860s, and at Forbury Park the first horse racing track was formed in the early 1870s.

Dunedin's earliest cemetery on Arthur Street was cleared and levelled in 1879. An obelisk commemorates those buried there. In the Southern Cemetery, opened in 1858, are the graves of many of Dunedin's early settlers, including William Cargill, Thomas Burns and Johnny Jones. In the Northern Cemetery are the graves of Thomas Bracken, author of 'God Defend New Zealand', and the Gothic mausoleum of William Larnach.

Excellent museums are also a feature of Dunedin. The Otago Museum has an important Maori collection, including the meeting house Mataatua, carved at Whakatane in the early 1870s. The Maritime Hall focuses on the Union Steam Ship Company, which was founded in Dunedin. The lives of Otago's early settlers are represented by household and other items from whaling, goldmining and pioneering days. The Museum building itself (1876–77)

is a fine old structure. The Hocken Library has large collections of maps, pictures and photographs of early New Zealand. The Early Settlers Association Museum and Portrait Gallery has exhibits which further illuminate Dunedin's early days. The Ocean Beach railway is a working steam railway on which early locomotives pull old wagons and carriages. Dunedin's old cable cars gave it a distinctive place in New Zealand transport history, but the last line closed in 1957. One car is held in the Early Settlers Museum. The Dunedin Public Art Gallery occupies a building constructed for the 1925–26 New Zealand and South Seas International Exhibition and contains much material of historic interest. There is a military museum housed in the Dunedin Army headquarters.

▲ *In the Dunedin Railway Workshops, 1893.* Alexander Turnbull Library

◄ *New Zealand's oldest university, Otago University opened its doors in 1871. Amid its many modern structures are sturdy stone buildings, some of which date back to the decade in which the university opened.*

PORT CHALMERS

The purchase of Otago was concluded at Port Chalmers in 1844 and the Otago settlers landed four years later. Plaques on Beach Street, opposite the museum, mark the sites of those events. One of the oldest items in the town is the signal flagstaff which was erected in 1862 and is possibly the mast of the *Cincinnati*, ship of the notorious Bully Hayes. The railway line between Dunedin and Port Chalmers was opened in 1872. The tunnel into Port Chalmers is an example of an early engineering achievement only a little younger than the Lyttelton Tunnel.

Notable old churches include Holy Trinity which was built in 1874–76, St Mary's Star of the Sea, 1878, and the Iona Presbyterian Church, which dominates the town centre. An older 1872 church survives as the hall of the Iona Church. Many early wooden and stone houses in Port Chalmers date from the 1880s and even earlier. Two interesting larger buildings also date from the 1860s — Chicks Hotel and the Masonic Hall — and two more from the 1870s — the Port Chalmers Hotel and the post office.

Like Lyttelton, Port Chalmers has connections with Antarctica. Scott made Port Chalmers his last port of call on both his *Discovery* and *Terra Nova* expeditions and a memorial to Scott, unveiled in 1914, stands above the town. Shackleton and Byrd also called at Port Chalmers. There is a memorial to the American Antarctic explorer Richard Byrd on the Unity Park Lookout in Dunedin.

From the Beach Street wharf the first cargo of frozen meat left New Zealand's shores in 1882. In Port Chalmers itself and at Deborah Bay the hulks of old ships are visible. One of the interesting graves in the town's two old cemeteries is that of the early missionary, the Rev. J.C. Reimenschneider.

OTAGO PENINSULA

The Otago Peninsula supported extensive Maori settlement from ancient times. The Maori church at Otakou, opened in 1941, stands more or less on the site of the main Maori village in the harbour at the time Europeans began to arrive in New Zealand. Within the church is a small but fascinating museum which can be visited by making enquiries locally. A meeting house opened in 1946 stands next to the church. Behind

◄ *New Zealand's finest monument to the days when railway was the country's premier means of passenger travel is the Dunedin Railway Station. The grandiose Edwardian building was opened in 1906.*

167

the church and meeting house is a cemetery in which are the graves of many leading Ngai Tahu chiefs, including Te Matenga Taiaroa and Karetai, both of the generation which fought against Te Rauparaha and witnessed the arrival of the Europeans.

Plaques on the foreshore at Otakou, near Wellers Rock, recall the early European history of the area, including the establishment of the Weller Brothers' whaling station on the site in 1831. Another records Bishop Pompallier's conducting the first Christian service held in Otago in November 1840.

Taiaroa Head, once the site of a pa, has two items of historic importance. The Taiaroa Head lighthouse, built in 1864–65, is one of the country's oldest. Nearby is an Armstrong 'disappearing' gun installed in 1888 as a result of the Russian scares of that decade. It is one of the most interesting relics of New Zealand's concern about its coastal defences and the Otago Peninsula Trust has made it easier to visit. The famed albatross colony is close by. There are also remains of old coastal fortifications — gun emplacements and a tunnel system — at nearby Harrington Point.

After the founding of the Otago settlement, the peninsula was taken up by farmers, most running cows on relatively small holdings. From these early, small-farming days, remain cottages and barns, many built of stone, and stone walls. Old post and rail fences can also be seen. Part of the peninsula's farming history is a stone farmhouse at Springfield, in which the country's first co-operative cheese factory was established in 1871.

At Broad Bay there is a pioneer cottage of the 1860s and a Catholic church which was built at Waihola in the 1870s and moved to Broad Bay only in 1949. The harbour wall by the road from Andersons Bay round to Portobello was built by prison labour between the 1860s and 1880s. Much of the original stonework is still in good condition. The island in the Otago Harbour between Portobello and Port Chalmers was a quarantine station from the 1860s into the 1920s, and a small cemetery and one or two buildings remain from those days. Interesting relics of pioneer industry on the peninsula are the spectacular nineteenth century Sandymount lime kilns. There is also an old schoolhouse at Sandymount, which was once a thriving dairying settlement.

One of the peninsula's best known historic places is Larnach Castle, a grand stone residence built in the early 1870s. The ballroom was added about ten years after the main building. Once fallen into disrepair, the castle has been carefully restored and is open to the public. The peninsula's other larger house to which the public has access is the kauri Glenfalloch homestead, begun in 1871 but later much altered. It is now the headquarters of the Otago Peninsula Trust and is surrounded by delightful gardens.

THE TAIERI

South of Dunedin, stretching from Mosgiel to Milton, is an extensive area of flat farmland, the Taieri Plain. On this plain are many old houses, farm buildings and churches dating back as far as the 1850s. The swamps of the plain were drained in the 1860s and farmers prospered by meeting the demand for supplies on the goldfields. An old horse-drawn scoop used to excavate earth for stopbanks can be seen at the Taieri Pumping Station.

The many interesting farmhouses and cottages of the area include Dunrobin (early 1850s), Duddingston (1864), Salisbury (1873), the Poplars (1876) and Clairinch (1878). Some of these are wooden and others brick. The Adam Guest House at Otokia dates from 1856. Most of these are private homes but can usually be viewed from the road. Some larger houses have been taken over by institutions. At the Invermay Research Centre, the homestead of 1862 is still in use. Many towns of the Taieri have old public and commercial buildings as well as houses and cottages that have stood unchanged for generations. Outram has three early bank buildings and some old railway buildings.

There are several churches of note on the Taieri Plain. The brick East Taieri Presbyterian Church was opened in 1870, with a manse built in the later 1870s. The nearby cemetery is also of interest. At Allanton there is an 1865 Presbyterian church and a Catholic church. A church at North Taieri dates from 1866 and the manse nearby from a year or two later. An 1864 school building is also still intact at North Taieri. At West Taieri is an 1875 manse and an old cemetery. In Milton are three nineteenth century churches.

Of interest among the many old farm buildings on the Taieri Plain are the imposing stables built in 1884 at Horseshoe Bush, just south of Lake Waihola, and the

◄ The Sandymount lime kilns on the Otago Peninsula, built in 1865, are among the oldest and also the best preserved in the country. In kilns like these limestone was burnt to provide lime for agricultural and building purposes.

farm buildings at Abbotsford, designed in 1870. At Ravenscliffe are the remains of a waterwheel used to drive a sawmill, and at Berwick the remains of old bread ovens. Berwick also has an old woolshed which has been converted into an information centre for the Berwick Forest. At Maungatua is an 1889 cheese factory now used as a woolshed.

At the Taieri Historical Park, Outram, farm machinery is on display and the restored and resited Outram Courthouse and old jail can be inspected. A museum in Milton is housed in a cottage of the late 1850s. In the hills to the west of the Taieri Plain, Waipori Falls was the goldfield closest to Dunedin and stamper batteries and other mining relics can still be seen there.

The island Moturata at Taieri Mouth was used intermittently as a shore whaling station in the late 1830s and early 1840s. In the 1860s it supported a pilot and signalling station for vessels heading up the river with passengers and goods for the goldfields.

BALCLUTHA

Balclutha grew up around the best river crossing, originally with a ferry, on the lower Clutha. The area was first settled in the late 1840s and early 1850s. The Telford Farm Institute in Balclutha is housed in a stone homestead built in 1869. Around Balclutha are several historic places. At Lovells Flat, on Highway 1 north of Balclutha, is a restored sod cottage furnished in pioneer style. East of Balclutha is the former coalmining town of Kaitangata. There are still some abandoned coalmining buildings and old houses and cottages there and a Presbyterian church which was built in the late 1870s.

The Port Molyneux cemetery overlooks the site of the port and town abandoned when the river mouth changed in 1878. Only the old town hall remains as a reminder of this now deserted town. Just south of Balclutha the small private Somerville Museum, which can be visited by arrangement, is housed in the buildings of an early flour mill. Further south again the Willowmead homestead, built of pit-sawn timber in the late 1850s, can be glimpsed from the road. On Inchclutha, the large island below Balclutha, is a kiln built in 1881 and used to dry chicory until about 1950. River steamers once plied the river as far as Tuapeka Mouth, where the Tuapeka punt is an example of working history.

CENTRAL OTAGO

Gold rushes and long years of goldmining have left Central Otago an area of great historic interest. Many buildings of goldmining days were built of stone, mud or clay and their survival has been helped by the dry climate of the region. The distinctive buildings of Central Otago, in quiet or even deserted townships, and the remnants of machinery used to recover gold or extract it from its ore, make it one of the country's most fascinating regions. Many of the historic places of Central Otago associated with the goldmining days are administered by the Department of Conservation as part of the Otago Goldfields Park. The department's office in Dunedin can provide detailed information about the many sites included in the park.

Central Otago was also an area of early sheep runs and there are groups of old farm buildings, most built of stone or earth, to be seen. Long before the coming of goldminers and sheepmen, the Maori hunted moa in Central Otago and a form of greenstone was collected from the head of Lake Wakatipu. Maori villages were established in many places.

LAWRENCE

Gabriels Gully, near Lawrence, was the scene of the discovery by Gabriel Read in May 1861 which triggered the Otago gold rushes. A monument, incorporating an old miner's pick and shovel, stands at the bottom end of Gabriels Gully in the general area of Read's discovery. Deep river gravels, deposited by floods in the past century, have greatly altered the appearance of the gully since the time of the discovery. The road to the old mining town of Blue Spur, where there are still a few old buildings, turns off the road to Gabriels Gully from Lawrence. A cairn on the old workings at Waitahuna, near Lawrence, marks where a second discovery of gold was made in July 1861.

Old buildings in the town of Lawrence include the post office, now somewhat dilapidated, built in 1866–67 as a courthouse. In 1876 a new courthouse, now a community centre, was built next door. Lawrence has two substantial old churches, some interesting old commercial buildings and many attractive old houses. The Lawrence and District Museum contains goldfield relics.

At Wetherstones, near Lawrence, the old Black Horse brewery, built in 1866 and closed in 1923, is a picturesque ruin. Around Beaumont can be seen the old formation of the railway line that once ran to Roxburgh.

ROXBURGH

Runs were taken up in the Roxburgh area in the 1850s, a few years before the gold rushes. One of the most impressive monuments to early pastoralism in the area is the Teviot woolshed, built in 1880 of stone with a barrel-vaulted roof. At the time it was the largest building of its kind in New Zealand. Burned out in 1924, it is now a majestic ruin on private property.

The Clutha River at Roxburgh was a rich source of gold from 1862 until the dredging

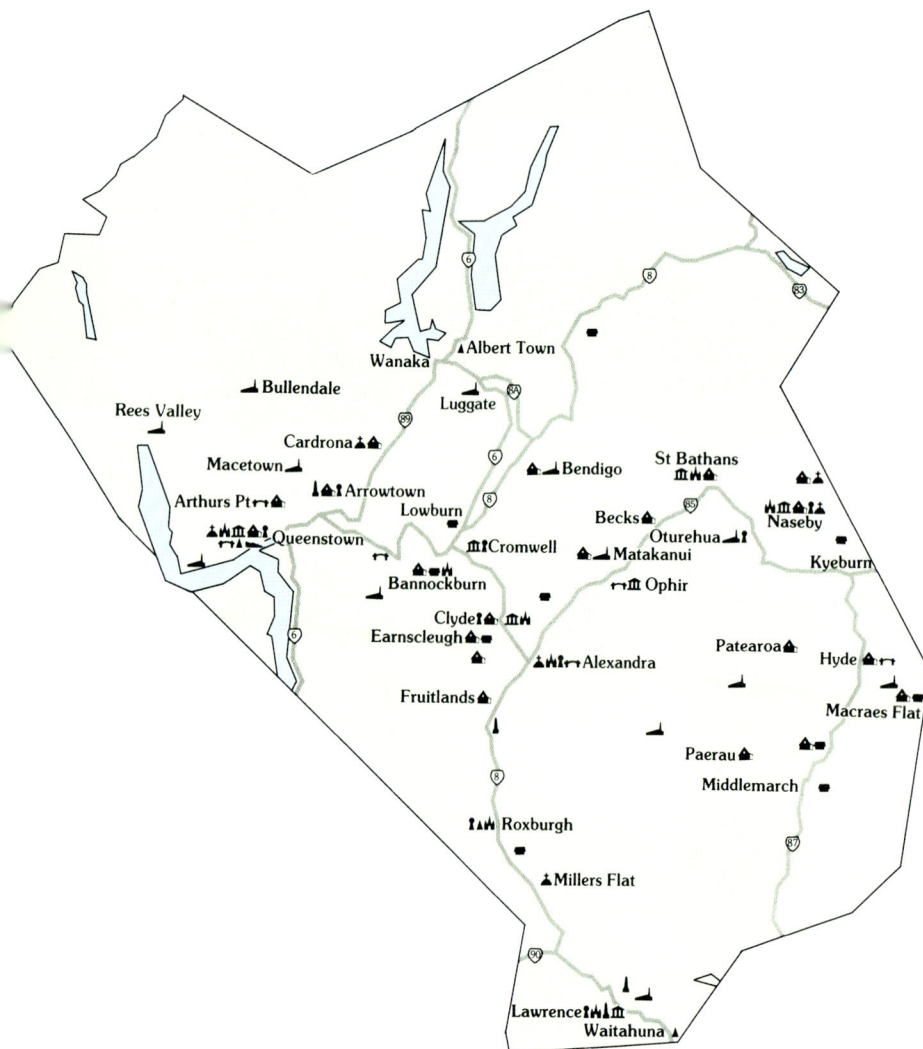

boom of early this century. A relic of dredging days is an anchor, mounted at the entrance to the Pinders Pond reserve, on the east bank of the Clutha. At Millers Flat a historic reserve protects the Lonely Graves, where in 1865, according to tradition, an unknown miner whose body had been found in the river was buried as 'Somebody's Darling' by another miner.

The stone churches at Roxburgh are most attractive. St James Anglican was built in 1872 and the Teviot Presbyterian church in 1880. The tiny stone Methodist church, 1872, houses a pottery. The stone piers of a bridge built in the late 1870s can be seen on the western bank of the river.

ALEXANDRA AND CLYDE

The year after gold was discovered at Gabriels Gully, new finds were made between Clyde (formerly Dunstan) and Cromwell. The towns of Alexandra, Clyde and Cromwell emerged to serve these rich Dunstan diggings. An era of dredging followed the initial years of panning and sluicing. Alexandra, at first eclipsed by nearby Clyde, prospered with a dredging boom of the 1870s.

In Alexandra's Graveyard Gully is a memorial to miners buried there in the 1860s. In Conroys Gully, the Chinese miners left their own memorial in the form of extensive stone walls built during their meticulous recovery of gold, often from the abandoned tailings of earlier miners. Notable old buildings in Alexandra include the Presbyterian and Anglican churches. Several historic suspension bridges are a feature of Central Otago. Beside the modern highway bridge in Alexandra are the substantial stone piers of the bridge built in 1882. A short distance up the Manuherikia River from its confluence with the Clutha the Shaky Bridge, for pedestrians only, was built in 1880.

Part of the Goldfields Park, Alexandra's historic Courthouse has been restored and is open to the public. Video programmes of historic court cases are shown in the building.

South of Alexandra the road to Roxburgh passes through the Fruitlands district where there are many old stone and earth cottages and other pioneer buildings, most now in ruins but some, including the old Cape Broome hotel, still in use as farm buildings. Mitchells Cottage, with its exceptionally fine stonework, was built at the turn of the century by a miner and stands in a delightful setting about 1½ km off the main road. South of Fruitlands, the Gorge Creek Memorial, in a roadside rest area, recalls the many miners who lost their lives attempting to cross the Old Man Range in the winter of 1863.

▲ *Several of Central Otago's swift rivers are crossed by nineteenth century, stone-towered suspension bridges. This one spans the gorge of the Kawarau River between Cromwell and Queenstown. Opened in 1880, it was on the main route linking important Central Otago goldfields with Dunedin. Superseded in the 1950s by a modern bridge, it has been preserved as a fine example of last century's bridge building.*

In Clyde, the 1864 stone courthouse is now the local museum, and the stone general store a restaurant; other buildings of the 1860s include the Town Hall, 1868–69, an old hotel and cottages. An old coaching inn, built of stone in the 1880s, is now known as Dunstan House. The Athenaeum was built in 1874 and St Michael's Church in 1877. There are many old stone cottages in the Clyde area; those in Blackmans Gully were built by Chinese miners.

On the west bank of the Clutha between Clyde and Alexandra stands the Earnscleugh Station, one of the oldest Central Otago runs. Its castle-like homestead and outbuildings were erected early this century and can be distantly viewed from the road. Near Earnscleugh are extensive tailings, left by gold dredges of 1890s.

CROMWELL

Cromwell, like Clyde, began its days as a gold rush town. Just below the town is a memorial to Hartley and Reilly who first discovered gold in the Clutha's gorges. Sadly, the site of old Cromwell was cleared for the filling of Lake Dunstan behind the Clyde dam. Some of its most important stone buildings have been saved for re-erection on a site above the new waterline. The 1872 courthouse is one of the few nineteenth century buildings to escape inundation.

In the hills around Cromwell are numerous deserted goldmining townships and mining sites. Much of the evidence of early goldmining is in the form of tailings, some in herringbone patterns, from sluicing. The town of Bannockburn, about 6 km from Cromwell, has a stone church, scattered old cottages and a former post office. Nearby is the cob Kawarau homestead, built in the late 1850s, and a stone woolshed. On the Carrick Range above Cromwell, the ruined cottages of Carricktown are an evocative sight with, nearby, the frame of an old quartz crushing battery. Carricktown can be reached only on foot. Also on the range is a huge waterwheel, 8 metres in diameter, erected in 1875 to power the quartz crushing batteries of the Young Australian Mine.

There are more tumbledown cottages and stone and cob buildings on the sites of the Bendigo and other old townships, along with old shafts, slag heaps and other traces of quartz mining. Bendigo also has an old battery, the Come-in-Time, re-erected in 1880 on its present site on the banks of Rise and Shine Creek. Visitors are reminded to watch for deep and partly concealed gold workings and shafts. At Lowburn there is an interesting group of old buildings on the Partridge farm providing evidence that farming has gone hand in hand with gold-mining since Central Otago's early days.

In the Clutha Valley there are local museums at Roxburgh, Alexandra, Clyde and Cromwell. All have collections and displays emphasising goldmining, but touch also on the early days of farming and fruit growing in the region.

THE MANUHERIKIA VALLEY

At Alexandra the Manuherikia River joins the Clutha. In the valleys of the Manuherikia and its tributary, the Ida Burn, are several interesting places. On the privately owned Galloway Station, just above Alexandra, are some fine stone farm buildings, built soon after the run was taken up in 1858. They include a stables, barn, chaff house and men's quarters. The Moutere Station, further up the other side of the valley, has a cob woolshed built in the early 1870s.

One route into the tiny town of Ophir leads over a grand stone-piered suspension bridge, opened in 1880. Ophir's lovely post office was built in 1886 of schist masonry with plaster quoins and still has its Victorian fittings. The historic old courthouse nearby is dilapidated.

At Matakanui, an almost deserted gold town, is a unique group of mud-brick buildings — a store, house, stable, bakery and hotel. On Highway 85 at Lauder is an interesting stone house and at Becks the remains of an old coaching run.

Towards the head of the Manuherikia Valley is St Bathans. Its best known building is the picturesque Vulcan Hotel, built in 1869, during the first rush to the area. Nearby is an old restored public hall, a stone cottage ruin and the restored former Bank of New South Wales gold office of 1893. The old St Bathans post office has also been restored. Both offices are open to the public. The 1892 Catholic church was built of mud brick and is still in use.

On the Ida Burn is the little township of Oturehua, with two interesting early industrial sites. The water-powered Ida Valley flour mill was housed in a square stone building, built in 1884. The Hayes Engineering Works is a remarkably intact rural workshop which provided engineering services and equipment to farmers. Much of the original plant is still in place inside the mud-brick and corrugated iron buildings. The Historic Places Trust, which owns the building, has brought the plant back into operation to show visitors how it worked.

North of Oturehua, a short walk into the hills off Reef Road, across private land (closed for lambing in September and October), leads to the Golden Progress mine. The reefs here were exploited from the mid-1860s to the 1890s and again later. A massive twin boiler stands by the 14 metre high poppet head and another boiler marks the site of the battery.

A huge waterwheel, the Serpentine, on an isolated site between the Poolburn and Manorburn Reservoirs, is another remote relic of goldmining days, high above the Manuherikia Valley.

THE MANIOTOTO

Naseby, at the head of the Maniototo Plains, is well known for its Victorian goldmining charm. It has buildings of gold rush days, made of sun-dried brick, among them St George's Anglican Church, 1875, the Welcome Inn (now a home) and the Briton Hotel, 1863. The tiny corrugated iron Athenaeum was built in 1865. In the 1878 County Council Chambers there is a local museum featuring goldmining relics and household items. An 1868 watchmaker's shop has been set up in authentic style. There are old diggings around the town and a cemetery containing many old graves. About 4 km from Naseby on the road

▲ *Old boilers and the poppet head (the wooden structure above the vertical mine shaft) still stand on the site of the Golden Progress Mine near Oturehua which was still being worked this century. This poppet head is the only one to have survived in Otago.*

to Dansey Pass is the Kyeburn Diggings cemetery.

On the old Hamiltons run, 15 km south-east of Ranfurly, is a cob woolshed, built in 1860 and still in use. At Patearoa there are cottages from goldmining days and an old hydraulic sluicing nozzle mounted by the town hall. On the Upper Taieri River the buckets and other machinery of a small barge-mounted dredge which spent more than 80 years under water have been raised and mounted on the river bank near the Stonehenge Station. At Paerau the Styx Hotel and stables date from 1861. Nearby is the jail, still with leg irons from the time when the township was a stopping point on the Old Dunstan Road, a now abandoned route into the Dunstan diggings.

Hyde, another gold rush town, has an attractive nineteenth century wooden

school building. The bridge across the Taieri River at Hyde was built in 1878. Just north of the town the river flows through a tunnel where a stone wall stands as a reminder of efforts to recover gold from the river bed. At Macraes Flat, between Hyde and Dunback, Stanley's Hotel was built of stone in the 1880s. Near it are stone stables and stone-walled paddocks. There are goldmining relics in the area at Deepdell Creek, where scheelite was mined in conjunction with gold, and at Nenthorn, a deserted township about 17 km south-west of Macraes Flat. North of Macraes Flat, at Golden Point, a reserve protects a stamper battery still in working order, and there are also several old miners' huts.

The Taieri Lake Station south of Hyde has an interesting group of historic buildings.

ARROWTOWN AND QUEENSTOWN

State Highway 6 crosses the Kawarau River, between Cromwell and Queenstown, at a suspension bridge with stone towers built in 1880. It is now a historic reserve.

Arrowtown has much historic charm stemming from its old buildings, particularly the much-photographed row of old cottages in Buckingham Street. The discovery of gold in the Arrow River brought thousands of miners into the area in the 1860s. A monument on the river bank about 800 metres upstream from the town records where gold was first discovered. Near the monument is an old Chinese miners' settlement which has been excavated and set up for public interpretation. The 1875 jail, with poky cells and heavy iron doors, is one of Arrowtown's more interesting older buildings. The Lake District Centennial Museum is housed in the former Bank of New Zealand, built of stone in 1875.

Up the Arrow River from Arrowtown the ruins of old stone buildings and a battery stand on the site of the abandoned township, Macetown, which can be reached only on foot or by 4-wheel-drive vehicle.

Runholders preceded goldminers to Queenstown and the pioneer runholder William Rees built a cottage there in the early 1860s. Its site is now occupied by another old cottage. There is a memorial to Rees at the foot of Ballarat Street on the waterfront wall.

Goldminers came hard on the heels of the runholders. The rushes to the Arrow and Shotover Rivers in 1862–63 gave Queenstown its initial boost. A lodge building of 1863 and a stone bridge on Ballarat Street remain from early gold rush days. The stone library was built in 1876–77, sharing a wall with the courthouse, built in 1875–76. Parts of Eichardt's Tavern date back to 1871.

A huge boulder in the Queenstown Gardens is a memorial to Scott of the Antarctic.

On the lake itself sails the vintage steamer, the *Earnslaw*, built in Dunedin in 1912 and assembled at Kingston. It is still in use, the only survivor of four steamers which once plied the lake's waters.

At Kawarau Falls, at the outlet to Lake Wakatipu, a dam was built in the 1920s in an attempt to recover gold from the dry river bed. The project failed but the dam remains as the road bridge and control structure. An old turbine from a flour mill is displayed on the knoll.

Up the One Mile Creek above Queenstown an old pipeline can be followed to a powerhouse, constructed in 1924 as the town's first source of electricity. At Bullendale, far up the Shotover River, are the remains of a much earlier hydro-electric power station. In 1885–86, on this remote goldfield 40 km from Queenstown, the Phoenix Goldmine Company installed a water-powered dynamo to drive the pump and stamper batteries at their goldmine. Today it is a three hour walk to the scattered relics at the sites of the powerhouse, mine and township.

Skippers is also an area of historic interest. The scenically impressive road to Skippers passes through mining areas with old tails and often ruined stone buildings. Other abandoned goldmines and townships, which can be reached only on foot or by horseback, are found up the Moke and Moonlight Creeks. At Arthurs Point is an old coaching inn, first built in 1862 but reconstructed after a fire in 1882. Above Arthurs Point the Edith Cavell Bridge, an early reinforced concrete arch structure, was built in 1919 and only later named after the British World War I heroine.

At Bobs Cove, on the road from Queenstown to Glenorchy, are the ruins of three nineteenth century lime kilns. Above Glenorchy on the site of the Invincible Mine in the Rees Valley is a battery and other machinery and equipment once used for the recovery of gold.

The road over the Crown Range follows, on the Wanaka side, the Cardrona Valley. In this valley are further relics of goldmining: tailings, rusting iron and ruined cottages. The Cardrona Hotel, built in 1870, is at the centre of the old goldmining settlement. An old hall, a cottage or two and a tiny cemetery have also survived.

There are historical displays in the Mount Aspiring National Park headquarters at Wanaka. At Luggate the old stone buildings of a closed-down flour mill are of historic interest. The Morven Hills woolshed, in the Lindis Valley, is one of the finest stone woolsheds in the country, built about 1873. Other interesting old farm buildings can also be seen on the Morven Hills run. The runholder's permission is needed to view these buildings.

SOUTHLAND

Southland's history has been similar to that of Otago, from which Southland was 'independent' for only a few struggling years in the provincial period. There was a sizeable population of Maori in pre-European times on the shores of Foveaux Strait where whaling first brought Europeans in any numbers. The main town of Invercargill was laid out and settled in the 1850s and still retains a number of nineteenth century buildings. Southland is also rather like the Wairarapa in having a history of farming development and in the Southland countryside it is old farmhouses and farm buildings which provide the points of greatest historical interest. Fiordland, occupying western Southland, has scenic rather than historic attraction but the story of its exploration is an interesting one. Remote Dusky Sound is one of the few places in the southern South Island with strong associations with Captain Cook.

THE CATLINS

The Catlins Coast stretches around the south-east corner of the South Island from Nugget Point to beyond Waipapa Point. It bounds an area of magnificent scenery and a fascinating history. In the early nineteenth century the indented coastline was frequented by sealers and whalers: there were whaling stations at Cannibal Bay, east of Owaka, on the Tautuku Peninsula, at Waikawa and at Fortrose, and traces of whaling days can still be found. At Cannibal Bay, on False Island, are the remains of a windlass used by whalers.

Today in the Catlins the proximity of virgin bush to cultivated farmland provides an impression of how farmland was won from bush throughout New Zealand. The decline of the rural population has left the Catlins with many half-derelict houses, cottages, churches and other buildings. In Owaka the exhibits of the Catlins Historical Society Museum illustrate early whaling and sawmilling in the area and the days of the now-closed Catlins Railway.

GORE

Mataura River and grew when gold was discovered nearby, at places like Waikaia. The site of an early accommodation house, Gore's first building, is marked near today's bridge. The land around was subdivided in the 1870s and Gore became a farming town. The Presbyterian church, opened in the 1880s, is the town's most interesting church, but other older buildings are worth seeking out, especially the library.

In the surrounding countryside are further historic buildings or sites. At Knapdale is an 1868 woolshed. Willowbank has one of the country's two remaining railway windmills, built to raise water for steam locomotives on the now closed Waikaka branch line.

Waikaka had its first gold rush in the 1860s and 1870s. At the turn of the century

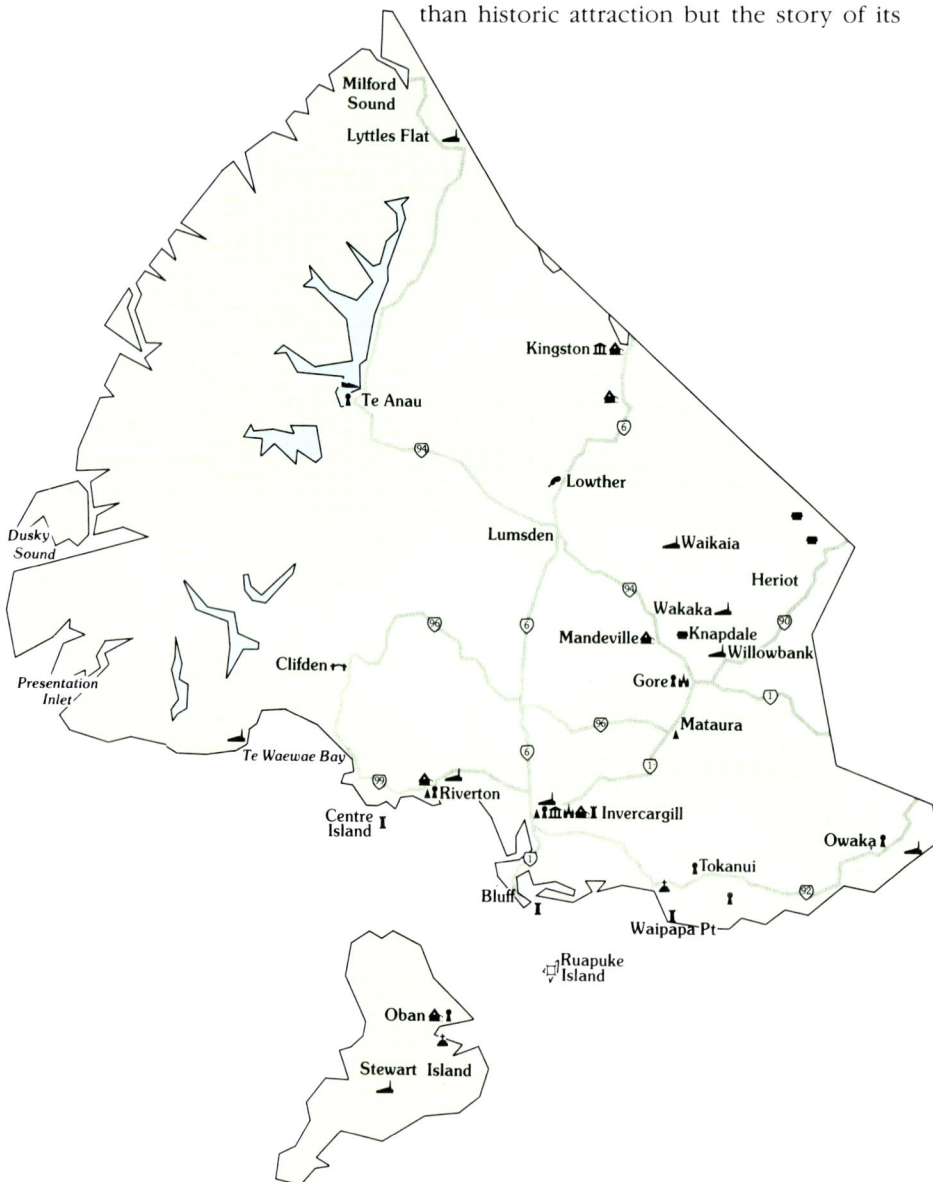

dredges worked the river but the only traces of the town's goldmining days are a few scrub-covered tailings and rusting dredge buckets. Waikaia too was a gold rush town. About 20 km north of Heriot, the shearing shed on the Moa Flat station and the nearby wooden Newstead stables are of historic interest. Both these buildings are privately owned. On the Dusky Forest Road, near Tapanui, is a stone culvert, hand-built by convicts in the 1890s.

The Hokonui Hills west of Gore were the scene of illicit distilling of 'moonshine' and an old still can be seen in Invercargill's Southland Museum. Along Highway 94, near Mandeville, the magnificent stone homestead, Wantwood House, can be seen from the roadside.

Mataura grew around the falls which provided water power for early industries — papermills in 1875, a dairy factory in

1887 and a meatworks in 1892. At Tuturau a Ngati Toa war party, after making an epic journey down the West Coast, was overwhelmed by Ngai Tahu. A memorial along the road to Wyndam marks the area.

INVERCARGILL AND BLUFF

The site of Invercargill was first settled in 1856 and surveyed in 1859. A plaque on the former Bank of New Zealand building marks where stores were landed for the first settlers in 1856. Another plaque on the ANZ bank recalls the first settler John Kelly and his family. Kelly's grave is marked in the Eastern Cemetery. The site of Invercargill was once swampy and the prospect of establishing a flax industry first brought Europeans into Bluff Harbour. Along the

▲ *The gracious stone homestead of the Wantwood run, near Mandeville, epitomises the importance of agriculture in Southland's past, and present. The substantial gabled and dormer-windowed house was built in the 1880s.*

▲ *Southernmost of the impressive Roman Catholic churches of architect F.W. Petre is St Mary's, Invercargill, built in 1894-95. Its dome is prominent on the Invercargill skyline.*

Waihopai Walkway are the derelict sheds of an old twinespinning mill, one of the few relics of the once important flax trade. (At Otaitai Bush are the remains of an old water-powered flax mill.)

Southland was an independent province between 1861 and 1870. One of Invercargill's most historic buildings is Kelvin Chambers, a humble building of 1864, used as a Provincial Council Chambers. Apart from the Canterbury Provincial Government Buildings in Christchurch, it is the only Provincial Council premises to survive. Two churches dominate Invercargill's skyline. First Church, with its tower, was built in 1915; St Mary's Basilica, with its dome, was built in 1894-95. Older than these is St John's Anglican Church, built in 1887.

Another historic structure which breaks the Invercargill skyline is the imposing brick water tower, built at the end of the 1880s.

The Anderson Park Art Gallery is housed in one of Invercargill's finest houses, the Georgian-style home of Sir Robert and Lady Anderson, built in 1924–25. A carved meeting house stands in the grounds. The city's other notable large house, Lennel, was built in the early 1880s by the country's first Surveyor-General, J.T. Thomson.

Invercargill is the home of Southland's major museum. The displays of Maori history emphasise the distinctive aspects of Southland's pre-European Maori culture. Furnished rooms give an idea of how an affluent household lived in the 1880s. Whaling and shipping on the Southland coast are featured in displays. Elsewhere in Southland there are local or district museums in Gore; in Waikawa, housed in the old Waikawa School and the Tokonui jail (shifted onto the site); and in Riverton.

Bluff's first European settler arrived as early as 1824. A sailor settled there and with his Maori wife made a living supplying whaling ships. In the mid-1830s a shore whaling station was established there but Bluff has few reminders today of its whaling origins.

From Stirling Point on the top of Bluff Hill can be seen the historic Dog Island lighthouse, built in 1865 of locally quarried stone. Beyond Dog Island is low-lying Ruapuke Island, site of a large Maori settlement when Europeans arrived in southern New Zealand and the home base of the nineteenth century Ngai Tahu chief Tuhawaiki. In 1843 the German Lutheran missionary J.F.H. Wohlers established a mission station on Ruapuke.

Another historic Foveaux Strait lighthouse is Centre Light, completed in 1878.

The Waipapa Point lighthouse, accessible by road, was built after the 1881 wreck of the S.S. *Tararua*. Victims of the disaster lie in the Tararua acre of the Fortrose cemetery.

RIVERTON

Riverton's founder, John Howell, established a whaling station there for Johnny Jones in the mid-1830s. Howell went on to become a large landholder while the whaling station became a sawmilling and farming centre. Howell's early cottage remains, cared for today by a descendant, and a memorial to him, flanked by trypots and an anchor, stands above the river mouth. Riverton has an interesting collection of old cottages, some dating back to the 1860s, and also an old Customs House.

Beyond Riverton, at the eastern end of Colac Bay, is an outcrop of argillite which was quarried by the Maori in prehistoric times. At the western end of Te Waewae Bay are the ruins of Port Craig, a sawmilling town which failed in the Depression. Farther west, Preservation Inlet and Dusky Sound are of historic interest because of their associations with Cook and early sealers. They are accessible only by foot, air or boat.

North of Tuatapere, at Clifden, an old road suspension bridge is being preserved by the Historic Places Trust. Near Lumsden, at Lowther, is the site of a battle fought between Ngati Mamoe and Ngai Tahu warriors in the early eighteenth century.

Southland fought hard to retain the celebrated vintage train, the Kingston Flyer. Between 1902 and 1937 the Flyer ran as a crack express between Gore and Kingston but it is now confined to a short stretch south of Kingston, where excursions are offered over the summer months.

Fairlight homestead, near Garston, is where Riverton's John Howell later settled.

On Lake Te Anau is another working survivor of a past age in New Zealand's transport history. In 1899 the S.S. *Tawera* was taken, in pieces, to the lake and assembled. Built as a lake steamer it is now a diesel launch, but in spite of the conversion still has a venerably historic air.

Most of the historic interest about scenic Milford Sound concerns the discovery and development of routes into the Sound. The pioneer Donald Sutherland settled at the Sound in 1877. The route of the famous Milford Track was discovered in 1888 and the track cut for tourists soon afterwards. Road access to Milford did not come until 1953, although the Homer Tunnel was pierced in 1940.

Remote Martins Bay, accessible only on foot, was the site of the ill-fated Jamestown settlement, established in the early 1870s but soon abandoned.

STEWART ISLAND

For such a wild, remote place, Stewart Island has a surprisingly long and varied industrial history, beginning in the early

nineteenth century, when the Island's harbours and bays became the haunt of sealers and whalers. Harold Acker's House, near Oban, is a humble building which has survived from whaling days. Sites associated with timber and flax milling, ship-building and mining for tin and gold are encountered in remote places on Stewart Island, but most are difficult for the ordinary visitor to reach. Visitors can, however, walk to the old Kaipipi shipyard from Oban.

More accessible is Ringaringa Beach, where the grave of and a memorial to the Rev. Wohlers, who established the mission on Ruapuke Island in the 1840s, stand on a small headland. Ulva Island in Paterson Inlet has historic interest as the home of Walter and Charles Traill, two early Island settlers. Ulva was for years the location of Stewart Island's post office. Old buildings and the graves of the Traills remain on the island, which can be visited by launch. In Oban is a small museum with displays touching on many aspects of Stewart Island history.

▲ *Invercargill's magnificent Edwardian Town Hall was designed by a local architect and opened in November 1906 as a combined city hall and civic theatre. It is one of the most imposing of the country's municipal buildings to be found in a secondary centre.*

WEST COAST

The places of historic interest on the South Island's rugged West Coast are associated with the exploitation, for centuries past, of the region's natural resources. In pre-European times the West Coast had only a small resident Maori population but was important as the major source of greenstone from which the finest weapons and ornaments were made. One source of the stone was the Arahura River where a plaque close to the road and rail bridge records the river's importance in bygone days.

Greenstone brought the Maori to Westland; gold brought the Pakeha, first in 1863, to an area with otherwise poor prospects for European settlement. The first West Coast gold workings were of alluvial deposits, but quartz veins were discovered which maintained gold production long after the first rushes were history. Old town sites, abandoned workings and overgrown cemeteries from gold rush days are to be found throughout Westland.

Coal and timber have been the West Coast's other important products. Coalmining also began in the 1860s and the working out of many mines has left ghost or semi-ghost towns and sites of industrial interest. There are fewer traces of the early days of the timber industry than of early gold or coalmining. Relics of old water and steam powered sawmills and of early bush tramways are among the few reminders of this once prolific enterprise.

Heavy rainfall means that much of the history of the West Coast is hidden in luxuriant bush. Efforts have been made to clear town sites and abandoned workings so that the public can enjoy and learn from them. Mitchells Gully is a reconstructed gold claim and Shanty Town, a recreation of a West Coast gold town, is popular with tourists.

Many of the West Coast's historic sites are on land controlled by the Department of Conservation which provides excellent leaflets covering many of the sites mentioned.

THE BULLER AND WESTPORT

The Buller River, which provides a route between Nelson and the West Coast, was explored in the late 1840s by Thomas Brunner who made one of the epic journeys of New Zealand exploration. A memorial to Brunner stands on an island in the Grey River at Brunner. Far to the south of the Paringa Bridge, on State Highway 6, another plaque records the furthest point reached by Brunner on his journey.

Murchison started life as a goldmining township. It has a small museum with material on early settlement of the district and a photographic record of the 1929 Murchison earthquake. There are traces of old gold workings and settlements up the now almost deserted Matakitaki Valley.

At Lyell, between Murchison and Inangahua, are the more accessible remains of a goldmining town founded in 1863. Lyell reached its heyday in the 1880s, when about 2000 people lived in the vicinity, then steadily declined. No buildings remain, but there are displays and a family memorial in the roadside picnic area and a 10 minute walk takes visitors to old cemeteries.

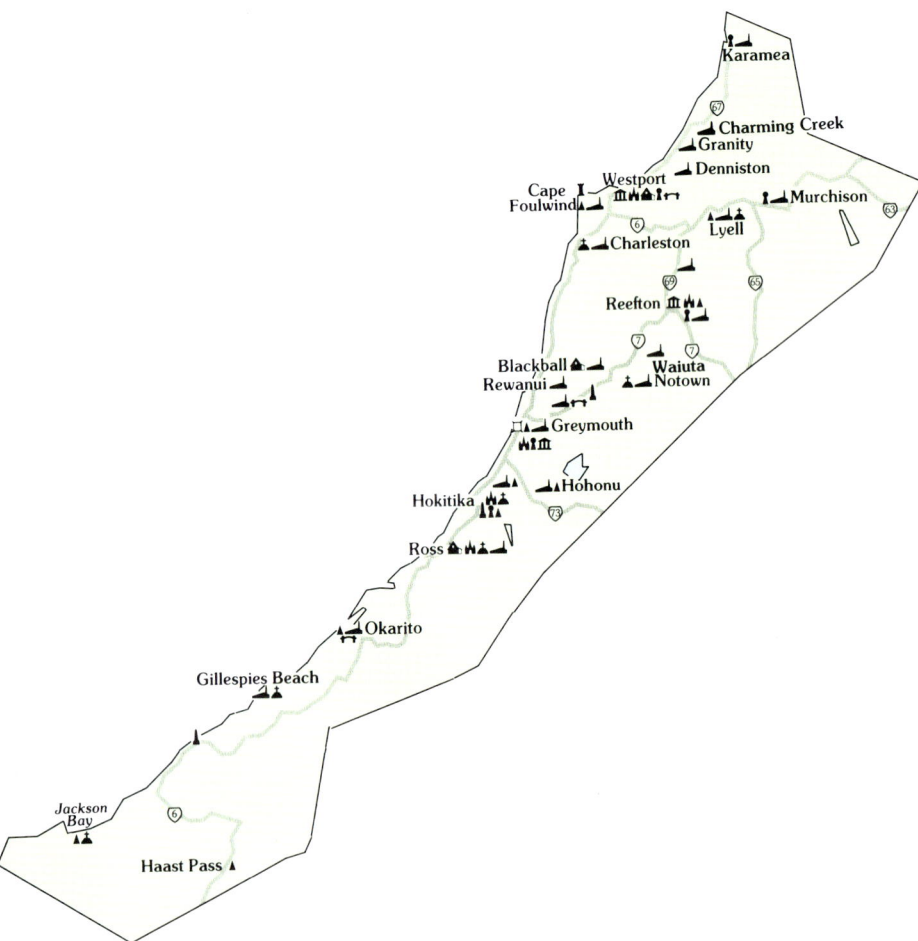

Another 45 minutes up the walkway, which follows an old dray road, is a restored stamper battery.

Westport first grew as a port for the early Buller goldfields. The town has a number of interesting older structures including its Bank of New South Wales building, St John's Anglican Church, the imposing Borough Council Chambers and old cottages and hotel buildings.

At Cape Foulwind is a memorial to Abel Tasman, a bronze replica of an astrolabe. Tasman anchored in nearby Tauranga Bay in December 1642. The present lighthouse on Cape Foulwind was erected in 1926. A railway was built to Cape Foulwind in the late 1880s to transport rock for the retaining walls of Westport Harbour. Some of the old formations can still be seen on a walkway, along with a tunnel (now collapsed), driven when the line was extended in 1914.

South of Westport, old goldworkings still exist at places like Bald Hill and Addisons Flat. Little more remains even at Charleston, the largest of the gold rush towns.

At Mitchells Gully, near Charleston, is a reconstructed working goldmine, including a stamper battery. The two cemeteries at Charleston have some interesting old graves. A 1½ hour walk along an old logging tram track up the Four Mile River, inland from Charleston, leads to the remains of an old timber mill.

Westport continued to prosper after the gold was mostly exhausted, on the basis of coal mined in the Buller fields north of the town. Coaltown, in an old Westport brewery building (of about 1890), traces the history of the coalmining industry from the first discovery of coal in the area through to modern mining methods. The displays include a model of the Denniston Incline and a 'working' underground mine which visitors can enter.

At the sites of some old coal mines, and in present day mining towns, buildings and structures like bins and screens are worth seeing.

The Denniston Incline, which conveyed coal 600 metres from a hilltop mine to a coastal railhead, was one of the steepest rail

▶ *Among Reefton's generally well cared for older buildings is the courthouse built in 1872. It remained in use for nearly one hundred years and has been retained as an important part of a precinct of older buildings.*

wagon inclines in the world. A self-acting railway, it was built in the late 1870s and closed in 1967. A walkway which follows the line of an old bridle track, built in the mid-1880s, provides views of the abandoned incline. Denniston, at the top, is a ghost town in the making, with many derelict houses. The remains of the old cottages and mining plant, and particularly the huge stone walls built in the late 1870s to form terraces on the steep site, are notable features.

At Ngakawau, the Charming Creek Walkway follows the route of an abandoned railway line, built in 1914, up the Ngakawau River. Near Granity, the Britannia Track provides a three hour walk into the old Britannia goldmine, where the stark remains of a stamper and other relics are located. Gold workings can also be reached by a two hour walk north of Karamea, an isolated settlement founded in 1874.

REEFTON

Reefton owes its existence, like many West Coast towns, to gold and coal. In the town is a precinct of old buildings identified by plaques placed by the local historical society. The buildings include the Court House, built in 1872, the old School of Mines, built in 1887, and two churches, Sacred Heart and St Stephen's, both built in 1878. Nearby is Oddfellows Hall and old bank and hotel buildings. The Reefton railway station is a good example of a small town station, and has a coal-loading facility.

Reefton lit the way for the rest of New Zealand when the first public hydro-electric station, using water from the Inangahua River, was built there in 1888. A plaque near the War Memorial records this 'first'. On the site of the powerhouse, on the river bank downriver from the town, are concrete foundations and a few scraps of plant.

At Blacks Point, just out of Reefton, a museum housed in a restored Wesleyan church, built of pit-sawn timber in 1876, has displays which illustrate colonial and goldfields life in the district. Quartz mining equipment, including an operating battery rebuilt from parts found nearby, is also exhibited. At Crushington, one of the mine buildings and some machinery of the Wealth of Nations mine can be inspected, as can the foundation of the huge Progress battery a short distance away on the opposite

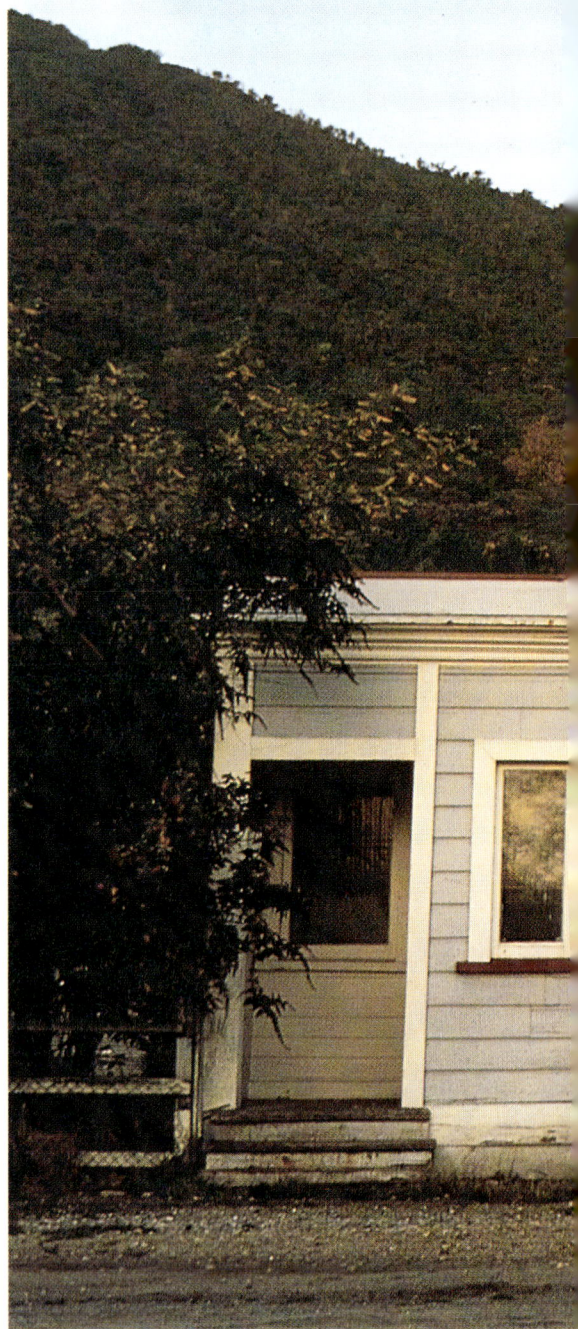

side of the river. The Big River mine was worked from the 1880s into the middle of this century. A poppet head, engine house and cyanide tanks remain on the site, a full day's walk from the road.

North of Reefton, towards Inangahua, the Larry Creek goldfield worked from the 1870s to the 1900s. Remains including an old steam engine, berdan and tunnels, can be reached by a one and a half hour tramp.

The ghost town of Waiuta, off State Highway 7 between Reefton and Ikamatua, came to life when a reef was discovered there at the beginning of the century. It closed in 1951. Some of the old workings remain on site.

The Murray Creek goldfield, near Blacks Point, began life as an alluvial field, then

gained a new lease of life when quartz reefs were discovered in 1870. Several mines were worked in the area and the vestiges of a winch, a boiler, batteries, winding wheels and cyanide tanks, along with tunnels and shafts, can be seen on the walking tracks which the Department of Conservation maintains. Coal was also mined in the area and the remains of winches used to extract the coal can be seen. The ghost town of Waiuta can be reached off State Highway 7 between Reefton and Ikamatua.

GREYMOUTH

Before Greymouth was founded, a Maori pa, Mawhera, stood at the mouth of the Grey River. In a park at the southern end of the Cobden Bridge a plaque marks the site of the pa, where James Mackay completed the deed of sale of Westland in May 1860. Gold was discovered near Greymouth in 1864 but its more recent prosperity has been based on timber and coal. The town has some interesting older buildings, but none dating from the time of the first gold rushes.

South of Greymouth is Shanty Town, a reconstructed goldfields town of the late nineteenth century. Some of the buildings are authentic, moved to Shanty Town from other parts of the West Coast, and include the old Notown Church and the Ross Borough Council Chambers. Visitors to Shanty Town can ride behind a bush locomotive or on a stage coach.

An exciting drive from Runanga up an old railway formation leads to Rewanui where a preservation society is working to retain old workshops, coal bins, a railway station and other relics of an important group of coalmines. North of Greymouth, the Point Elizabeth Walkway has historic associations, following for part of its length an old mining road and water race.

THE GREY VALLEY

Commercial production of coal at the Brunner Mine, near Taylorville, began in 1864, exploiting a seam first reported by the explorer Thomas Brunner in 1848. The mine became one of the most productive in New Zealand. In 1896, 65 workers were killed in an explosion in the mine, the country's worst mine disaster. Most of the victims are buried in a mass grave in the Stillwater cemetery where a monument stands in their memory.

A fine old suspension bridge gives foot access to the Brunner Mine site from State Highway 7, between Stillwater and Dobson. Coke-making and brick-making were also undertaken on the site and some of the most interesting remains are those of the old coke ovens, including two rows of rare beehive ovens. A programme of preservation and stabilisation has been carried out by the Historic Places Trust.

Blackball was first a gold then a coalmining town. Some old cottages, the substantial mine manager's house and an old hotel are among buildings of historic interest there. The Blackball miners' strike of 1908 was an important episode in New Zealand union history, but nothing in the town specifically recalls it.

For the energetic, tracks behind the town lead into old goldmining areas. Gold was taken from 1865 on, by both alluvial and quartz-crushing methods. On the Croesus Track there is a restored quartz battery at Garden Gully in Dugout Creek (a 2 ½ hour walk from the carpark). Up the Moonlight Track are the remains of old water races and tailings, the sites of old huts and the fragmentary remains of another quartz-crushing battery.

On the southern bank of the Grey River, at Notown, up a side road from State Highway 7 north of Stillwater, are old tunnels built by the early goldminers, a derelict school and an old cemetery. Control of water is a key to large-scale alluvial mining

◀ *The restored mine manager's house in Blackball now serves as a community centre. Its size and style mark it out from the humbler cottages occupied by the families of the miners, many of which are also still standing. The contrast highlights the class structure of Blackball, a key town in the history of New Zealand's trade unions.* Frank Simpson

for gold and at Lake Hochstetter is a dam and control gates built in 1876 to supply the miners' water races.

At the Mawhera picnic area between Stillwater and Ngahere are the remains of an old logging locomotive. Nelson Creek, in from Ngahere, has further old gold mining remains.

SOUTH OF GREYMOUTH

Between Greymouth and Hokitika are many reminders of old goldmining sites and townships. Gold was first discovered in payable quantities on the coast at Greenstone in 1864 and a plaque at the start of the Revell Terrace track near Hohonu Junction, near Kumara, records this discovery. Also in the vicinity are sluicing and dredge tailings, and the carefully stacked tailings of Chinese miners. There are similar workings at Woods Creek, east of Dunganville.

Goldsborough, reached through Stafford or Dillmanstown, has remains of gold workings, although little is left on the site of the township itself. Near Stafford is an old cemetery and, close by, the forlorn remains of a dredge which worked in the area from about 1938 to 1948. Both Woods Creek and Goldsborough have walking tracks.

The township of Kumara has a small historic reserve on its main street. A plaque identifies it as the place where the famous politician, Richard John Seddon, Premier from 1893 to 1906, had his home until he moved permanently to Wellington in 1895. Hokitika has a statue of Seddon, erected in 1910, in front of the old Government Buildings.

HOKITIKA

The goldmining metropolis of more than 4,000 people (with hundreds more living on nearby diggings) established at the end of 1864 is now a quiet town, still with the rough and ready air of its goldmining origins. Its most prominent building, St Mary's Catholic Church, was built in 1914.

Hokitika possesses a splendid array of monuments besides its statue of Seddon. A cairn at the corner of Revell Street and Gibson Quay recalls its goldfield beginnings. A Heritage Hokitika project is under way to reconstruct part of the old wharf to

portray Hokitika's importance as a trading port. An old wooden custom house has been restored. A statue of a digger was erected in 1914 to mark the 50th anniversary of the opening of the West Coast goldfields. The memorial clock tower in the centre of the main street was built in 1901–02 to commemorate both the Boer War and Edward VII's coronation. Other statues are of Robbie Burns (1923) and 'Summer', celebrates the British and Intercolonial exhibition of the same year.

Near the entrance to the cemetery an obelisk records the names of four early surveyors and explorers who were killed in the 1860s. The cemetery has other fascinating memorials and the base of a lighthouse, disused since 1925, stands on the terrace edge by the entrance to the cemetery.

The West Coast Historic Museum in Hokitika focuses on the Maori recovery and working of greenstone as well as the discovery and exploitation of gold in European times.

Lake Kaniere, inland from Hokitika, was the scene of an early hydro-electric development. The race which serves the present powerhouse was constructed in 1906–07 using parts of an even earlier race. At the intake weir are old gear wheels and winches which control the flow of water. A walkway follows the race, passing a restored raceman's cottage. The powerhouse still has the old plant inside a new building and has interpretative panels for public viewing.

Mahinapua Creek and Lake Mahinapua once provided a water route part of the way between Hokitika and Ross. Paddle steamers were first used on the route in 1867. A steamer built in 1883 in Hokitika and used to carry supplies to the Lake Mahinapua gold dredge was scuttled when the railway line to Ross was completed in 1906. It was raised and partly restored in 1977 and is now on show under cover in a recreation area on the lake shore. A walkway which starts four kilometres before the lake follows an old logging tramway past the sites of old sawmills.

ROSS

The Ross goldfield was long-lasting, partly because the field had very deep alluvial deposits which required mining techniques not used elsewhere in New Zealand. Gold was still being extracted at the beginning of this century and in 1909 New Zealand's largest nugget, the 'Honorable Roddy', was found at Ross. It was later presented to George V as a coronation gift.

A miner's cottage of the mid-1880s now serves as a display centre at the start of two walkways which can be used to explore the old workings. Races, shafts, dam sites, fluming, tunnels, tailings and rusting old machinery can all be seen. One of the walkways takes visitors to the town's original cemetery and past a replica miner's hut in the bush. An old fire bell tower, with an even older bell, and other mining relics stand next to the cottage. Other buildings of historic interest in Ross are St Patrick's Church, built in 1866, and the City Hotel, built some time after 1868, and later rebuilt.

SOUTH WESTLAND

Minerals, timber and tourism have drawn people to remote South Westland. Maori greenstone gatherers settled this area some 800 years ago. The valuable stone was recovered from hills and valleys to the south of Jackson Bay. The tiny coastal township of Okarito enjoyed a brief heyday in 1866 as a gold rush town. A memorial stone in the township commemorates the early diggers, who won gold from the black sand beaches. At the Three Mile and Five Mile, south of Okarito, are goldmining relics. An old pack track including old bridges and logs laid as 'corduroy' links these township sites with Okarito. At the Three Mile are the remains of an old ferryman's cottage and at the Five Mile the rusting remains of a dredge and the pipeline which supplied it with water.

In the National Park headquarters at Franz Josef a major display concentrates on the history of transportation and settlement in the area. Nearby is the historic Defiance Hut, brought down from a site high above the Franz Josef Glacier to give visitors a taste of mountaineering history. An early hydro-electric power scheme was constructed on the Tartare River near Franz Josef and visitors can walk through the tunnels of the scheme.

Gillespies Beach, like Okarito, was a coastal goldmining settlement. Today a cemetery, an old dredge lying around in bits and a miners' track, including a walking tunnel, remain from its early days.

At the Karangarua Bridge, south of Fox Glacier, a noticeboard records the journeys of explorer Charles Douglas, up the valleys

of South Westland between about 1868 and 1900.

The road through the Haast Pass, connecting South Westland with Otago, was completed in 1965. At the summit of the pass a plaque records the use of this old Maori route by two early explorers, Charles Cameron and Julius von Haast. At the head of the Windbag Creek, just before Lake Moeraki, a noticeboard marks where the old cattle track leaves the line of the new highway. The track was used for many years before the opening of the highway to drive stock from the isolated settlements further south.

Jackson Bay was the scene in 1875–76 of an attempt to found a settlement. A plaque near the shore records this ill-fated effort to settle this far corner of New Zealand. Near the present-day settlement is the Arawhata Pioneer Cemetery.

▲ *Deaths by drowning and other accidents were common when gold and then coal were being extracted from the physically wild West Coast. At the now abandoned goldmining town of Gillespies Beach a few graves are almost all that remains of past settlement there.*

INDEX <small>* (A selective listing.)</small>

MONUMENTS AND STATUARY

PUBLIC BUILDINGS 🏛

FARM BUILDINGS 🏠